DICKENS
AND THE
GROTESQUE

MICHAEL HOLLINGTON

CROOM HELM
London & Sydney

BARNES & NOBLE BOOKS
Totowa, New Jersey

© 1984 M. Hollington
Croom Helm Ltd, Provident House, Burrell Row,
Beckenham, Kent BR3 1AT

Croom Helm Australia Pty Ltd, First Floor, 139 King Street,
Sydney, NSW 2001, Australia

British Library Cataloguing in Publication Data

Hollington, Michael
    Dickens and the grotesque.
    1. Dickens, Charles, *1812-1870* — Criticism
    and interpretation   2. Grotesque in literature
    I. Title
    823'.8   PR4592.G7

    ISBN 0-7099-1261-7

First published in the USA 1984 by
Barnes & Noble Books, 81 Adams Drive,
Totowa, New Jersey, 07512

Library of Congress Cataloging in Publication Data

Hollington, Michael.
    Dickens and the grotesque.

    Bibliography: p. 247
    Includes index.
    1. Dickens, Charles, 1812-1870 — Criticism and in-
terpretation.   2. Grotesque in literature.   I. Title.
PR4592.G7H6   1984   823'.8   83-27302
ISBN 0-389-20457-9

Printed and bound in Great Britain

CONTENTS

For Arthur Sale, in gratitude for many years of friendship, advice and support.

PREFACE

This book is about an aesthetic and a rhetoric that
are present (it is argued) in the work of Charles
Dickens. The aesthetic is that of the grotesque,
and in the opening chapter and elsewhere, some
relevant aspects of its theory and history are
sketched in. The rhetoric is an ironic application
of this aesthetic for satiric purposes, in
criticism of a society which, by and large,
disapproved of the grotesque.
    The book's aim is to try to gain recognition
of the importance of these procedures and
strategies in Dickens's writing. In an attempt to
suggest the range and prominence of a 'rhetoric of
the grotesque' it has something to say about all
the major works, and several of the minor ones.
Yet it is in no sense an attempt at a comprehensive
or exhaustive survey of the field of the grotesque
in Dickens.
    Nor is it a chronological account of Dickens's
development as a grotesque artist. Because of its
convenience and familiarity, the sequence of
Dickens's novels, in the order of their appearance,
provides the main basis for the arrangement of the
book's chapters, and certainly this stimulates the
elaboration of arguments about the progress from
one book to another. Yet other relationships
between the works in the Dickensian canon are also
explored, in part to counteract any impression of
an inexorable linear logic.
    Instead, the book might best be seen as a
series of related essays (in a fairly literal sense)
exploring various aspects of Dickens's relation to
the grotesque, each one of which could be developed
further, and extended to focus upon other phases of
Dickens's career. Thus, after an initial chapter
attempting to locate Dickens in relation to some

strands of the tradition of grotesque art, chapter
two focusses upon a favourite paradox of the 1830s'
emergence from romanticism - the idea that 'real
life' is more grotesque and fantastical than
anything the artistic imagination can produce -
that is obviously to recur in Dickens's later work.
Chapter three, for instance, develops it in relation
to the representation of the city as the site of
monstrous human juxtapositions in *Oliver Twist* and
Nicholas Nickleby, though clearly, again, the city
is a major focus for the grotesque throughout
Dickens's career.

Chapters four to seven then develop the
inherent binary structure within this paradox (real
vs. fantastic, classical vs. grotesque, etc.) along
two axes. The first is temporal: *The Old
Curiosity Shop* and Dickens's two historical novels
seem to work through ironic comparison of supposedly
contrasting phases of time (pre- and post-
revolutionary, pre- and post-industrial, etc.) to
show the persistence of the discredited, old
'grotesqueness' of the past in the present. The
second (already apparent in *A Tale of Two Cities*,
of course) is spatial, centring on a supposed
geographical contrast between enlightened and
benighted societies - America vs. England, England
vs. Italy, etc. - that is shown to be highly
insecure. Again, an ironic 'rhetoric of the
grotesque' strives to undermine complacent
fantasies of progress and utopia.

Then, focussing upon some relatively neglected
minor writings, chapter eight attempts to explore
the impact of the grotesque upon Dickens's
narrative technique, examining how, as the writer's
career develops, increasing use is made of fractured
and distorted narrative perspectives, and how a
harmonious, classical vision of the whole (e.g. of
the city) is progressively abandoned. Following
this, chapters nine to twelve focus upon the rôle of
the grotesque in Dickens's late, major novels
(though nine, in fact, concerned with *David
Copperfield* and *Dombey and Son*, continues to focus
upon 'point of view' by stressing the importance of
the child in Dickens as a privileged perceiver of
grotesque realities unnoticed by adults). Ten
develops some of the concerns of chapter one, with
particular reference to Ruskin's theory of the
grotesque, which may have some relevance to
Dickens's novels, particularly those (like *Hard
Times*) that Ruskin admired; eleven concerns *Great
Expectations* ("a grotesque, tragicomic conception",

according to Dickens) and explores the relationship
between the grotesque and tragicomedy in what may
be Dickens's finest novel; and finally, in chapter
twelve, some of the continuities between Dickens's
last two novels are highlighted through a study of
the rôle of the grotesque in each.

On the last page of *Edwin Drood*, indeed, the
function of the grotesque in Dickens seems to be
particularly clearly revealed. There stands the
Princess Puffer, "as ugly and withered as one of
the fantastic carvings on the under brackets of the
stall seats", to exemplify countless ironically
subversive juxtapositions in Dickens's work, and
testify to the tenacity with which the grotesque
manages ceaselessly to metamorphose itself into new
forms.

ACKNOWLEDGEMENTS

Many colleagues and friends over a number of years have helped in a number of ways in the development and production of this book. Though I shall probably neglect some important debts, I should like to mention a few of their names. In America, I think of Graham Barker-Benfield, John Callahan, Royal Gettmann, David Paroissien, and Robert Patten; in Germany, of Kurt Otten, Peter Steiger, and Christian Thomsen; in Norway of Andrew Kennedy, Ulf Lie, and Jim Voss; and in Australia, of David de Giustino, Gareth Griffiths, Jane Novak, Richard Yeo and Nick Zurbrugg.

In England the names are particularly numerous and the risk of inadvertent omissions particularly great. In Norwich I think of Jonathan Cook, Thomas Elsaesser, George Hyde, George MacLennan, Lorna Sage, Vic Sage, Jennifer Searle, and Bod and Thom Wright; in Leicester, of Philip Collins; in Cambridge, of Su Kappeler, and the old pro(-) and con(-) Dickensian, Arthur Sale, to whom this book is dedicated.

For substantial financial help with the preparation of the manuscript I am indebted to the Research Committee of the School of Humanities of Griffith University, Nathan, Brisbane, Australia. For the work involved I should like to thank Diane Forgan and, in particular, Robyn Pratten, who did a great deal of editorial work on the text, as well as typing it up in its final form. Any errors that remain, however, are entirely my own responsibility.

Nevertheless, in the end all these debts are subservient to that to my wife Barbara and to my children, Barnaby and Lucy. Without their co-operation and support I should not have got to the stage of writing acknowledgements.

A NOTE ON ABBREVIATIONS AND QUOTATIONS OF DICKENS'S WORKS

Standard formulae are used to refer to Dickens's
works: e.g., *SB* = *Sketches by Boz*, *OT* = *Oliver
Twist*, etc., etc. All quotations refer to the
Oxford Illustrated Dickens, and give part and
chapter numbers as well as page numbers. The
Pilgrim House edition of the letters (5 volumes to
date) is used wherever possible, and abbreviated as
'Letters'; where another edition is used, fuller
references are given.

Chapter One

THE GROTESQUE TRADITION, ANCIENT AND MODERN

To write about Dickens and the Grotesque is to
approach a quite central feature of the novelist's
art, one that has been recognised and commented
upon, admiringly or disparagingly, by almost every
critic who ever wrote on Dickens.[1] Fundamental
originality is therefore not to be expected, nor,
perhaps, desired; yet a persistent, concentrated
focus upon the grotesque in Dickens may be able to
emphasise some relatively neglected aspects of his
art and its relationship to other European writing
in the nineteenth century and beyond.
    Any such undertaking must inevitably commence
with a consideration of the meaning of the term
'grotesque', and of the usefulness of available
theories of its nature. One does not need to read
very far into the subject to discover the pre-
eminent contemporary importance and influence of
two books - Wolfgang Kayser's *Das Groteske: seine
Gestaltung in Malerei und Dichtung*, published in
1957 and translated as *The Grotesque in Art and
Literature* in 1963, and Mikhail Bakhtin's
Tvorchestvo Fransua Rable, translated as *Rabelais
and his World* in 1968.[2] In that they also manifest
markedly contrasting approaches (Bakhtin's book is
in part intended as a criticism of Kayser's), these
indispensable starting-points can be seen to
dramatise some of the dynamic tensions within the
concept - how grotesque art may provisionally be
said to be an essentially mixed or hybrid form, like
tragicomedy, its elements, in themselves heterogenous (human forms, animal forms, the natural, the
supernatural, the comic, the monstrous and misshapen),
combining in unstable, conflicting, paradoxical
relationships - and to represent poles in relation
to which, perhaps, any theory of the grotesque is
likely to orient itself.

Kayser's book begins by tracing the origin of the word 'grotesque' in the early Mannerist phase of the Renaissance. He relates how the word (deriving from the Italian *grotta*, cave) refers to what were thought to be underground paintings excavated beneath the baths of Titus in the 1480's; painters like Ghirlandaio, Pinturicchio and Filippino Lippi, came, saw and scratched their names, and the fantastic ornamental style soon became a feature of the borders of their frescoes. He quotes the first recorded use of the term in a commission for the Piccolomini library in Siena dating from 1502, commanding the painter Pinturicchio to decorate its ceilings "with such fantastic forms, colours, and arrangements as are now called grotesques (... *che oggi chiamano grottesche*)."[3]

Yet immediately the problematical nature of the concept suggests itself: does the term 'grotesque' and its history (since chronicled in exemplary fashion by Frances Barasch[4]) adequately convey the phenomenon it is held to represent? Leo Spitzer argues in an influential review[5] against Kayser's preoccupation with the mere word, claiming that the grotesque must be seen as a psychic constant with a continuous existence stretching back to remotest antiquity. The temptation to agree is perhaps bolstered by the Piccolomini document itself (nowadays they are called 'grotesques', but they have been appreciated for a long while), but may be motivated primarily by the greater relevance of the longer historical perspective for the study of a nineteenth century writer. Dickens, we shall see, did not think of the grotesque merely as a post-Renaissance phenomenon; and Thomas Wright, an important English theorist of the grotesque and contemporary of the novelist, finds his earliest examples, in his *History of Caricature and Grotesque* of 1865,[6] in ancient Egypt.

Locating such an origin, it is perhaps not surprising that Kayser views the grotesque as an expression of a peculiarly modern *angst* and alien-ation, and emphasises its sinister, disturbing features throughout his book. He describes how he first came to think about the grotesque, in Spain, in the Prado, in 1942 - a time and place that may go part of the way to explain Kayser's severity with those who neglect the monstrosity and horror he associates with the concept. The classicizing Goethe is censured for his frivolous approach to Raphael's *loggie* (he thought they should be regarded as 'arabesques'): "When describing Raphael's

in other words — myth / timelessness
history vs.

grotesques in this manner. Goethe overlooked the sinister quality inherent in even this playful world". A definition in Richelet's *Dictionnaire français* of 1680, characterising the grotesque as "that which has something pleasantly ridiculous", is dismissed: "Here the grotesque has lost all its sinister overtones and merely elicits a carefree smile". And it is the loss of "... belief in demonic or mythical attitudes", the decline of "... a strange, ominous and abysmal quality" in fantastic humour, that "... helps explain why the word 'grotesque' has lost its status as a technical term and is currently used in a rather vague and non-committal manner".[7] Bakhtin is certainly able to find some evidence to support his critical view that "Kayser's definitions first of all strike us by the gloomy, terrifying tone of the grotesque world that alone the author sees".[8]

Thus Kayser's "final interpretation of the grotesque" as "AN ATTEMPT TO INVOKE AND SUBDUE THE DEMONIC ASPECTS OF THE WORLD"[9] is challenged by attempts (by Bakhtin and others) to construct an alternative tradition of the grotesque, at once more ancient and more benign. Their argument tends to dissolve the category "demonic" altogether, treating it as a function of the Christian campaign against the lingering remains of pre-Christian beliefs in medieval Europe, exemplified for instance in Bernard of Clairvaux's diatribe against grotesque art.[10] The devils are not in themselves sinister and terrifying, according to this argument, until Christianity declared them so: "Die hybriden Zwischenformen, die antiker Spieltrieb und Formensinn geschaffen (Ovid, der im Mittelalter 'moralisiert' wird), sind von der christlichen Spekulation zu Damonen umgebildet worden, bei denen Menschen 'das Lachen vergeht', die den Menschen zu schrecken bestimmt sind - sie steigen auf aus dem Abgrund des Ungeformten oder Missbildeten."[11] And they live on in popular tradition as attractive images of subversive power, according to Bakhtin: ... "in the parodical legends and the *fabliaux* the devil is the gay ambivalent figure expressing the unofficial point of view."[12]

Implicit in this approach is a theory of the origins of the grotesque essentially drawn from Fraserian anthropology. Invoking in Greco-Roman antiquity an alternative strand that contrasts with the classical ethos of calm, heroic repose, "... un monde des êtres fantastiques aux origines complexes, venus souvent de très loin, mêlant des corps et des

natures hétérogènes", Jurgis Baltrusaitis emphasises
its fundamental preoccupation with matter in
metamorphosis, and hence with a vegetal cycle of
growth and decay;[13] declaring their belief that
"medieval grotesque art stems directly from earlier
pagan beliefs, that the representations are pagan
deities dear to the people which the Church was
unable to eradicate", Ronald Sheridan and Anne Ross
perceive Celtic influence everywhere in medieval
church grotesques, "memories of human sacrifice and
tree worship" and traces of "divine power - prophecy,
fertility, speech, song and hospitality" in the
monstrous heads and members they disport.[14]

At the same time, many of these large
historical constructs display unmistakeable symptoms
of ideological assumptions. An interesting case in
point is Dickens's contemporary, Thomas Wright; his
view of the grotesque as the expression of a
fundamental "need for laughter which was human and
natural",[15] forever exercising itself in history
despite repression and prohibition, betrays a
version of bourgeois radicalism that bears a number
of similarities to Dickens's own. For Wright, art
originates in caricature - mocking one's enemies,
drawing them on rock; irreverence is part of the
essential nature of the art of antiquity ("It is
astonishing with how much boldness the Greeks
parodied and ridiculed sacred subjects" (17)). The
best grotesque art is thus political: whereas Greek
new comedy, forbidden to express controversy, seems
to be in decline, Roman art is distinguished by its
irreverent "readiness to turn into burlesque the
most sacred and popular legends of the Roman mythology.(15)"[16]

Wright also displays the rudiments of a sociology of the grotesque, lacking in Kayser but later to
be one of the most noticeable features of Bakhtin's
theory. Because of its irreverence, grotesque art
is fundamentally social in character: "caricature
and burlesque are naturally intended to be heard and
seen publicly."(51)[17] Because of its broad popular
appeal, it has a long and tenacious history: "The
popular institutions of the Romans were more
generally preserved to the middle ages than those of
a higher and more refined character" (106; elsewhere
Wright comments on "... the pertinacity with which
the popular stories descend along with peoples
through generations from the remotest ages of
antiquity" (111)). And because of its historical
nature, it expresses the particular class relationships of succeeding social structures. Under

feudalism, according to Wright, grotesque art dealt only on personal satire and individual vendetta. But with the dawn of bourgeois democracy in the later middle ages the grotesque emerges in more developed, consciously political guises; in *Piers Plowman*, for instance, a nascent English radicalism can be felt: "Political satire in the middle ages appeared chiefly in the form of poetry and song, and it was especially in England that it flourished, a sure sign that there was in our country a more advanced feeling of popular independence, and a greater freedom of speech, than in France or Germany." (183)

Wright is thus the apologist of liberal England and its superior democratic institutions - freedom of speech, freedom of the press, etc., and their significance for grotesque art. Yet with his continual awareness of how, for instance, medieval carnivals like the Festival of Fools are "... political, and ... constantly directed against the ecclesiastical order" (207), Wright undoubtedly anticipates Bakhtin, for whom the essential social matrices of the Rabelaisian grotesque are the carnival and the market-place. Bakhtin shows Rabelais as "closely and essentially linked to popular sources",[18] and grotesque art is for him a popular anti-classical tradition, "ambivalent and contradictory ... ugly, monstrous, hideous from the point of view of 'classic' aesthetics, that is, the aesthetics of the ready-made and the completed".(25) Rabelais as an artist of the grotesque is someone with an awareness of historical change, his art an art of matter in the process of formation, and Bakhtin relates the revitalised interest in the grotesque to the Renaissance sense of history - it is the means "for the artistic and ideological expression of a mighty awareness of history and of historic change which appeared during the Renaissance" (25), being in its very nature "opposed to all that is finished and polished, to all pomposity, to every ready-made solution in the sphere of thought and world outlook."(3) Rabelais's preoccupation with the body and its functions is also progressive in character, antipathetic as it is held to be to any idea of the body as a "strictly completed, finished product" (29), or of "the body and its physiology in the modern sense of these words, because it is not individualised." (19)

But of particular relevance, perhaps, to the study of Dickens and the grotesque is Bakhtin's identification of a tradition of "grotesque realism" stemming from Rabelais: "the entire field of realistic literature of the last three centuries is strewn with the fragments of grotesque realism, which at times are not mere remnants of the past but manifest a renewed vitality." (24) Bakhtin sees this realist tradition, with its aim "to consecrate inventive freedom" (34), as qualitatively superior to that "classic realism" that Colin McCabe identifies (questionably, perhaps) as the dominant style of the nineteenth century:[19] "Realism of grand style, in Stendhal, Balzac, Hugo and Dickens, for instance, was always linked directly or indirectly with the Renaissance tradition. Breaking away from this tradition diminished the scope of realism and transformed it into naturalist empiricism." (52) It is for him a marketplace, open air kind of realism in contrast to the "realism of eavesdropping and peeping which reached its climax in the nineteenth century." (106)[20]

Valuable as these suggestions may prove to be, it should be stressed that Bakhtin's approach, as much as Kayser's, suffers from exaggeration and limitation. Whereas Kayser is invariably not amused by the grotesque, Bakhtin has great difficulty checking his risibility, so that the idea of the grotesque seems often to contain for him the principles of all comic art. In particular, he espouses a myth of the fall of the grotesque from its pristine comic splendour in the work of Rabelais that makes it difficult for him to perceive merit in later grotesque art (in this he is reminiscent, oddly enough, of another major Victorian writer on the grotesque, of John Ruskin). Romantic humour, and the Romantic grotesque, for instance, are given inadequate, schematic attention: "no grotesque, even the most timid, is conceivable in the atmosphere of absolute seriousness. But laughter was cut down to cold humour, irony, sarcasm. It ceased to be a joyful and triumphant hilarity." (30)

Yet "a joyful and triumphant hilarity" might well be an appropriate phrase to describe Dickens's early comedy, itself significantly affected by Romanticism. Arnold Kettle's important essay, "Dickens and the Popular Tradition", might in fact be seen as a sketch of Dickens's essential relation to Bakhtin's grotesque tradition.[21] Kettle praises Dickens for "his refusal to be drawn into a way of thinking that sees 'material' and 'spiritual' as opposites"[22] and also recognises Dickens's capacity to fuse heterogenous elements of popular tradition - fairytale, chapbook romance, popular gothic, etc. - into an integrated representation of the industrial society he was faced with. It is worth remembering, too, that Dickens himself regarded his artistic mission as in part a "holding of popular literature through a kind of popular dark age",[23] and that this task would involve the art of grotesque heightening.

However, Kettle's essay, though of considerable theoretical and polemical value, does little to flesh out the bones of the popular tradition upon which Dickens might have drawn. The main purpose of this chapter will be to provide a slightly clearer, ampler sketch of that tradition. All of it has been presented elsewhere in some degree of detail; some of it has been presented elsewhere in a great degree of detail; but it has perhaps not been brought together all that frequently in an attempt to focus upon Dickens's relation to the tradition of the grotesque.

———

The first thing to stress is that such a tradition, if it exists, should be conceived of as European in scope and not as something sharply delimited by national boundaries. Dickens's reputation as a specifically English writer has tended to obscure his extensive relations with European culture and even perhaps, to limit appreciation of his stature; whilst it is possible to construct a purely English tradition of the grotesque (and Arieh Sachs and Christian Thomsen have done it[24]), to think of Dickens in relation to the grotesque is almost inevitably to stray freely and frequently across national boundaries ("[es] wäre eine rein nationalliterarisch ausgerichtete Darbietungsweise bei kaum einem Untersuchungsgegenstand weniger angebracht als beim Grotesken" warns Thomsen).[25]

Secondly, it is useful to keep in mind an outline of the history of popular culture in the nineteenth century - of how, following the Romantics' discovery and enthusiastic championing of a tradition of popular culture (so that the very concepts associated with it have their origin in this period) the mid-nineteenth century saw a reaction, in Britain and elsewhere, in the name of middle-class propriety and a 'raising of standards'. Peter Burke's *Popular Culture in Early Modern Europe* comments on this trend ("I should like to launch the phrase 'the reform of popular culture' to describe the systematic attempt by some of the educated (henceforth described as 'the reformees' or 'the godly') to change the attitudes and values of the rest of the population, or as the Victorians used to say, to 'improve them'"[26]) and labels it 'the petty-bourgeois ethic';[27] it is important to see how Dickens is one of the most significant figures in that century to define himself in opposition to it.

These points established, it would be convenient to divide Dickens's debt to the grotesque popular tradition into three areas which, despite considerable overlapping, can be considered separately: 1) his relation to the tradition of popular theatre (the *commedia dell'arte* and pantomime in particular, but also the puppet theatre), 2) his relation to the tradition of visual satire, and 3) - mediate rather than direct in its contact with popular sources - his relation to literary tradition (in particular German romanticism and Gothic fiction).

"Their origins are ancient, and they will live for ever", writes Duchartre of the characters of the *commedia dell'arte*, lamenting that "all forms of popular art have, as a general thing, been regarded by men of letters and historians as unimportant and beneath their notice".[28] The reason for their longevity is perhaps that they represent types rather than individuals - and it is to these types that Dickens's characters are profoundly indebted. "The ancestor of Pantaloon, and his son Harpagon, is Pappus, the lecherous old miser of the *Atellanae*"[29] - Arthur Gride, of course, yet he originates in Atella, between Naples and Capua. There were fixed masks - Maccus the fool, Bucco the glutton or braggart, Pappus the old man, Dossensus the swindler and clever hunchback, Manducus "who was represented as constantly eating or champing his jaws in a grotesque manner"[30] (Mrs. Brown). The masks originated in the impersonation of animals ("the fact that so many choruses of fifth-century Attic comedy were disguised as animals implies that the animal-masquerade lies at the very basis of Old Comedy"[31]) - and here too, the ultimate origins of Dickens's habitual comparisons of human and animal appearance and behaviour may lie. At any rate, to draw such parallels is by no means original, as an anonymous, imperialistic reviewer (comparing the British and Roman Empires) writing in 1891 in the *Quarterly Review* attests:

> Plautus popularized, vulgarized, if you like, the sentimental comedy of Greece; and he became the national dramatist of Rome, and the father of the modern drama, if any one individual can

claim to have originated it. Charles Dickens popularised, many will have it vulgarized, the English novel; but he vulgarized it in such sort that he is the undisputed favourite of the English Race all over the globe. And it is in the writings of Dickens that we find the best parallels to the *importunae uxores* ... When Samuel Weller is assisting Mr. Winkle to elope with his beloved Arabella, Dickens is unconsciously treading in the beaten track of the Latin comedy. When he makes Sam Weller rescue Mr. Pickwick from the pound, he is also, without knowing it, narrating over again the rescue of Menaechmus of Epidaurus by Messenio. The promptness of Mr. Weller's action, and his exultation in his own success, are both reflected in the conduct and words of Messenio.[32]

The *commedia dell'arte*, descendant of the old *fabulae Atellanae* and the new comedy, was brought to England as the pantomime. According to John Weaver, an early eighteenth century dancing master, "the first entertainment that appeared on the English stage, where the representation and story were carried on by dancing, action and motion only, was performed in grotesque characters, after the manner of the modern Italians, such as Harlequin, Scaramouche, etc."[33] According to Frances Barasch, "'grotesques' became the term for the characters of the *commedia dell'arte* in England";[34] gradually they and their plots, their gestures, their acrobatic tricks became absorbed into the native pantomime. A fairy-tale was grafted on to a harlequinade - they were linked by a transformation scene, in which the fairy godmother turned the fairy characters into the 'grotesques' of the *commedia dell'arte* - and gradually swallowed up its parent as the modern pantomime evolved.

Everywhere what was praised in early nineteenth century pantomime was the mixed art - comic, serious, playful, monstrous - of the grotesque. An English speciality, the clown, became established amongst the stock characters, with Joseph Grimaldi its paramound exponent. Contemporary witnesses declared him the quintessence of the grotesque: Leigh Hunt wrote in 1817 of the way in which "the grotesque mimicry of Mr. Grimaldi has its proper force; and the bullies and coxcombs who he occasionally imitates come in one respect nearer to the truth than in the best dialogue".[35] Another commentator

9

describes a mingling of laughter and tears: "When he sang 'An Oyster Crossed in Love', such touches of real pathos trembled through its grotesqueness as he sat in front of the footlights between a cod's head and a huge oyster that opened and shut its shell in time to the music, that all the children were in tears."[36] And Thackeray, echoing Dickens in his appropriation of the pantomime as a metaphor for life itself, describes the Hanoverian court as a grotesque amalgam of contradictory spectacles: "it is grave, it is sad; its theme most curious for moral and political speculation; it is monstrous, grotesque, laughable, with its prodigious littleness, etiquette, ceremonials, sham moralities; it is as serious as a sermon, and as absurd and outrageous as Punch's puppet-show".[37]

Axton's *Circle of Fire* is the crucial study of Dickens's indebtedness to pantomime, a book that has not, perhaps, received the attention it deserves. His suggestion that Dickens's famous 'animistic' sense of matter, noted long ago by Dorothy van Ghent,[38] might have its origin in pantomime, where "properties commonly played upon grotesque incongruities in scale or context, and comic animism was a favourite device"[39] (Harlequin's wand, for instance, was used "to animate innocent furnishings, chairs, wine casks, and decorative ornaments to torment and perplex Columbine's pursuers"[40]) will be explored later. Axton focusses upon an early occasional essay, "The Pantomime of Life", where Dickens develops the topos of life as a piece of grotesque theatre, as a representative key to Dickens's work as a whole, in which "the characters are stereotypes borrowed from the playhouse: elderly lechers and gormandizers in the mould of Pantaloon; swaggering military types like Grimaldi's hussar; slightly tarnished ladies patterned after Columbine; and palpably extravagant frauds in the broad, gestic manner of pantomime clowns".[41] He takes the central aspect of Dickens's art to be the grotesque ("if this welter of forms may be said to have any governing spirit, however, it was that of grotesquerie, considered not only in the figurative sense associated with "bizarre" - that is, extravagant, fantastic, caricatural, or capricious - but as a mode or structure with its own distinguishing elements" (28)) and offers an interesting account of its strategic purpose: "Dickens's ultimate intention was not, I believe, to mediate any existential or metaphysical alienation so much as it was to revivify his readers' sensibilities, to awaken a sense of the liveliness and interest of the familiar world. However that may be, the novel [*Pickwick Papers*] remains pleasantly subversive in the way that theatrical burlesque was subversive: it indicates the presence of the discrepant, incongruous and ambivalent, even sinister." (83)

Thus, though his intentionalism may be a bit crude, Axton seems to echo Bakhtin in his sense of the way in which grotesque art may have political significance, particularly since he seems also to be aware of the Russian formalist concept of *ostranenie*, that 'making strange' of the familiar world which may serve to renew and radicalise automatic or stereotyped perception of reality (and Dickens's continued championing of the pantomime vision of the world takes on added significance in the post-Reform Bill Era, when, according to Leigh Hunt, "Pantomimes seem to have become partakers of the serious spirit of the age, to be waiting for the settlement of certain great questions and heavy national accounts, to know when they are to laugh and be merry again."[42]) If what Axton writes about Dickens and pantomime can be taken seriously, one begins to see Dickens rather differently, perhaps, as a writer comparable to Gogol, a link between Romantic irony and modernism, with consequences even for his placing and stature.

However this may be, before leaving Dickens and the tradition of popular theatre it may be useful to mention briefly the impact of the puppet theatre, and especially of the Punch-and-Judy show, upon his mind and art. Again Punch is a figure of ancient pedigree, and again his fundamentally mixed appeal, compounded of attraction and repulsion, may have to do with the stern prohibition of popular preferences: "the old gods, outlawed by the conversions of the West, went underground and survived in such characters as the Devil; the Church accorded them the recognition of enmity. Seen through Christian eyes the anarchy of paganism appeared as the grotesque, and as such it is perpetuated in the gargoyles of cathedral gutters and the medieval drama. Perhaps Punch is such a perpetuation of the pagan world; Doctor Johnson asserted that he was the descendant of the Vice of the morality plays, who is in turn a descendant of the devil."[43]

As a *commedia dell'arte* figure, Punch flourished at the San Carlino theatre in Naples from the middle of the eighteenth century until the last quarter of the nineteenth; and there Dickens went to see and celebrate him, as *Pictures from Italy*

11

records, in a passage that exhibits his characteristically Bakhtinian understanding of the meaning of
realism in art: "... for astonishing truth and
spirit in seizing and embodying the real life about
it, the shabby little San Carlino Theatre - the
rickety house one storey high, with a staring picture
outside: down among the drums and trumpets, and the
tumblers, and the lady conjurer - is without a rival
anywhere" (PI, 423). The Punch and Judy show came
to England at the end of the 18th century, brought
by a man called Piccini - Mayhew was to interview a
street puppeteer who had bought out his stock-in-
trade. Thus, as Steed puts it, "the memory of the
medieval and early Renaissance drama lingered among
the most illiterate and despised section of the
showfolk until the time when the fairs declined and
were lost amid the grimy wilderness of Victorian
industrialism".[44] And Dickens's indebtedness to
this "whispering gallery in which linger the voices
of centuries of popular entertainment" is plain -
not only in the countless references to Punch but
in the habit of perceiving characters as wooden
automata impelled by forces outside their control.
    Grimaldi was called the "Hogarth of action"[45] -
sufficient reason, perhaps, for linking the pantomime quite closely with the next major source of
influence on Dickens's grotesque art, that of visual
satire. R.H. Horne made the point long ago, in a
frequently quoted passage: "Anyone who would
rightly ... estimate the genius of Mr. Dickens,
should first read his works fairly through, and
then read the Essays by Charles Lamb and by Hazlitt,
on the genius of Hogarth -"[46] to which one might add
that some further consideration of Hogarth's place
within the European tradition of grotesque art might
be useful as a corrective to Hogarth's own classicizing aesthetics, for as Antal claims, "even in his
most realistic works - the cycles - he employed
means to bring out the unusual, fantastic, grotesque
potentialities in human figures as well as in
inanimate objects."[47]
    Yet Dickens's relationships with visual
grotesques begin, perhaps, in a more distant past.
"Loathsomely contorted grotesques disport on the
Perp W Porch above and below an image-niche", writes
John Newman in the West Kent and Weald volume of the
Buildings of England series,[48] describing Chalk
Church near Gravesend; it was a favourite landmark
for Dickens - he spent his honeymoon there, and,
according to Forster, the Guermantes way from Gads
Hill Place was "to walk through the marshes to

Gravesend, return by Chalk Church, and stop always
to have a greeting with a comical old monk who for
some incomprehensible reason sits carved in stone,
cross-legged with a jovial pot, over the porch of
that sacred edifice".[49] Interestingly, Hogarth had
also passed that way during his 'peregrination'
through Kent, and may have used one of the carvings
as the basis of a design that accompanies an account
of his travels. "It is possible," writes Charles
Mitchell, "that the memory of a bodyless monster
carved over the west door of Chalk Church, which he
passed on the road to Rochester, went into the
crucible of his invention, as it was later to
fascinate Dickens."[50]

That figure above the niche is a 'nobody', a
favourite *jeu d'esprit* of medieval grotesque
sculpture, with colleagues all over Europe, as Ronald
Sheridan and Anne Ross (among others) suggest;[51] and
he may serve to introduce a whole gallery of
Dickensian motifs drawn from visual sources.
Whether he began life as a Celtic magic head, or
whether (to quote Beckett) in the beginning was the
pun, a tradition of verbal satire exploiting the
ambiguity of the concept quickly developed, as far
back as Homer's *Odyssey*, where Ulysses gives his
name to Polyphemus as 'nobody'. Joke medieval
prayers to the subversive St. Nemo are lovingly
recorded by Mikhail Bakhtin;[52] Renaissance satires
involving 'nobody' and 'somebody' (with 'nobody' a
constant, convenient scapegoat) are exhaustively
documented by Charles Mitchell and Gerta Calmann.[53]
This is the tradition, revitalised by Hogarth and
Cruikshank,[54] within which one can situate Dickens's
extensive play with the idea of 'nobody' - Captain
Nemo in *Bleak House* is one example, of course, but
above all there is the 'Nobody's Fault' theme of
Little Dorrit where, just as in popular tradition,
'nobody' is the abstract fiction upon whom all the
ills of society are blamed.[55]

But there are many other areas of specific
overlap between Dickensian themes and the subjects
of visual satire. Holbein's *Dance of Death* is a
major example, ubiquitously present in Dickens's
work in an ironic modern version which stresses the
superior ghastly grotesquerie of death in the nineteenth century city.[56] The January and May theme,
the grotesque juxtaposition of the old lecher and
the young wife, with its long tradition (from
Chaucer to Lorca) in European culture, enjoys a
simultaneous vitality in Dickens's early work
(*Nicholas Nickleby* in particular) and the caricatures

13

of Rowlandson. Or there is Gillray's John Bull, resurfacing in *Barnaby Rudge* as John Willet, the landlord of the Maypole, whose porch is itself "quaintly and grotesquely carved"; or figures like Mr. Bumble the beadle and Mr. Fang the magistrate, beloved of English caricature from Hogarth to Dickens; or the powerful visual counterparts, in Goya and elsewhere, of those grisly ladies like Mrs. Skewton and Lady Tippins, who dress up for the bridal suite 'till death do us part'.[57]

A second and strangely neglected aspect of Dickens's relation to grotesque visual art is the significance he gives, along with visual satirists, to human physiognomy as an index of character. "I hold phrenology, within certain limitations, to be true; I am much of the same mind as to the subtle expressions of the hand; I hold physiognomy to be infallible; though all these sciences demand rare qualities in the student," declares the Uncommercial Traveller (*UT*, 333); and in "Hunted Down" the narrator assures us that "there is nothing truer than physiognomy, taken in connexion with manner." (*RP*, 667) These passages make it plausible to argue a relation between the standard descriptions of appearance that accompany the introduction of each character in Dickens's novels and the 'science' of physiognomy as practised by visual satirists. Hogarth is again a pivotal figure, Antal suggesting that "in the 1770's and 1780's the physiognomic studies Hogarth had largely helped to promote, became the most topical theme for theory and art alike, and under Hogarth's auspices it was to a large extent in Germany, with its sensitive intellectual climate, that the battle of physiognomy was fought out."[58]

But again, physiognomy is of ancient origin, resting as it does on that perception of formal similarities between human and animal features (and apportioning moral qualities according to an emblematic taxonomy of species) that also informed early caricature and mime. Again too it surfaces with renewed vitality in the mannerist phase of the Renaissance, above all in Leonardo's grotesque heads, the source, according to writers like Gombrich and Antal, of countless derivations (among them Hogarth's 'Chorus of Singers').[59] All that the Romantic era did, in the person of Lavater, was to systematise physiognomy according to new scientific principles, making it available for instruction and education (so that, as Draper Hill informs us, "we are safe in supposing that Gillray was trained to

classify forms in terms of a personality spectrum"[60])
and to confer upon its practitioners a new and
radical moral significance. Physiognomy was a means
of unmasking hypocrisy and deceit, revealing the
truth about someone's moral nature; so that Lavater
wrote menacingly of its powers ("let the Genius of
Physiognomy awake and exert its power, and we shall
see those hypocritical tyrants, those grovelling
misers, those epicures, those cheats who under the
mask of Religion are its reproach, branded with
deserved infamy"[61]) and his disciple, Mrs. Wilfer in
Our Mutual Friend, imagines herself equipped to unveil the criminality inscribed in Mrs. Boffin's
countenance (*OMF*, 113, 207, 312, etc.).

The supposed resemblance between human faces
and animal heads - in physiognomical thought, people
endowed with particular physiognomies are imagined
to have the slyness of a fox, the servility of a dog,
the ferocity of a tiger, etc. - finds its counterpart in Dickens's regular habit, already commented
upon, of developing animal analogies as indices of
moral natures (in *Oliver Twist*, for instance, Fagin
is lynx-eyed, Mrs. Sowerberry of a vixenish countenance, and Monks like a vampire in appearance).
And one may speculate whether the caricaturist's art
of grotesque exaggeration and underlining to produce
these analogies had any direct influence on Dickens,
when as a young man working as a reporter in the
House of Commons, he witnessed with the passing of
the Reform Bill of 1832 the dying throes of the
great age of English caricature. Constant references
throughout Dickens's work to the sculptural qualities of the human head (in *Sketches by Boz*, "A
Parliamentary Sketch" describes an MP with "the
appearance of a figure in a hairdresser's window, if
his countenance possessed the thought which is
communicated to those waxen caricatures of the human
face divine" (*SB*, 154); in *Edwin Drood*, Mr.
Grewgious is described as bearing "certain notches
in his forehead, which looked as though Nature had
been about to touch them into sensibility or refine-
ment, when she had impatiently thrown away the
chisel, and said: 'I really cannot be worried to
finish off this man: let him go as he is'" (*ED*,84))
suggest some acquaintance with the caricaturist's
practice of working from a wax model or "charge" of
his victim's head; Daumier's are the most striking
to have survived.[62] At any rate, Dickens's
characterizations may surely be approached as a
means of giving his figures that degree of visual
definition and memorability achieved by the great

caricaturists of the preceding age, or (to quote John Dixon Hunt) "of our 'picking them out' of the crowd, like the Whig Candidates in Hogarth's *Election Entertainment*".[63]

We may conclude this section on Dickens the visual satirist by considering very briefly the still-repeated charge that Dickens was a caricaturist, to which there is surely only one reply: he was indeed, and a very great one at that. Reaction against caricature set in at about the same time as reaction against the grotesque, a writer of 1796 marking perhaps the origins of this change of taste ("the taste of the day leans entirely to caricature. We have lost our relish for the simple beauties of nature ... We are no longer satisfied with propriety and neatness, we must have something grotesque and disproportioned, cumbrous with ornament and gigantic in its dimensions"[64]), and a writer of 1874, damning the feeble 'decadent' caricaturist HB with faint praise, signalling the firm entrenchment of Victorian attitudes and assumptions about caricature: "HB's sketches are not exaggerated. They are simply faithful renderings of the men with whom our own recollections of the last thirty years have made us familiar."[65] Living in such a period. his own public attitudes towards caricature tainted, perhaps, by such a climate of opinion,[66] Dickens found this aspect of his art under frequent attack from the exponents of 'classic' realism.

Though Dickens criticism is still not free of such prejudices, twentieth-century taste has shifted once more. Draper Hill comments acutely on how the Mannerist vogue of caricature represents a reaction amounting almost to boredom with the harmonious proportions of Renaissance figures ("once the representation of the human form no longer presented a challenge, artists began to experiment with distortion"[67]), and Gombrich clearly understands caricature as an expression of psychic health, the instinct for free, unrepressed play that has its ideological significance too: "the license given to humorous art, the freedom from restraint allowed the masters of grotesque satire to experiment with physiognomies to a degree quite impossible for the serious artist."[68] Earlier in the century Eduard Fuchs, compiler of a vast survey of the history of caricature, introduces his work with the promise of a carnival world from which everyday logic is banished:

Es ist ein gar wunderseltsames Reich, in das

wir den Leser einführen wollen. Die Begriffe
scheinen darin förmlich auf den Kopf gestellt,
Die Gesetze, nach denen sich sonst alles bewegt
und handelt, haben hier keine Gültigkeit.
Tiergestalt mischt sich mit Menschengestalt,
das Leben mit dem Unorganischen. Technische
Vorrichtungen erscheinen als Glieder des
menschlichen Körpers, eine Nase wird zur Flute,
ein Baumast zum unheimlichen langen Arm und ein
ganzer Mensch zum mächtigen Suppentopf.[69]

Dickens, in whose work such metamorphoses are
familiar and who thought it his "infirmity to fancy
or perceive relations in things which are not
apparent generally",[70] may perhaps be seen as one of
the most important of the nineteenth century artists
who keep the tradition of caricature alive.

In turning to the third area of relationship
between Dickens and the grotesque, his relation to
literary tradition, it is necessary to emphasise
that popular culture will appear in this section in
a rather less foregrounded way than hitherto. No
attempt will be made here to link Dickens to what
Peter Burke calls the 'chap-book culture' or to the
tradition of fairy stories (this latter task already
magisterially performed by Michael Kotzin and Harry
Stone[71]); instead the major focus will be on
Dickens's relationship to German romanticism and
Gothic fiction - both areas where popular elements
play a not considerable but hardly dominant role.
Part of the purpose in choosing this focus is to
effect an eventual return to the theoretical con-
siderations with which this chapter opened.

It is hardly contentious to claim that German
romanticism is the original source of the modern
revaluation of the grotesque. In this period,
writes Frances Barasch, "the grotesque would be
shown as an inherent taste and a compelling need of
mankind ... Wieland's analysis emphasized the
psychological effect of the grotesque on the
perceiver";[72] and Wieland is also revered by
Champfleury as the originator of the renewed taste
for caricature ("le doux philosophe Wieland eût
l'idée que l'art antique n'était pas seulement celui
qui prêchait Winckelmann, et que les anciens avaient
connu la caricature"[73]). His influence has been
discernible ever since - in Friedrich Schlegel's
claim that the grotesque "is the most ancient form
of fantasy";[74] in Thomas Wright's belief that the
grotesque was an essential human need;[75] and still
in Kayser's work, where the emphasis on the psych-

ological impact of the grotesque is paramount.[76]

The German Romantic interest in the grotesque is closely connected with philosophical idealism, and therefore antipathetic to any materialist approach to real phenomena. Friedrich Schlegel condemned the English realist novelists of the eighteenth century, including even Fielding, for their prosaic acceptance of the material world;[77] he reserved his enthusiasm for the grotesque artists Swift and Sterne, and their European disciples, Diderot in *Jacques le Fataliste*, and above all Jean Paul, whose "Grotesken and Bekenntnisse noch die einzigen romantischen Erzeugnisse unsers unromantischen Zeitalters sind."[78] The tradition to which German Romantic writing wished to align itself resembles Bakhtin's tradition of 'grotesque realism' - as Wellek remarks, "Hoffmann in his fairy tales seems ... to have learned from Gozzi and the tradition of the *commedia dell'arte*."[79] The work of these artists strives to manifest the imagination's freedom from the constraints of material reality ("there is nothing so fanciful, verbally inventive, and absurdly grotesque as some of Brentano's fairy tales."[80])

At the same time the really crucial innovation of the German Romantics was a focussing of the idealising, transcendentalising power of the imagination upon the here and now of everyday reality. Novalis announced his intention of 'making strange' the familiar world: "Indem ich dem Gemeinen einen hohen Sinn, dem Gewöhnlichen ein geheimnisvolles Ansehn, dem Bekannten die Würde des Unbekannten, dem Endlichen einen unendlichen Schein gebe, so romantisiere ich es."[81] The Romantics discovered the aesthetics of ugliness - how beauty could be constructed, paradoxically, from the most intractible materials, including, most importantly, the unpleasant but fantastic realities of a new urban and incipiently industrial society. They discovered the city as a fit subject for imaginative treatment, according to Marianne Thalmann, and explored how the artist's powers of heightening and 'romanticising' might create urban phantasmagorias capable of outdistancing traditional representations of the marvellous and supernatural ("... es hier nicht um die Wunder des Übernatürlichen geht, sondern um die Wunder der gewöhnlichen Wirklichkeit in einer grossen Stadt").[82]

The operation of such grotesque imaginative vision of the world involved a special kind of ironic consciousness (what came to be known as

18

'romantic irony') of the paradoxicality and
incongruity it implies. According to Wellek, it
was Schlegel who introduced the term 'irony' into
modern literature with far-reaching consequences
for art and criticism; for Schlegel himself it
meant "an insight into the ... nothingness of
aesthetic illusion."[83] Such an insight depended on
a sense of the teasing interplay of reality and
illusion, perpetually generating paradox and logical
contradiction, such as that which Novalis possessed:
"nothing is more romantic than what we usually call
the world and fate. We live in a colossal novel."[84]
Wellek goes on to explore how such an ironic
consciousness generated the striking 'modernity' of
much German Romantic writing: "today it is
frequently forgotten that devices considered
strikingly modern were common among the German
Romantics: the deliberate breaking of illusion,
the interference of the author, the manipulation of
the conventions of the novel or the play."[85]

This book will attempt to show some similarities between these theories and the role of the
grotesque in Dickens's novels, particularly in
establishing ironic perspectives on the 'realities'
they record. But it is not easy to establish any
direct connections between Dickens and German
Romanticism. Opinions on the subject vary between
those who are skeptical about Dickens's capacity to
absorb such influences[86] and those who, like Una
Pope-Hennessy, have no doubts that

> ... there is something distinctively German
> about his excursions into the world of fantasy.
> He had certainly read Hoffman's *Tales*, and *The
> Golden Pot* in particular, for we may notice
> that the knocker in *A Christmas Carol* which
> changes into Marley's dead-alive face, and yet
> remains a knocker, has its counterpart in this
> tale. His friend Carlyle had translated some
> of the *Tales* and was for ever talking to anyone
> who would listen, of Germany and German
> literature.[87]

Though this may be rather on the rash side,
there are certainly passages in Dickens's work that
indicate a general indebtedness to German romantic
writers or their imitators. This passage from a
Christmas Story of 1850, describing childhood
reading, is probably autobiographical, and certainly
ironical:

Legion is the name of the German castles, where
we sit up alone to wait for the Spectre - where
we are shown into a room, made comparatively
cheerful for our reception - where we glance
round at the shadows, thrown on the blank walls
by the crackling fire - where we feel very
lonely when the village innkeeper and his
pretty daughter have retired, after laying down
a fresh store of wood upon the hearth, and
setting forth on the small table such supper-
cheer as a cold roast capon, bread, grapes, and
a flask of old Rhine wine - where the reverb-
erating doors close on their retreat, one after
another, like so many peals of sudden thunder -
and where, about the small hours of the night,
we come into the knowledge of diverse supernatural mysteries. Legion is the name of the
haunted German students, in whose society we
draw yet nearer to the fire, while the school-
boy in the corner opens his eyes wide and
round, and flies off the footstool he has
chosen for his seat, when the door accidentally
blows open (*CS*, "A Christmas Tree", 17).

An even more interesting discussion of German
Romantic themes and conventions occurs in a review
of Catherine Crowe's *The Night Side of Nature* (a
compilation of ghost stories) published in the
Examiner in February 1848, where Dickens follows
Poe in claiming "that terror is not of Germany, but
of the soul.":[88]

And it may be fairly urged that this influence
of habit and education on kind of spirit that
is popular in this place, or in that, is
hardly taken into fair consideration by Mrs.
Crowe, with reference to the general probabil-
ities. For example, here is the Doppelgänger,
or Double, or Fetch, of Germany. This
Doppelgänger, it appears, is so common among
learned professors and studious men in Germany,
that they have no need of the Kilmarnock
Weaver's prayer for grace to see themselves as
others see them, but enjoy that privilege
commonly. Here is one good man who sees himself knock at his own door, take a tangible
tallow candle from his own maid, and go upstairs to his own bed: he himself looking on,
very much disconcerted from over the way. But
how does it happen that one little spot of
earth is famous for these particular occurr-

ences? If there is no immediate contagion of
the imagination, and no influence of education,
in the case, why not more Doubles, in England,
France, India, Sarawak? It certainly is
difficult to believe that spirits, like wines,
are of so peculiar a growth as to become
indigenous to certain patches of soil, and
that the Doppelgänger and the Hockheimer
necessarily flourish together.[89]

Here the ironic rhetoric certainly has something in common with Schlegel's insights, for it
would be Dickens's purpose in his works to show the
teeming presence of such phenomena as doubles from
ground from which they had supposedly been
exorcised: the great industrial cities of Victorian
England.[90] A passage in *Pickwick Papers*, reflecting
on how close at hand the marvellous and monstrous
may be ("Talk of your German universities ... Pooh,
pooh! there's romance enough at home without going
half a mile for it; only people never think of it"
- *PP*, XXI, 280) suggests how early Dickens adopted
this perception, and how constantly he refined it.
But although it may be hard to pin down
Dickens's connection with the German grotesque in
any very precise way, it is a simple task to
identify within Dickens's milieu and social connection very direct and significant links. There was a
vogue of German literature during Dickens's youth,
disseminated in a climate where Romanticism
dominated taste through figures like Scott, whose
important if hostile essay of 1827 on Hoffmann, *On
the Supernatural in Fiction*, displays unmistakeable
command of the essential terminology:

> In fact, the grotesque in his compositions
> partly resembles the arabesque in painting,
> in which is introduced the most strange and
> complicated monsters, resembling centaurs,
> griffins, sphinxes, chimeras, rocs, and all
> other creatures of romantic imagination,
> dazzling the beholder, as it were, by all
> the unbounded fertility of the author's
> imagination, and sating it by the rich
> contrast of all the varieties of shape and
> colouring, while there is in reality nothing
> to satisfy the understanding or reform the
> judgement.[91]

After Scott, Carlyle took up the watch on Germany,
and his awareness of the significance of the

grotesque in the Romantic era was tempered with no
such coolness, on his enthusiastic celebration of
Tieck's *Der Gestiefelte Kater* attests:

> Among these Volksmährchen, one of the most
> prominent, is *Der gestiefelte Kater*, a
> dramatised version of *Puss in Boots*; under
> the grotesque masque of which, he had laughed
> with his whole heart, in a fine Aristophanic
> vein, at the actual expense of literature; and
> without mingling his satire with personalities,
> or any other false ingredient, had rained like
> a quiet shower of volcanic ashes on the cant of
> Illumination, the cant of Sensibility, the
> cant of Criticism, and the many other cants of
> that shallow time, till the gumflower products
> of the poetic garden hung draggled and black
> under their unkindly coating. In another
> country, at another day, the drama of *Puss in
> Boots* may justly be supposed to appear with
> enfeebled influences; yet even to a stranger
> there is not wanting a feast of broad joyous
> humour in this strange phantasmagoria, where
> pit and stage, and man and animal, and Earth
> and air, are jumbled in confusion worse
> confounded, and the copious, kind, ruddy light
> of true mirth overshines and warms the
> whole.[92]

Two points of interest surface here, both of
them stemming ultimately from Carlyle's German
mentor, Jean Paul.[93] The first concerns wit and
language: for Carlyle, all language was metaphoric
in origin, depending upon the perception of likenesses; and wit (like the word 'gumflower' here) a
particularly prestigious instance of language in
its purest form, for it creates fresh likenesses
out of unlike things, its best flashes a manifestation (and here the model is Novalis) of the
infinite in the finite. We may return to Dickens's
central confession to Bulwer Lytton ("I think it is
my infirmity to fancy or perceive relations in
things which are not apparent generally") and
speculate whether any mutual consciousness of
Carlyle's German-inspired theory of wit and
language played through it.

But of course the more obvious point concerns
grotesque humour itself. It is apparent that
Carlyle, unlike Bakhtin, sees no absence of
"joyful and triumphant hilarity" in romantic irony,
and in his third essay on Jean Paul of 1830, divides

Richter's humour into the idyllic and the grotesque, giving the palm to the latter.[94] Humour at its best, according to Richter and Carlyle, contrasts the finite with the infinite in such a manner that the finite is annihilated, creating thereby a kind of "inverse sublimity". If we may follow Wellek, and agree that Carlyle "determined in many ways the thought and the art of the English nineteenth century",[95] it is instructive indeed to find John Forster (no champion of the grotesque), summing up in his biography the quintessential characteristics of its outstanding creative genius ("his leading quality was humour") and leaning upon Carlyle for a definition of what Dickens pre-eminently possessed: "... the property which in its highest aspects Carlyle so subtly described as a sort of inverse sublimity, exalting into our affections what is below us ...".[96]

To turn to Dickens's relations to Gothic Fiction is to record a similar pattern of influence.[97] The taste for the grotesque and the taste for the Gothic were very much intertwined in the late 18th and early 19th centuries, so that for a time at least, as Frances Barasch points out, the word 'grotesque' is used, more or less as a synonym of 'picturesque', to describe the appropriate land-scape setting for the Gothic atmosphere: "By the second half of the century, as interest in Gothic antiquities, ruins, and literature increased, and the English came to identify more closely with their Teutonic origins, appreciation of the Northern landscape school also increased. The word 'grotesque' came to mean pleasing though irregular"[98] (*Nicholas Nickleby* contains an isolated use of the word in this sense when it describes Nicholas and Smike on their way to Portsmouth passing through "... undulations, shapely and uncouth, smooth and rugged, graceful and grotesque" (*NN*, xxii, 276). Moreover, reciprocally as it were, the grotesque figures prominently in Gothic fiction, both as a general atmosphere (a 1786 reviewer of *Vathek* praised the novel for possessing "the sombrous grotesque of Dante"[99]) and as a term of approbation for pleasing effects - *The Mysteries of Udolpho* contains "a rude kind of tent, round which many children and dogs were playing, and the whole formed a picture highly grotesque"[100] and Old Melmoth, dying in the opening pages of *Melmoth the Wanderer*, bears on his face an expression of "grotesque fierceness".[101]

Yet it is the conception of mixed aesthetics,

of an art compounded of opposite and indeed contradictory sensations, that provides the most valuable
link between the Gothic grotesque and the Dickensian
counterpart. The idea of the "mixed charm of
repulsion and attraction" (Mario Praz's phrase,
echoing Ippolito Pindemonte's "orror bello che
attristando piace"[102]) finds a very direct echo in
Dickens's writing; as Philip Collins has demonstrated,
the phrase "the attraction of repulsion" was a
favourite of his, and he believed in its psychological truth, as a passage on public hanging attests:
"The attraction of repulsion being as much a law of
our moral nature, as gravitation is in the structure
of the visible world..."[103] In particular (again
according to Collins[104]) Dickens felt this mixture
of sensations in relation to the experience of
London - the centre of crimes and horrors, monstrosities and delights that he was fond of polemically
placing (especially in his early work) much above
those to be encountered in Gothic fiction. "The
Bloomsbury Christening" of April 1834, for instance,
describes London in the rain, so that "Cabs whisked
about, with the 'fare' as carefully boxed up behind
two glazed calico curtains as any mysterious picture
in any one of Mrs. Radcliffe's castles ..." (*SB*,
471); "The Old Bailey" of October 1834 (renamed
"Criminal Courts" in the second version of *Sketches
by Boz*) goes one better, placing Gothic horrors
beneath prison realities: "We have a great respect
for Mrs. Fry, but she certainly ought to have
written more romances than Mrs. Radcliffe." (*SB*,
197); and "Mr. Robert Bolton: The Gentleman
Connected with the Press" (one of the Mudfog Papers
of 1837-9) tells a grotesque London murder story in
the pub, of which it is claimed that "The whole
horrible ideality of the Mysteries of Udolpho,
condensed into the pithy effect of a ten-line paragraph, could not possibly have so affected the
narrator's auditory" (*SB*, 685).

Thus we encounter again a very important inter-
section of Dickens's work, where the romantic, the
fantastic or the gothic comes into collision with
the 'real' world of the city to produce the paradoxically mixed and contradictory art of the
grotesque. Yet it should be stressed that in this
respect and others Dickens bears a clear resemblance
to a number of other writers in the 19th century,
whose relationship to the city is explored in Donald
Fanger's brilliant *Dostoevsky and Romantic Realism*.[105]
Oddly enough, too (though Tolstoy's name is not
amongst them) these writers turn out to be amongst

the very greatest nineteenth century novelists -
Balzac, Dickens, Gogol, Dostoevsky - which may
suggest that the term 'classic realism' as a slogan
for the dominant or characteristic style of the
nineteenth century novel may be inappropriate, and
that an equally important tradition of 'fantastic'
or 'romantic' realism, its aesthetic written in the
German Romantic period by Schlegel, Novalis and
others, its influence unmistakeably felt in the
modernist period, must be taken into any serious
account of the history of the novel. What
Baudelaire wrote of Daumier might apply to any of
its protagonists, and certainly to Dickens:

> Feuilletez son oeuvre, et vous verrez défiler
> devant vos yeux, dans sa réalité fantastique
> et saisissante tout ce qu'une grande ville
> contient de vivant monstruosités. Tout ce
> qu'elle renferme de trésors effrayants,
> grotesques, sinistres et bouffons, Daumier
> le connaît.[106]

NOTES

   1. There seems little point in instancing
critics who draw attention to the grotesque in
Dickens, since they are so numerous; a thorough
investigation of how the concept has affected
Dickens criticism might constitute a study of its
own (for some early critical responses to the
grotesque in Dickens see M. Hollington, "Dickens's
Conception of the Grotesque", *The Dickensian LXXVI*
(Summer, 1980), 91-99). But it may be worth
recalling the essential passages in Forster's
biography, in the ninth book, assessing Dickens's
characteristics as a writer. "His leading quality
was Humour", writes Forster, but he goes on to
qualify his praise: "All humour has in it, is
indeed identical with, what ordinary people are apt
to call exaggeration; but there is an excess beyond
the allowable even here, and to "pet" or magnify
out of proper bounds its sense of what is droll, is
to put the merely grotesque in its place." In
Dickens's case, according to Forster, there were
times when "humour was not his servant but his
master: because it reproduced too readily, and
carried too far, the grotesque imaginings to which
great humourists are prone" (John Forster, *The Life
of Charles Dickens*, ed. A.J. Hoppé (London, J.M.
Dent and Co., 1966: 2 vols.), II, 272, 273, 278).
   2. Kayser's book was first published by

Gerhard Stalling Verlag, Oldenburg und Hamburg; the translation is by Ulrich Weisstein, and was first published by Indiana University Press, then reprinted as a McGraw-Hill paperback in 1966. Bakhtin's work was first published in Moscow (Khudozhestvennia Literatura), translated by Hélène Iswolsky, and published by M.I.T. Press. In both cases references cite the paperback edition.

3. *op. cit.*, p. 20 (Kayser's italics).

4. In *The Grotesque: A Study in Meanings* (The Hague, Mouton, 1971).

5. In *Göttingische Gelehrte Anzeigen CCXII* (1958), 95-110.

6. See in particular the Unger reprint edition (New York, 1968), with an excellent introduction by Frances K. Barasch. This edition is cited here throughout.

7. Kayser, *op. cit.*, pp. 21, 27, 103.

8. Bakhtin, *op. cit.*, p. 47.

9. *op. cit.*, p. 188 (Kayser's capitals).

10. In *Apologia ad Guillelmum Sancti - Theoderici Abbatem*; he asks 'quid facit illa ridicula monstruositas, ac formas deformitas?' (what profit is there in that ridiculous monstrosity, a marvellous kind of deformed beauty and beautiful deformity?). For a translation of the whole passage, see *A Medieval Garner*, ed. G.G. Coulton (London, 1910), pp. 71-2; for a discussion of St. Bernard and the grotesque, see Willard Farnham, *The Shakespearean Grotesque* (Oxford, OUP, 1971), pp. 1-5. It is instructive that St. Bernard expresses himself in oxymoron.

11. Spitzer, *op. cit.*, 99: "Those mixed, hybrid forms created out of the ancients' love of play and sense of form (Ovid, who was 'moralised' in the middle ages) were transformed by Christian speculation into demons to wipe the smile off mens' faces, their aim to terrify people - they come up out of the abyss of the misshapen or deformed."

12. *op. cit.*, p. 41.

13. Jurgis Baltrusaitis, *Le Moyen Age Fantastique* (Paris, 1955), p. 1: "a world of fantastic beings with complex and often very remote origins, mingling their bodies and heterogenous characters."

14. Ronald Sheridan and Anne Ross, *Grotesques and Gargoyles: Paganism in the Medieval Church* (Newton Abbot, David and Charles, 1975), pp. 8, 15.

15. Frances Barasch, Introduction to Wright, *op. cit.*, xix. The succeeding page references are to Wright.

16.   Yet Wright perceives that this kind of parody does not imply blasphemy or loss of faith - as Christian commentators often suggested - but that it is in fact kind of *contrapposto* or 'inverse sublimity' (Wright himself perhaps affected by Carlyle and German Romanticism).

17.   Wright also makes the interesting suggestion that the public naming of children with desired animal or other qualities expresses a spirit of caricature: "The Anglo-Saxon love of caricature is shown largely in their proper names, which were mostly significant of personal qualities that parents longed they would possess." (52)

18.   Bakhtin, *op. cit.*, p. 2. All the succeeding page references are to Bakhtin.

19.   In *James Joyce and the Revolution of the Word* (London, MacMillan, 1978), pp. 15ff.

20.   Particularly interesting in relation to Dickens, because of his constant fascination with secrecy and for the possibility of "a good spirit who would take the house-tops off" (*DS*, xlvii, 648) in the manner of Lesage's *Diable Boiteux*. For a discussion of the significance of this topos for narration in 19th century fiction, see Jonathan Arac, *Commissioned Spirits: The Shaping of Social Motion in Dickens, Carlyle, Melville and Hawthorne* (New Brunswick, Rutgers University Press, 1979).

21.   Originally published in *Zeitschrift für Anglistik and Amerikanistik III* (1961), it is reprinted in David Craig, ed., *Marxists on Literature* (Harmondsworth, Penguin, 1975), pp. 214-244.

22.   *Ibid.*, p. 242.

23.   Forster, *op. cit.*, p. 279.

24.   In *The English Grotesque* (Jerusalem, Israel Universities Press, 1969) and *Das Groteske und die Englische Literatur* (Darmstadt, 1977) respectively.

25. Thomsen, *op. cit.*, p. 2: "There is hardly any object of research for which a mode of representation in terms purely of national literatures is less suited than the grotesque."

26.   Peter Burke, *Popular Culture in Early Modern Europe* (London, 1978), p. 207.

27.   *Ibid.*, p. 213.

28.   Duchartre, *The Italian Comedy* (New York, Dover Press, 1966; first published 1929), pp. 18, 25.

29.   *Ibid.*, p. 17.

30.   See George E. Duckworth, *The Nature of Roman Comedy: A Study in Popular Entertainment*

(Princeton, N.J., Princeton University Press, 1952)
pp. 10-12.

31. *Ibid.*, p. 20.

32. Review of Reinhardstettner's *Plautus*,
Quarterly Review 173 (1891), 37-69, quoted in
Duckworth, *op. cit.*, p. 432.

33. Quoted by M. Willson Disher in *Clowns and
Pantomimes* (New York, Blom reprints, 1968; first
published in 1925), p. 229.

34. Barasch, *op. cit.*, p. 81.

35. *The Examiner* 26/1/17, quoted in David
Mayer, *Harlequin in His Element: The English
Pantomime 1806-36* (Cambridge, Mass., Harvard
University Press, 1969), p. 10.

36. Quoted in Gyles Brandreth, *Discovering
Pantomime* (Aylesbury, Shire Press, 1973), p. 7.

37. In *The Four Georges*, pp. 107-8, quoted in
Mayer, *op. cit.*, pp. 14-15.

38. In "The Dickens World: A View from
Todgers", *Sewanee Review LVIII* (1950), 419-43;
reprinted in *The Dickens Critics* ed. George H. Ford
and Lauriat Lane, jr. (Ithaca, N.Y., Cornell
University Press, 1961), pp. 213-232.

39. William F. Axton, *Circle of Fire:
Dickens's Vision and Style and the Popular Victorian
Theatre* (Lexington, Ky., University of Kentucky Press,
1966), p. 19.

40. Mayer, *op. cit.*, p. 30.

41. *Op. cit.*, p. 41 (Axton is writing here
specifically about *Sketches by Boz*). The remaining
page references in this paragraph are to Axton.

42. Writing in *The Tatler* 28/12/31; quoted in
Mayer, *op. cit.*, p. 69.

43. Quoted from Philip John Steed, *Mr. Punch*
(London, 1950), p. 16.

44. *Ibid.*, p. 46.

45. According to Friedrich Antal in *Hogarth
and his Place in European Art* (London, 1962), p.191.

46. Writing in *A New Spirit of the Age*
(London, 1844); quoted in Antal, *op. cit.*, p. 190.

47. Antal, *op. cit.*, p. 128.

48. (Harmondsworth, Penguin Books, 1975), p.
191.

49. Forster, *op. cit.*, II, 215.

50. Charles Mitchell, ed., *Hogarth's
Peregrination* Oxford, Oxford University Press, 1952),
p. xxix.

51. Sheridan and Ross, *op. cit.*, p. 113: "As
with so many other grotesque representations, the
Nobodies are to be found all over Europe. If our
other Celtic analogies are to be maintained it would

not be unreasonable to suppose that there would be a connection here between Celtic worship of the severed head and what could be seen as a sort of 'severed head spirit'."

52. Bakhtin, *op. cit.*, pp. 413-5.

53. Mitchell, *op. cit.*, and Gerta Calmann, "The Picture of Nobody: An Iconographical Study", *Journal of the Wartburg and Courtauld Institutes LX* (1960), 60-104.

54. English caricatures containing a 'Nobody' figure are listed and discussed in Calmann, *op. cit.*, 97-99.

55. cf. also, among many other references, the battered girl in *Sketches by Boz* ("I did it myself - it was nobody's fault - it was an accident"); ("The Hospital Patient", *SB*, 243); "Nobody's Story", the 1853 Christmas Story (*CS*, 61-66); and "Nobody's Son" in *The Lazy Tour of Two Idle Apprentices* (*CS*, 701).

56. See M. Hollington, "Dickens and the Dance of Death", *The Dickensian LXXIV* (May, 1978), 67-75.

57. For John Bull, see Dorothy George ed., *Catalogue of Political and Personal Satires preserved in the Department of Prints and Drawings in the British Museum* vol. IX (London, 1949), xxiii; for the Goya caricature see F.D. Klingender, *Hogarth and English Caricature* (London, 1941), illustration no. 33; for magistrates and beadles by Cruikshank and others see (e.g.) nos. 14598 and 16350 in the British museum catalogue.

58. Antal, *op. cit.*, p. 207.

59. See *ibid.*, p. 130 and Ernst Gombrich, "Leonardo's Grotesque Heads: Prolegomena to their Study", in A. Marazza ed., *Leonardo, Saggi & Richerche* (Rome, 1954), pp. 199-219.

60. In *Mr. Gillray the Satirist* (London, 1965), p. 4.

61. Quoted in José López-Rey, "Goya's Caprichos: Beauty, Reason, and Caricature", in Fred Licht, ed., *Goya in Perspective* (Englewood Cliffs, N.J., Prentice Hall, 1973), p. 117.

62. See Howard P. Vincent, *Daumier and His World*, (Evanston, Ill., Northwestern University Press, 1968), for an account of the techniques of caricature.

63. See John Dixon Hunt, "Dickens and the Tradition of Graphic Satire" in *Encounters: Essays on Literature and the Visual Arts* (London, Studio Vista, 1971), p. 127.

64. Quoted from the *Morning Chronicle* 1/8/1796 in Draper Hill, *op. cit.*, p. 1.

65. Paget, *Paradoxes and Puzzles* (London,

1874), quoted in M.D. George, ed., *Catalogue of Political and Personal Satires Preserved in the Department of Prints and Drawings in the British Museum*, XI, xlv.

66. Dickens in fact wrote disparagingly of Regency caricature in an article on John Leech:

> "It is to be remarked of Mr. Leech that he is the very first English caricaturist (we use the word for want of a better) who has considered beauty as being perfectly compatible with his art .... If we turn back to a collection of the works of Rowlandson or Gillray, we shall find, in spite of the great humour displayed in many of them, that they are rendered wearisome and impleasant by a vast amount." (See "Leech's 'Rising Generation'", *The Examiner* 30/12/1848, quoted in Michael Steig, "Dickens, Hablôt Browne, and the Tradition of English Caricature", *Criticism II* (1969), 219-33).

67. Draper Hill, *op. cit.*, p. 3.
68. See *Art and Illusion* (London, Phaidon Press, 1962), p. 296.
69. Eduard Fuchs, *Die Karikatur der Europäischen Völker vom Altertum bis zur Neuzeit* (Berlin, A. Hofmann, 1901), p. 1.
70. Forster, *op. cit.*, II, 273.
71. Michael C. Kotzin, *Dickens and the Fairy Tale*, (Bowling Green, Ohio, Bowling Green University Popular Press, 1972) and Harry Stone, *Dickens and the Invisible World* (London, Macmillan, 1980).
72. Barasch, *op. cit.*, p. 147.
73. Champfleury, *Histoire de la Caricature antique* (Paris, N.D.) p. x.
74. Quoted from Bakhtin, *op. cit.*, p. 41.
75. See above, p. 3.
76. Christian Thomsen, *Das Groteske im Englischen Roman des Achtzehnten Jahrhunderts* (Darmstadt, Wissenschaftliche Buchgesellschaft, 1974), p. 10, makes this point about Kayser, and also emphasises Kayser's indebtedness to the existentialism of the 1950's.
77. See René Wellek, *A History of Modern Criticism* (New Haven, Yale University Press, 1955-1966: 5 vols.), II, 99. Yet Thomsen has shown in *Das Groteske im Englischen Roman des Achzehnten Jahrhunderts* how important the grotesque is in writers like Fielding and Smollett.

78. Friedrich Schlegel, 'Brief über den Roman'. The similarity of phrasing to Dickens's "the very holding of popular literature through a kind of popular dark age" is noteworthy.

79. See *Confrontations: studies in the intellectual and literary relations between Germany, England and the United States during the nineteenth century* (Princeton, N.J., Princeton University Press, 1965), p. 16.

80. *Ibid.*, p. 16.

81. Quoted from Lilian R. Furst, ed., *European Romanticism: Self-Definitions* (London, Methuen, 1980), p. 3. Her translation reads: "By investing the commonplace with a lofty significance, the ordinary with a mysterious aspect, the familiar with the prestige of the unfamiliar, the finite with the semblance of infinity, thereby I romanticise it."

82. Marianne Thalmann, *Romantiker entdecken die Stadt*, (Munich, 1965), p. 27. "It's not a question here of the marvels of the supernatural, but of the marvels of everyday reality in a large town."

83. See Wellek, *A History of Modern Criticism*, II, 16 and *Confrontations*, 21.

84. Quoted in Wellek, *A History of Modern Criticism*, II, 84.

85. Wellek, *Confrontations*, p. 21.

86. See Kotzin, *op. cit.*, p. 36 for a useful survey of views (Helmut Viebrock is amongst the skeptics).

87. Una Pope-Hennessy, *Charles Dickens* (Harmondsworth, Penguin Books, 1970), p. 337, Originally published in 1945.

88. Poe's Preface to *Tales of Grotesque and Arabesque*, quoted in Kayser, *op. cit.*, p. 76.

89. See Philip Collins, "Dickens on Ghosts: An Uncollected Article", *The Dickensian LIX* (January, 1963), 5-14.

90. See M. Hollington, *Dickens and the Double*. Ph.D. Thesis (Ann Arbor, Mich., University Microfilms, 1967).

91. Quoted from *Sir Walter Scott on Novelists and Fiction*, ed. Ioan Williams (London, RKP, 1968), p. 335.

92. Quoted from 'Tieck' in 'Preface and Introductions to the Book called German Romance', *Critical and Miscellaneous Essays* (London, Chapman and Hall, 1903; 3 volumes), I, 245.

93. The next two paragraphs are indebted in general ways to G.B. Tennyson, *Sartor Called Resartus* (Princeton, N.J. Princeton University Press,

1965) and Michael Goldberg, *Carlyle and Dickens* (Athens, Georgia, University of Georgia Press, 1972). Goldberg's chapter on the Grotesque is one of the indispensable contributions to this subject in relation to Dickens.

94. For a discussion of Richter's theory of comedy in his *Vorschule der Aethetik*, see Kayser, *op. cit.*, pp. 54-6; for Carlyle's essay, see *Critical and Miscellaneous Essays*, ed. cit., II, 1-61.

95. *Confrontations*, p. 81.

96. Forster, *op. cit.*, II, 273.

97. Two general studies of the connection of the gothic and the grotesque (apart from Frances Barasch's indispensable book) can be mentioned: Christian Thomsen's chapter on the subject in *Das Groteske im Englischen Roman des Achtzehnten Jahrhunderts* and Maximilian Novak's "Gothic Fiction and the Grotesque", *Novel XI* (Fall, 1979), 50-67.

98. *The Grotesque: A Study in Meanings*, p. 116.

99. Quoted in Thomsen, *op. cit.*, p. 305.

100. Ann Radcliffe, *The Mysteries of Udolpho*, ed. Bonamy Dobrée (Oxford, Oxford University Press, 1970) p. 40.

101. Charles Maturin, *Melmoth the Wanderer*, ed. Alethea Hayter (Harmondsworth, Middx, Penguin Books, 1977), p. 49.

102. In the introduction to *Three Gothic Novels* ed. Peter Fairclough, (Harmondsworth, Middx, Penguin Books, 1968), p. 16.

103. This passage from Dickens's 1846 letter on public execution to the *Daily News* is quoted from Philip Collins, *Dickens and Crime* (London, Macmillan, 1965; 2nd edition), p. 248.

104. See Philip Collins, "Dickens and London", *The Victorian City: Images and Realities*, eds. H.J. Dyos and Michael Wolff (London, Routledge and Kegan Paul, 1973; 2 vols.), II, 537.

105. *Dostoevsky and Romantic Realism: A Study of Dostoevsky in Relation to Balzac, Dickens and Gogol* was first published by Harvard University Press, Cambridge, Mass., in 1965.

106. Charles Baudelaire, 'Quelques Caricaturistes Français', *Oeuvres Complètes*, ed. Ruff (Paris, du Seuil, 1968), p. 383. Quoted in English in Walter Sorell, *The Other Face: The Mask in the Arts* (London, Thames and Hudson, 1973), p. 207: "Look through his works, and you will see parading before your eyes all that a great city contains of living monstrosities: in all their

fantastic and thrilling reality. There can be no item of the fearful, the grotesque, the sinister or the farcical in its treasury, but Daumier knows it."

Chapter Two

THE ROMANCE OF REAL LIFE:
SKETCHES BY BOZ AND *PICKWICK PAPERS*

> "La vie parisienne est féconde en sujets
> poétiques et merveilleux. Le merveilleux nous
> enveloppe et nous abreuve comme l'atmosphère;
> mais nous ne le voyons pas."
>   Baudelaire, *De l'héroïsme de la vie moderne.*[1]

> "He was but like many others - men, women, and
> children - alive to distant, and dead to near
> things."
>   Gaskell, *North and South.*[2]

"A joyful and triumphant hilarity" - Bakhtin's
phrase is worth retaining for its possibilities of
application to the grotesque in Dickens's early
writing. Yet it should be emphasised straight away
that some critics are unwilling to connect Dickens's
first work, *Sketches by Boz*, with the grotesque at
all, and that the terms in which they make this
exclusion are instructive. "Veracity I take to be
the high merit of these sketches" writes Gissing,
"Dickens has not yet developed his liking for the
grotesquely original; he pictures the commonplace,
with no striving for effect";[3] he seems to imply
that realistic reportage and grotesque heightening
can have no commerce. Recently Duane De Vries has
qualified that view, emphasising how even Dickens's
early parliamentary reporting, entirely 'factual' in
content, contains grotesque touches that shape the
material into fiction, and recalling that even the
mature grotesque cannot be simply disentangled from
the effects of realist writing.[4] Yet perhaps even
this does not go far enough to describe what this
chapter hopes to demonstrate, that the 'inimitable'
interpenetration of the marvellous and the mundane
is the very hallmark of Dickens's characteristic
'romantic realism'.

34

To begin with, it may be useful briefly to invoke the literary milieu in which Dickens began writing in 1833. There is general agreement that in many countries, and especially in England and Germany, the main impetus of Romanticism was spent by the 1830's, but rather less certainty about what happened to the kind of grotesque art it had fostered (Byron's death in 1824 is a favourite marker for the date of demise). Kayser's view is that it suffers a relative eclipse, but Lee Byron Jennings, for one, challenges this ("It will be shown that this secondary phase of the grotesque ... flourishes tenaciously, well into the realistic period, and that it is by no means certain that the post-Romantic nineteenth century contains so little grotesquerie, and that of such an innocuous nature, that the period may be "hastened through" (as Kayser puts it) in a historical treatment of the grotesque."[5]) And J.C. Reid, writing of the immediate post-Romantic period in England, in fact defines this era in terms close to Kayser's definition of the grotesque:

> In the 1820's the Romantic energy peters out in spiritual and imaginative exhaustion, vulgarity creeps in where once refined sensibilities ruled and poetry becomes uneasily betrothed to journalism. Interwoven with all this is the energetic expression of a freakish vision, sometimes merely whimsical or grotesque, yet quite often full of compulsive horror, a cathartic disgust, and a sense of nightmare that are more likely to be appreciated by a generation that has read Kafka and Samuel Beckett than one reared on Arnold Bennett and John Galsworthy.[6]

A number of writers are frequently instanced as representative of the period (besides the writing of Dickens himself, Christian Enzensberger lists works by Lamb, De Quincey, Beddoes, Poe, and Ebenezer Elliot as examples of the grotesque in the 1830's;[7] René Wellek describes Beddoes as the English counterpart of Jean Paul at this time),[8] but the general consensus seems to be that if one figure can be said to create and disseminate the taste for the grotesque in the 1830's it is Thomas Hood.

Hood thought of himself as a grotesque writer - the preface to *Hood's Own* of 1839 (recommended by Dickens in a letter to George Cattermole)[9] makes prominent mention of those "Grotesques and Arabesques

and droll Picturesques that my Good Genius ...
charitably conjures up to divert me from more sombre
realities";[10] and Poe praised Hood's "glowing
grotesquerie, uttered with a rushing *abandon* vastly
heightening its effect."[11] Besides ill health, Hood
suffered from severe financial difficulties that
forced him to live after 1834 in Germany, where he
furthered his acquaintance with German Romantic
writing and in particular with that highly self-
conscious 'romantic irony' that is a feature of his
poems. From there he followed Dickens's career with
warm interest and (after initial revulsion against
Pickwick Papers) enthusiasm, claiming Dickens as a
grotesque writer in (for instance) his review of *Old
Curiosity Shop*, which Dickens prized very highly and
which may (as we shall see) have influenced the
novel in its final version.

Thus the attempt to establish Hood as the most
significant and representative writer of the 1830's
is bound to reflect upon the way in which Dickens's
early work should be approached. At the same time,
it should be made clear that Dickens seems to have
disapproved to some extent, at least, of the
extravagance of Hood's grotesque art, especially in
a passage to Forster describing Hood's Sternian
novel *Tilney Hall* as "the most extraordinary jumble
of impossible extravagance, and especial cleverness
I ever saw"[12] which he later seems to refer to in
the Preface to the first cheap edition of *Old
Curiosity Shop* in 1848 in his insistence that Nell
was intended to be surrounded by "grotesque and wild,
but not impossible, companions." (*OCS*, xii). Hood's
almost compulsive habit of punning to establish
connections between heterogenous, disparate spheres
of experience and reality - Thomas Wainwright,
critic and later poisoner, called him "our new Ovid"
for his powers of metamorphosis, and Douglas Jerrold
commented on his characteristic "commixture of, what
the superficial deem, incongruous elements"[13] - has
its counterpart in the habit of simile quite unmistakeable in Dickens's writing from the outset ("I
think it is my infirmity to fancy or perceive
relations in things which are not apparent
generally"). Yet the degree of transformation may
be differentiated - for Dickens, perhaps, likeness
does not imply identity.

At any rate, it is within these relationships
and differences that an approach to the grotesque in
Sketches by Boz and *Pickwick Papers* may be found.
The brilliant Grimaldian one-liners of that
"specimen of London Life",[14] Sam Weller, whose

introduction in July 1836 marked the beginning of
that enormous fame and success that never deserted
Dickens for the rest of his life, must surely
represent its most characteristic manifestation:

> Here's your servant, sir. Proud o' the title,
> as the living Skellinton said, ven they show'd
> him (*PP*, xiv, 207)
> ... I think he's the victim o' connubiality, as
> Blue Beard's domestic chaplain said, with a
> tear of pity, ven he buried him. (xx, 273)
> Business first, pleasure arterwards, as King
> Richard the Third said ven he stabbed t'other
> king in the Tower, afore he smothered the
> babbies. (xxv, 339)
> There; now we look compact and comfortable, as
> the father said ven he cut his little boy's
> head off, to cure him o' squintin' (xxviii,
> 384)
> (Tony Weller) I'm pretty tough, that's vun
> consolation, as the wery old turkey remarked
> ven the farmer said he was afeerd he should be
> obliged to kill him for the London market
> (xxxiii, 451)
> I only assisted natur' ma'am; as the doctor
> said to the boy's mother, arter he'd bled him
> to death (xlvii, 664)

Deaths, murders and corpses (living or dead)
provide the staple material for a revitalising of
stale everyday clichés, linking them associatively
with incongruous and remote situations. But the
formula and its humorous effects are only the most
striking and successful products of a habit of black
humour, very reminiscent of Hood, prevalent throughout Dickens's earliest writings. In the very first
story he published the central figure is a middle-
aged bachelor who "was not unamiable, but he could,
at any time, have viewed the execution of a dog, or
the assassination of an infant, with the liveliest
satisfaction." ("Mr. Minns and his Cousin", *SB*,
312). He is succeeded a few months later by a more
comprehensive misanthropist who "adored King Herod
for his massacre of innocents" ("The Bloomsbury
Christening", *SB*, 467) and who speaks at moments of
violent feeling "in a voice like Desdemona with the
pillow over her mouth" (478). In between the two,
early in 1834, Dickens had published a story about
amateur theatricals in which "every sofa in the
house was more or less damaged by the perseverance
and spirit with which Mr. Sempronius Gattleton, and

Miss Lucina, rehearsed the smothering scene in 'Othello'." ("Mrs. Joseph Porter", 421)

These jokes express the barely suppressed violence of the ambitious, upwardly mobile lower middle classes - clerks, tradesmen and their like - who are the subject of Dickens's early 'tales'. They are observed engaged in their characteristic leisure pursuits - dining at Poplar Walk in 'Mr. Minns and his Cousin' or at Oak Lodge in 'Horatio Sparkins' (their preferred habitat is clearly a Horatian shady bower, in anticipation of Mr. Boffin), amateur theatricals in 'Mrs. Joseph Porter', a ball in 'Sentiment', a christening party in "The Bloomsbury Christening"; habitually these occasions are ruined by some deliberate or unconscious social gaffe, and by their participants' powerful capacity for embarrassment (their narrative structure displaying a kind of *Schadenfreude*, perhaps).[15] Two male inhabitants of Mrs. Tibbs's Boarding-house are described "amusing themselves in the drawing-room, before dinner, by lolling on sofas, and contemplating their pumps" ("The Boarding-House", 278); three female inmates of the same establishment "gambled at libraries, read books in balconies, sold at fancy fairs, danced at assemblies, talked sentiment - in short they had done all that industrious girls could do ...". (281) They inhabit a world of property, of objects (particularly metallic) expressive of the new technology of the Industrial Revolution, and their intensest relationships may be said to be towards these possessions. Watkins Tottle has a "kitchen-pokerness of carriage" ("A Passage in the life of Mr. Watkins Tottle", 431); Mr. Calton a face like "a chubby street-door knocker, half-lion half-monkey" ("The Boarding-House", 280); and several figures, in an image that will recur throughout Dickens's career,[16] are, like Mr. Tibbs in "The Boarding-House", "like a figure in a Dutch clock, with a powerful spring in the middle of his body." (281). Such objects govern the habits of their lives - Tottle's money runs out each fortnight "about a day after the expiration of the first week, as regularly as an eight-day clock" (431); Mr. John Dounce has habits "Regular as clockwork- breakfast at nine - dress and tittivate a little - down to the Sir Somebody's Head - a glass of ale and the paper" etc. ("The Misplaced Attachment of Mr. John Dounce", 245). Within such constrained, monotonous, empty lives gestures of violence are formed - Dumps, suffering from 'nerves', delivers a christening toast that is more like a curse, and Tottle,

suffering from shyness and intense reserve, throws
himself into the Regents' Park Canal.

Implicitly such failures are contrasted with an
active habit of observation that is the narrator's
means of transcending the milieu he observes (and
from which he may be thought to originate). Whereas
the characteristically dilettantish Mr. Tomkins in
"The Boarding-House" has "a wonderful eye for the
picturesque" and can "see how splendidly the light
falls upon the left side of that broken chimney-pot
at No. 48" (298, 299), the professional writer Boz
employs microscopes, telescopes and such aids to
perception of grotesque forms[17] in order to seize
more essential imaginative truths. Horatio Sparkins,
in a cancelled passage, had displayed price-figures
with "a seven with a little three-farthings in the
corner, something like the aquatic animalculae
disclosed by the gas microscope, 'perfectly invisible
to the naked eye'";[18] an M.P.'s spoilt child is
dressed up to look "like a robber in a melodrama,
seen through a diminishing glass" ("Sentiment", 325
- an early instance of Dickens's perception of how
respectability and criminality resemble one another).
And as soon as the tales give away to the Sketches
(in September 1834, with the first of the 'Street
Sketches') a cardinal Dickensian image for the
ephemeral life of the city makes its appearance:
"The passengers change as often in the course of one
journey as the figures in a kaleidoscope, and though
not so glittering, are far more amusing."
("Omnibuses", 139)

Such passages intensify in Dickens's later work
- the view from a stage-coach in *Nicholas Nickleby*
makes the London scene "flit by in motley dance like
the fantastic groups of the old Dutch painter" (*NN*,
xxxii, 409), and Fanny's tears in *Little Dorrit* "had
the effect of making the famous Mr. Merdle, in going
down the street, appear to leap, and waltz, and
gyrate, as if he were possessed by several Devils"
(*LD*, II, xxiv, 701) - but their essential principle
is already established in *Sketches by Boz*. There is
no such thing as a purely neutral observer, reporting or observing 'reality'; observation depends upon
a psychological attitude, a capacity for romantic
vision, and above all for the imaginative perceptions
of relation between one object and another. The
narrator 'Boz' is thoroughly conscious of how he
depends upon such vision, especially when it fails
him, as in "The Parlour Orator": "by some means or
other, we were not in a romantic humour; and although
we tried very hard to invest the furniture with

39

vitality, it remained perfectly unmoved, obstinate, and sullen." (*SB*, 239)[19] And when it is operating normally, the prose is punctuated by a continuous series of visual resemblances (thus in "A Bloomsbury Christening", Mr. Dumps is seen "looking as grim as the figure-head of a man-of-war" (477); little Kitterbell is seen covered with "various particles of sawdust, looking like so many inverted commas, on his expressibles" (478); and there appears at the party "a little coquette with a large bustle, who looked like a French lithograph" (480)).

Moreover, it is important to recognise the major spheres from which these analogies are drawn. In the first instance, in the Tales in particular, relationships are established between human characters and puppets or stage figures, with the effect of establishing a "romantic irony" similar to Hood's. There is no question, in these early works, of 'realistic' character-portrayal; these are deliberately one-dimensional figures, caricatures and stereotypes with one hobby-horse which (to paraphrase "Mrs. Joseph Porter", 421) they proceed to mount and refuse to dismount. Thus their individuality is absorbed by the established archetypes they descend from: Mr. Simpson, dressing "according to the caricatures published in the monthly fashions" is "in society what walking gentlemen are on the stage" ("The Boarding-House", 278), and so resembles, in "Sentiment", the "fat mammas, who looked like the stout people who came on in pantomimes for the sole purpose of being knocked down" (329); Mr. Hicks speaks "in a voice like a Punch with a cold" ("The Boarding-House", 285).

The grotesque comparisons have the effect of emphasising the material nature of these creatures - how they are made of wood or metal or some other animal, vegetable or mineral substance. Mrs. Tibbs, coming from cooking, looks "like a wax doll on a sunny day" (278),[20] and Mrs. Kitterbell has a countenance that may "recall to one's mind the idea of a cold fillet of veal" ("A Bloomsbury Christening, 475). The imaginative observer's habit of perceiving connections thus involves not only a perception of the "pantomime of life" but also a sense of principles informing matter and the way it behaves. Electricity is the key force - the "magnetism which must exist between a man and his knocker" ("Our Next-Door Neighbour", 41) informing all relations between animate and inanimate matter, the human creature and his environment. Mr. Minns, horrified by Mr. Budden's dog and its attack upon his curtains,

40

"leaped from his seat as though he had received the discharge from a galvanic battery" ("Mr. Minns and his Cousin", 315); when the London stage coach arrives at the Winglebury Arms "up started the ostlers, and the loungers, and the post-boys, and the ragged boys, as if they were electrified ..." ("The Great Winglebury Duel", 405); and Mr. Hicks in agitation has "hair standing on end as if he were on the stool of an electrifying machine in full operation." ("The Boarding-House, 285).

To turn from these very early tales to the sketches proper is to encounter the grotesque in a somewhat different context, and yet a very similar emphasis upon "the romantic side of familiar things".[21] The observer presents himself as a Baudelairian *flâneur*,[22] roaming the streets and practising his eye, and scorning those who fail to perceive the immanent vitality of things:

> What inexhaustible food for speculation do the streets of London afford! We never were able to agree with Sterne in pitying the man who could travel from Dan to Beersheba, and say that all was barren; we have not the slightest commiseration for the man who can take up his hat and stick, and walk from Covent Garden to St. Paul's Churchyard, and back into the bargain, without deriving some amusement - we had almost said instruction - from his perambulation. ("Shops and their Tenants", 59)

Again, such pleasures are contrasted to those who cannot enjoy their leisure, who "grow suspicious of everybody, and do the misanthropical in chambers" ("Thoughts about People", 217).

"Criminal Courts" (originally entitled "The Old Bailey", and first published in October 1834) might be taken as a representative example of how such observation is achieved. It is dependent, first of all, on the leisured gait of the *flâneur* - the narrator is "walking leisurely down the Old Bailey" (197), practising an old habit ("Often have we strayed here ..."; "we used to gaze on the exterior of Newgate" - 196). At such a pace he 'speculates' or muses or wonders - an important word, here as in the Gothic fictions of Mrs. Radcliffe,[23] being 'curiosity' (196, 198). Such mental processes are not simple or single, but compounded of multiple, contradictory emotions, "mingled feelings of awe and respect" (196) and a state of "wondering how the hackney-coachmen on the opposite stand could cut jokes in the presence of such horrors". (196)

This, then, is the mixed "attraction of repulsion" of Gothic fiction, yet tales of terror, so much in mind here, are placed in rhetorical subordination to the marvels and horrors of real life ("We have a great respect for Mrs. Fry, but she certainly ought to have written more romances than Mrs. Radcliffe" - 197).[24] To perceive these latter requires above all a capacity for sympathetic projection - the narrator is struck by the "calm indifference with which the proceedings are conducted" (198) in the Old Bailey courts, and which prevents anyone seeing the drama that is played out there in any fresh or accurate way. "But turn your eyes to the dock; watch the prisoner attentively for a few moments" (198), and what you see is a man about to be condemned to death "forming all sorts of fantastic figures with the herbs which are strewed upon the ledges before him" (198), the marvellous and terrifying being revealed in the little fragmentary epiphany or illumination. Moreover, the juxtaposition of another case (again pronounced superior to any contrivance of art - "No imaginary contrast to a case like this could be as complete ..." - 199), in which a thirteen-year old boy attempts to conquer his circumstances through the exercise of a comic imagination ("It's all a howen to my having a twin brother, vich has wrongfully got into trouble, and vich is so exactly like me that no vun ever knows the difference atween us" - 200) provides another epiphany, a manifestation of the essential discontinuity of city life, grotesque, fragmentary, incomplete, unavailable to stereotyped perception.

Such a conception governs the habitual relish for zeugma in *Sketches by Boz*. Pub-names in which heterogeneities are yolked together by violence - the Blue Lion and Stomach-Warmer at Winglebury (408), the Pig and Tinder-Box, the Black-Boy and Stomach-Ache and the Boot-Jack and Countenance at Mudfog (627, 646) - are obvious examples. Likewise the turns of phrase in imitation of eighteenth century wit - Mr. Augustus Cooper has "a little money, a little business, and a little mother" (256), a young lady sits behind a shop counter "in a blaze of adoration and gaslight" - mingling animate and inanimate, abstract and concrete categories of thought. Matter in London is an indiscriminate cornucopia which language can generate through alliteration and association, as at Seven Dials, where Broker's shops are accompanied by "dirty men,

filthy women, squalid children, fluttering shuttle-
cocks, noisy battledores, reeking pipes, bad fruit,
more than doubtful oysters, attenuated cats, dressed
dogs, and anatomical fowls" ("Seven Dials", 72) or
at Ratcliff Highway, "that reservoir of dirt,
drunkenness and drabs: thieves, oysters, baked
potatoes, and pickled salmon" ("Brokers' and Marine-
Store Shops", 180).

The world of *Sketches by Boz* is thus dynamic,
electric and alive in its startling juxtapositions
and incongruous transitions, its chronicler revelling
in his newly discovered powers of realising it in
appropriate language. At Greenwich Fair, "ginger-
beer corks go off in volleys" (111) and the pea-and-
thimbles man sells his tricks with "Here's the sort
o'game to make you laugh seven years after you're
dead" and "such variations as the speaker's
exuberant fancy suggests". (112-3) "Charles
Dickens, Resurrectionist", according to one story,[25]
was one mode of styling himself that their author
chose at this stage of his career. And "a joyful
and triumphant hilarity" often seems in evidence,
even when, as in the Houses of Parliament, it
operates on intractable material like members of
parliament:

> You see this ferocious-looking gentleman, with
> a complexion almost as sallow as his linen, and
> whose large black moustache would give him the
> appearance of a figure in a hairdresser's
> window, if his countenance possessed the thought
> which is communicated to those waxen caricat-
> ures of the human face divine. He is a
> militia-officer, and the most amusing person in
> the House. Can anything be more exquisitely
> absurd than the burlesque grandeur of his air,
> as he strides up to the lobby, his eyes rolling
> like those of a Turk's head in a cheap Dutch
> clock? ("A Parliamentary Sketch", 154)

It is the narrator's vision - treating his subject
as the expression of a single 'idea', collapsing
distinctions between head and body, body and clothes,
playing upon the romantic irony of relationships
between the human body and artefacts like puppets
and dolls - that creates the 'exquisite absurdity'
of the puffed-up chauvinist who turns out to look
like the cheap effigy of a blackamoor in a foreign
clock. That such revitalising of perception should
involve a dehumanising of its object is only one of
the paradoxes of the Dickensian grotesque.

Pickwick Papers is also concerned, in an
essential way, with observation. "Philosopher, sir?"
asks Mr. Jingle, and Pickwick replies, "An observer
of human nature." (*PP*, ii, II). The book is to
present the Pickwickians' vision of things, gained
through observation, and augmented through the
regular contributions of others, and their writings.
And at an early stage, part of the learning process
involves a recognition of the extraordinariness of
everyday life. Dismal Jemmy offers Mr. Pickwick a
'curious' manuscript -- "observe, not curious
because wild or improbable, but curious as a leaf
from the romance of real life" (v, 58); he echoes the
terminology of "Criminal Courts", with its 'placing'
of Mrs. Radcliffe, and anticipates the phrasing of
the 1848 preface to *The Old Curiosity Shop*. His
first contribution to the stock of Pickwickian
wisdom ("The Stroller's Tale") had begun by
deprecating the taste for the marvellous ("There is
nothing of the marvellous in what I am going to
relate ... there is nothing even uncommon in it. Want
and sickness are too common in many stations of life
to deserve more notice than is usually bestowed on
the most ordinary vicissitudes of human nature" -
iii, 35) and then discovering it in the "grotesquely
ornamented" appearance of a dying pantomime clown:
"The spectral figures in the Dance of Death, the
most frightful shapes that the ablest painter ever
portrayed on canvas, never presented an appearance
half so ghastly." (36) And the narrator of "The
Tale of the Queer Client" begins his introduction
with the same emphasis, drawing out the secrets that
inhere in the old premises of lawyers:[26] "There is
not a panel in the old wainscotting, but what, if it
were endowed with the powers of speech and memory,
could start from the wall, and tell its tale of
horror - the romance of life, sir, the romance of
life!" (xxi, 279).
    The emphasis and phrasing would be the same
many years later in "Hunted Down" in 1859, where the
narrator declares his intention "to recall one of
these Romances of the real world" (*RP*, 667). The
fantastic invades the everyday run of the Pickwickians' adventures, as when they are pursued by a
horse: "It's like a dream ... a hideous dream. The
idea of a man's walking about, all day, with a
dreadful horse that he can't get rid of." (*PP*, v,
64) Boz had likewise been "haunted by a shabby-
genteel man ... bodily present to our senses all day",
who is far more terrifying than any supernatural or
imaginary visitation: "The man of whom Sir Walter

Scott speaks in his Demonology, did not suffer half
the persecution from his imaginary gentleman-usher
in black velvet, that we sustained from our friend
in quondam black cloth." ("Shabby-Genteel People",
SB, 263). And Job Trotter, contorting his face to
avoid being recognised by Sam Weller when they
encounter each other again, puts imaginary
representations of monstrosity into the shade: "The
most extraordinary thing about the man was, that he
was contorting his face into the most fearful and
astonishing grimaces that ever were beheld. Nature's
handiwork never was disguised with such extraordinary
artificial carving, as the man had overlaid his
countenance with in one moment." (*PP*, xxiii, 316-7)
    The 'black humour' of *Pickwick Papers* is
clearly a related manifestation of the marvellous
in everyday life. Mr. Jingle's patter, for instance,
clearly resembles Sam Weller's - and Thomas Hood's,
puns and all[27] - in its laconic notation of disaster:
"Terrible place - dangerous work - other day - five
children - mother - tall lady, eating sandwiches -
forgot the arch - crash - knock - children look
round - mother's head off - sandwich in her hand - no
mouth to put it in - head of a family off - shocking,
shocking!" (ii, 11). The cannibal jokes of which
Dickens was so fond[28] abound in this novel, as Mr.
Pickwick discovers in his observation of Bob Sawyer
and his surgeon-friends:

> 'Nothing like dissection, to give one an
> appetite', said Mr. Bob Sawyer, looking round
> the table.
> Mr. Pickwick slightly shuddered.
> 'Bye the bye, Bob,' said Mr. Allen, 'have you
> finished that leg yet?'
> 'Nearly,' replied Sawyer, helping himself to
> half a fowl as he spoke. 'It's a very muscular
> one for a child's.' (xxx, 408)

And the Fat Boy at times also strikes notes of
monstrosity, as when he enthusiastically applauds
his master's gentlemanly habits:

> "Oh, that he is! said the fat boy, joining in
> the conversation; 'don't he breed nice pork!'
> The fat youth gave a semi-cannibalic leer at
> Mr. Weller, as he thought of the roast legs
> and gravy." (xxviii, 390)

However, for much of its course, the main vehicle of
the grotesque in *Pickwick Papers* is the gothic inset

stories. These stories are not of great literary merit: they appear to be offshoots of work contained in *Sketches by Boz*, stories like 'The Black Veil' and 'The Drunkard's Death', late additions to the first volume of sketches published in 1836, which were much admired at the time for their capacity to compete in a more direct way with the fashionable sensationalism of melodrama and gothic. Their narrators, for instance, sport an unintentionally ludicrous ghastliness of appearance, marked by the overindulgence of sensational adjective and adverb - Jack Bamber, who narrates 'The Tale of the Queer Client', is a case in point:

> There was a fixed grim smile perpetually on his countenance; he leant his chin on a long skinny hand, with nails of extraordinary length; and as he inclined his head to one side, and looked keenly out from beneath his ragged grey eyebrows, there was a strange, wild shyness in his leer, quite repulsive to behold.

Yet the stories contain important elements of the Dickensian grotesque that the novelist later learnt to accommodate within an integrated fictional structure. 'The Bagman's Story' is an interesting case; it concerns the portentous encounter of a travelling salesman Tom Smart (he parallels the Pickwickians) with a carved wooden chair at an inn where he puts up one night. The chair is one of the medieval grotesques that inhabit Dickens's early work,[29] "carved in the most fantastic manner" (xiv, 183); Tom has a few glasses of Punch before retiring, and is awakened from his sleep to witness the chair in extraordinary metamorphosis: "The carving of the back gradually assumed the lineaments and expression of an old shrivelled human face; the damask cushion became an antique, flapped waistcoat; the round knobs grew into a couple of feet, encased in red cloth slippers; and the old chair looked like a very ugly old man, of the previous century." (183-4) It addresses Tom and tells him where to find a letter that will enable him to marry the handsome, Mrs. Lupin-style landlady. Everything turns out as the chair commands - yet in the morning it becomes clear, to sober eyes, that the chair's transformation has depended on creative perception: "... it was a fantastic and grim-looking piece of furniture, certainly, but it must have been a remarkably ingenious and lively imagination, that could have discovered any resemblance between it and an old man." (187-8)

Yet such an imagination was Dickens's 'infirmity', and the story reveals itself as a teasing piece of 'romantic irony'. It has very evident literary references: like *Northanger Abbey*, it parodies Gothic conventions like the discovery of mysterious manuscripts (here it turns out to be a letter about something as mundane as bigamy and six undeclared children). Yet it is not simply an expression of rational skepsis - the 'romantic' vision of reality, dependent (as in 'The Parlour Orator' in *Sketches by Boz*) upon the powers of a perceiving mind, has its level of reality too. Like Scott's *Letters on Witchcraft and Demonology*[30] the story oscillates between skepsis and superstition, for the chair turns out to be telling the truth. The story is neither simply comic nor horrific, realist nor supernatural; holding these elements in dynamic tension, it has the aim of instilling that appreciation of the "romance of real life" that is part of the Pickwickians' philosophic quest.

A related, less convincing but still interesting story, anticipating *A Christmas Carol*, is "The Story of the Goblin who Stole a Sexton". Its hero, a sexton named Gerald Grub, is again a drinker, this time a morose and solitary one. Digging a grave one Christmas eve, he is about to swig his favourite concoction when a goblin appears to chide him for his misanthropy and remove him to a hall of underground goblins where a synoptic vision of human suffering is to be had. What right has Gerald to be glum when so many shoulder their burdens cheerfully?

Grub repents, leaves town, and returns many years later, old, ragged, and rheumatic, but content. We are teased again about the status of his experience: was it a real supernatural occurrence or the projection of the vapours of his Hollands Gin? Whatever we decide about this, the story once again has a valid fictional reality through its relation to the issue of the Pickwickian quest, that determination to make the best of things which is also grotesquely reflected in Sam Weller's proud living skeleton and his father's tough old turkey. With a semiconscious philosophical vocabulary ("At first he began to doubt the reality of his adventures, but the acute pain in his shoulders when he attempted to rise, assured him that the kicking of the goblins was certainly not ideal" - xxix, 404) the story explores the interpenetration of psychology and matter, and how the action of the one upon the other may indeed effect transformations.

But as *Pickwick Papers* progresses, the inset
stories become scarcer, as the overall structure of
the novel becomes more concentrated, less episodic,
and their themes are absorbed into it. The central
factor here is the development of the Bardell plot,
and Mr. Pickwick's incarceration. The grotesque,
hitherto sporadic, an effect of isolated black jokes
and ghoulish tales, becomes immanent in the world of
the prison. "'Which is twenty-seven, my good
fellow?'" asks Mr. Pickwick when he arrives, and he
gets a very Wellerian reply from a potboy ("Five
doors further on ... There's the likeness of a man
being hung, and smoking a pipe the while, chalked
outside the door" - xlii, 590). Pickwick now
inhabits the same world of experience as those who
have hitherto been the material of framed narratives
- like the "tall, gaunt, cadaverous man, in an old
great-coat and slippers" (593) who tells him of his
miseries: "If I lay dead at the bottom of the
deepest mine in the world; tight screwed down and
soldered in my coffin; rotting in the dark and
filthy ditch that drags its slime along, beneath
the foundations of this prison; I could not be more
forgotten or unheeded than I am here." (594)
Affected by the prison, and the intense personal
memories touched off by it, Dickens's prose takes
on new accents and rhythms that anticipate the
"miracle of poetic prose" to be achieved in the
later novels. And the philosophical investigations
take darker turns as relationships between the
microcosm of the prison and the macrocosm of the
world outside are uncovered: "... the three chums
informed Mr.Pickwick, in a breath, that money was,
in the Fleet, just what money was out of it; that
it would instantly procure him almost anything he
desired" (592, the precision of the 'almost'
prefiguring that later discussion between Paul
Dombey and his father in which the inadequacies of
money-values are laid bare).

So the prison experience is the essential
formative one for Mr.Pickwick, the equivalent of
that 'eddication' so much vaunted by Mr.Weller
senior, and the basis of his son's 'philosophy':

Yes - the dry arches of Waterloo Bridge. Fine
sleeping-place - within ten minutes' walk of
the public offices - only if there is any
objection to it, it is that the sitivation's
rayther too 'airy. I see some queer sights
there.'
'Ah, I suppose you did,' said Mr.Pickwick, with

an air of considerable interest.
'Sights, sir,' resumed Mr. Weller, 'as 'ud
penetrate your benevolent heart, and come out
on the other side ... it's generally the worn-
out, starving, houseless creatures as rolls
themselves in dark corners o' them lonesome
places - poor creatures as an't up to the twopenny rope." (xvi, 210)

- which is also the reflection of Dickens's own
traumatic spell at Warrens's blacking-factory. This
discovery and experience of human misery is
reflected in Sam's jokes - the parrot who declaims
that it's a case of "addin' insult to injury ... ven
they not only took him from his native land, but
made him talk the English langwidge arterwards"
(xxxv, 493) might be a slave, the anonymous headless
victim of Turkish carelessness ("It's over and
can't be helped, that's one consolation, as they
always say in Turkey, ven they cuts the wrong man's
head off"- xxiii,315)a candidate for similar treatment
in pre-Victorian England. The 'inverse sublimity'
of the grotesque registers its effects in ways denied
to pathos or melodrama, causing us to question the
'normality' of those mundanities it treats, and
threatens to transform into monstrosities.

NOTES

    1.   Quoted from G. Robert Stange, "The
Frightened Poets", *The Victorian City*, ed. Dyos and
Wolff, II, 480.
    2.   Quoted from the Oxford Paperback edition,
ed. Angus Easson (Oxford, OUP, 1977), p. 419.
    3.   See George Gissing, *Charles Dickens: A
Critical Study* (London, Blackie and Son, 1898), p.
41.
    4.   See *Dickens's Apprentice Years: The
Making of a Novelist* (Hassocks, Harvester Press,
1976), p. 63.
    5.   In *The Ludicrous Demon: Aspects of the
Grotesque in German Post-Romantic Prose* (Berkeley,
Cal., University of California Press, 1963), p. 49.
    6.   J.C. Reid, *Thomas Hood* (London, Routledge
and Kegan Paul, 1963), p. 4.
    7.   See his article "Die Fortentwicklung der
Romantik am englischen Beispiel", *DVjS* 1964, 534-60.
    8.   In *Confrontations*, p. 20.
    9.   See Letters, I, 576; to George Cattermole,
21/8/39.
    10.   *Hood's Own; or Laughter from Year to Year*

(London, 1839), pp. 2-3. Quoted by Enzensberger, *op. cit.*, 551.

11. Quoted in J.C. Reid, *op. cit.*, p. 247. See M. Hollington, "Dickens's Conception of the Grotesque", *The Dickensian LXXVI*, 91-99, for some additional documentation of the grotesque in the post-Romantic period.

12. See Letters IV, 581; to Forster 3/7/46.

13. See Enzensberger, *op. cit.*, 548.

14. Thus Dickens announces Sam Weller in a letter to John Macrone of 30/6/36 (Letters I, 154), urging "particular regard" for him.

15. Virgil Grillo has some useful comments on the structure of these early tales in his *Charles Dickens's 'Sketches by Boz'* (Boulder, Colo., University of Colorado Press, 1974). He analyses them in terms of a conflict of thesis and anti-thesis, generated by the idiosyncrasies of the characters.

16. Some examples:

> Mr. Quilp in *The Old Curiosity Shop*: "And with that, he darted in again with one jerk and clapped the little door to, like a figure in a Dutch clock when the hour strikes." (*OCS*, xlviii, 356);
>
> Betsy Trotwood in *David Copperfield*: "Miss Betsey, looking around the room, slowly and inquiringly, began on the other side, and carried her eyes on, like a Saracen's Head in a Dutch clock, until they reached my mother." (*DC*, i, 4);
>
> Bitzer in *Hard Times*: "But on winter evenings, when he has fallen asleep at his table, I have heard him, what I should prefer to describe as partially choke. I have heard him on such occasions produce sounds of a nature similar to what may be sometimes heard in Dutch clocks." (*HT*, II, viii, 182);
>
> Mrs. Wilfer in *Our Mutual Friend*: "Bella playfully setting herself about the task, Mrs. Wilfer's impressive countenance followed her with glaring eyes, presenting a combination of the once popular sign of the Saracen's Head, with a piece of Dutch clockwork, and suggesting to an imaginative mind that from the composition of the

salad, her daughter might prudently omit
the vinegar." (*OMF*, III, xvi, 612-3).

17. It has long been recognised that, just as
the rise of the self-portrait and autobiography are
connected with the development of adequate mirrors,
so appreciation of the grotesque owes a lot to
optical instruments like the microscope and tele-
scope. Flögel in the 18th century, for example,
compares the effects of grotesque exaggeration in
art with the effects of magnifying glasses ("so wie
man durch ein Vergrösserungsglas Kleinigkeiten viel
deutlicher sieht" - see Thomsen, *Das Groteske und
die Englische Literatur*, p. 32). Swift and Sterne
offer excellent examples of how grotesque effects
may be achieved through the adoption of a close-up,
microscopic view of everyday phenomena which are
thereby 'made strange' (see M. Hollington, *Günter
Grass: The Writer in a Pluralist Society* (London,
Marion Boyars Publishing, 1980) for a discussion of
similar effects in a contemporary writer). Even
the 'classic realist' Turgenev is aware, in *A
Sportsman's Notebook*, that the reality he sees
through his hunter's field glasses is a distortion
with some grotesque features (caused essentially by
the social relations between the wielder of the
field glasses and the people he observes).
18. See John Butt and Kathleen Tillotson,
Dickens at Work (London, Methuen, 1957), p. 60.
19. Specifically, what Boz wants is for the
walls and furniture to speak about the past they
have witnessed: "The ancient appearance of the
room - the old panelling of the wall - the chimney
blackened with smoke and age - would have carried us
back a hundred years at least, and we should have
gone dreaming on, until the pewter-pot on the table,
or the little beer-chiller on the fire, had started
into life, and addressed to us a long story of days
gone by." (*SB*, 239)
This is one of Dickens's favourite ways of
making the familiar strange - old objects are
constantly on the verge of recounting sensational
crimes, secrets etc. *Sketches by Boz* offers a
number of instances, e.g. -

What an interesting book a hackney-coach might
produce if it could carry as much in its head
as it does in its body! The autobiography of
a broken-down hackney-coach would surely be as
amusing as the autobiography of a broken-down
hackneyed dramatist; and it might tell as much

of its travels *with* the pole, as others have of their expeditions *to* it. How many stories might be related of the different people it had conveyed on matters of business or profit - pleasure or pain! And how many melancholy tales of the same people at different periods! The country-girl - the showy, over-dressed woman - the drunken prostitute! The raw apprentice - the dissipated spendthrift - the thief! ("Hackney-Coach Stands", 84)

We love to walk among these extensive groves of the illustrious dead, and to indulge in the speculations to which they give rise; now fitting a deceased coat, then a dead pair of trousers, and anon the mortal remains of a gaudy waistcoat, upon some being of our own conjuring up, and endeavouring from the shape and fashion of the garment itself, to bring its former owner before our mind's eye. We have gone on speculating in this way, until whole rows of coats have started from their pegs, and buttoned up, of their own accord, round the waistcoats of imaginary wearers; lines of trousers have jumped down to meet them; waist-coats have almost burst with anxiety to put themselves on; and half an acre of shoes have suddenly found feet to fit them, and gone stumping down the street with a noise which has fairly awakened us from our pleasant reverie, and driven us slowly away, with a bewildered stare, an object of astonishment to the good people of Monmouth Street, and of no slight suspicion to the policemen at the opposite corner. ("Meditations in Monmouth Street", 75)

20. Doll images are to be frequent and important expressions of the grotesque in Dickens. Amongst others in *Sketches by Boz* may be mentioned the Miss Crumptons ('Sentiment'), "who were dressed in amber, with long sashes, like dolls" (329), and Mrs. Gabriel Parsons, who has a complexion" ... as clear as that of a well-made wax doll" and a "face as expressive" (437).

21. These words are of course from the Preface to *Bleak House* (*BH*, xiv). The romantic realism of *Bleak House* has been studied in Robert Newsom's *Dickens on the Romantic Side of Familiar Things: Bleak House and the Novel Tradition* (New York, Columbia University Press, 1977), but the book, whilst interesting in its approach to that novel, seems unaware both of the relevance of that famous

phrase to Dickens's work as a whole and of the
important comparative work on 19th century romantic
realism by Donald Fanger and others (cf. Bill
Overton's review in *The Dickensian LXXIV* (May, 1978),
109-110).

22. In his essay on Constantin Guys,
Baudelaire develops the concept of the '*flâneur*',
the street-observer, as the archetype of the modern
artist, mingling amongst the crowd and observing, in
the fleeting images that pass by, the essence of
modern urban life: "Pour le parfait flâneur, pour
l'observateur passionné, c'est une immense jouissance
que d'élire domicile dans le nombre, dans l'ondoyant,
dans le mouvement, dans le fugitif et l'infini."
Guys, like Dickens, is said to despise anyone who
can't find intense occupation simply by walking in
the streets: "tout homme ... *qui s'ennuie au sein
de la multitude*, est un sot! un sot! et je le
méprise!" ("Le Peintre de la Vie Moderne", *Oeuvres
Complètes*, 552). For some ways in which the concept
may be applied to Dickens, see M. Hollington,'Dickens
the Flâneur', *The Dickensian* (LXVII, Summer, 1981).

23. See Maximilian Novak, *op. cit.*, pp. 62,
65.

24. For a discussion of the fictional device
of "truth stranger than fiction" on a comparative
basis see M. Hollington, "The Fantastic Paradox:
An Aspect of the Theory of Romantic Realism", in
Comparison No. 7 (Spring, 1978).

25. See Letters I, 77n.

26. Cf Fn. 19 above, and Tom Pinch in the
Temple in *Martin Chuzzlewit*: "Every echo of his
footsteps sounded to him like a sound from the old
walls and pavements, wanting language to relate the
histories of the dim, dismal rooms; to tell him what
lost documents were decaying in forgotten corners of
the shut-up cellars, from whose lattices such mouldy
sight came breathing forth as he went past ..."
(*MC*, xl, 618).

27. See Christian Enzensberger, *op. cit.*, 556,
where Mr. Jingle's discourse is quoted and analysed.

28. The very frequent association of human
flesh with food may originate in a childhood memory.
An interesting autobiographical sketch in *The
Uncommercial Traveller* recalls a childhood visit to
some dead infants which had the effect of "reminding
me by a homely association, which I suspect their
complexion to have assisted, of pigs' feet as they
are usually displayed at a neat tripe-shop."
("Dullborough Town", *U7*, 119). The memory appears
to be echoed in *Nicholas Nickleby*, when Mrs.

Nickleby relates how pork was taboo in their house:
"Roast pig! I hardly think we ever had one, now I
come to remember, for your papa could never bear the
sight of them in the shops, and used to say that
they always put him in mind of very little babies,
only the pigs had much fairer complexions" (*NN*, xli,
529).

    29. Most particularly in *The Old Curiosity
Shop* and *Barnaby Rudge*, where Dickens employed
George Cattermole (see Letters, I, 277) as a special
illustrator for antiquarian subjects.

    30. Which Dickens had certainly read - see fn.
24 above.

Chapter Three

'THEY ALWAYS DIE WHEN I'M AT MEALS':
OLIVER TWIST AND *NICHOLAS NICKLEBY.*

It was Smithfield that they were crossing,
although it might have been Grosvenor Square
for anything Oliver knew to the contrary. The
night was dark and foggy. The lights in the
shops could scarcely struggle through the heavy
mist, which thickened every moment and shrouded
the streets and houses in gloom; rendering the
strange place still stranger in Oliver's eyes;
and making his uncertainty the more dismal and
depressing. (*OT*, xvi, 109)

Now, the first ideas called up in Mrs.
Nickleby's mind by the words milliner and
dressmaker were connected with certain wicker
baskets lined with black oilskin, which she
remembered to have seen carried to and fro in
the streets; but, as Ralph proceeded, these
disappeared, and were replaced by visions of
large houses at the West end, private carriages,
and a banker's book; all of which images
succeeded each other with such rapidity, that
he had no sooner finished speaking, than she
nodded her head and said 'Very true', with
great appearance of satisfaction. (*NN*, x, 120)

Whatever hesitation that might be felt, in
Sketches by Boz and *Pickwick Papers*, in naming
London as the principal focus and instigation of
Dickens's perception of the grotesque, is dispelled
by the two novels that follow these works. Sam
Weller's "queer sights", Horatio Sparkins's "animalculae", and the kaleidoscopic effects of "Omnibuses"
receive, in *Oliver Twist* and *Nicholas Nickleby*,
their first elaborated expression within a manifestation of the marvels of a "most fantastic city"[1]
designed to challenge the innocence, ignorance or

55

indifference of these novels' readership. "Within such walls" as those of Mr. Fang's Magistrates' Court "... enough fantastic tricks are daily played to make the angels blind with weeping" (*OT*, xi, 74); within the space enclosed by the city are to be found such places as Jacob's Island "... the filthiest, the strangest, the most extraordinary of the many localities that are hidden in London, wholly unknown, even by name, to the great mass of its inhabitants". (1, 381)[2]

Of paramount significance in these novels' analysis of the urban grotesque is the experience of incongruous juxtapositions, associations, continuities and discontinuities. It was Walter Bagehot who first noticed this aspect of Dickens's manner of presenting urban psychology:

> London is like a newspaper. Everything is there and everything is disconnected. There is every kind of person in some houses but there is no more connection between the houses than between the neighbours in the lists of 'births, marriages, and deaths'. As we change from the broad leader to the squalid police-report we pass a corner and we are in a changed world. This is advantageous to Mr. Dickens's genius. His memory is full of instances of old buildings and curious people and he does not care to piece them together. On the contrary, each scene, in his mind, is a separate scene - each street a separate street.[3]

Yet one should perhaps qualify Bagehot by stressing that at the same time Dickens is fascinated by the *contiguity* of separate streets and scenes. In *Nicholas Nickleby*, as in *Sketches by Boz* and *The Uncommercial Traveller*,[4] the representation of Newgate emphasises the thin spatio-temporal boundaries between condemned criminals and the crowded life of the street outside: "... within a few feet of the squalid tottering houses - upon the very spot on which the venders of soup and fish and damaged fruit are now playing their trades - scores of human beings ... have been hurried violently and swiftly from the world, when the scene has been rendered frightful with excess of human life" (*NN*, iv, 29). Contemplation of London shop-windows emphasises the startling and tragic contrast of inside and outside, and their narrow separation: "... pale and pinched-up faces hovered about the windows where was tempting food; hungry eyes wandered over the profusion guarded by one thin sheet of brittle glass - an iron wall to them ..." (xxxii, 409). And the pauper burial ground that Ralph Nickleby passes on the way to his death contains corpses set only marginally apart from the city above ground: "And here, in truth, they lay, parted from the living by a little earth and a board or two - lay thick and close - corrupting in body as they had in mind - a dense and squalid crowd. Here they lay, cheek by jowl with life ..." (lxii, 802).[5]

The consequence of such juxtapositions for the art of the novel are reflected upon in the well-known "streaky bacon" passage in *Oliver Twist*, which justifies sudden narrative trasitions and discontinuities as fit aesthetic expressions of "The transitions in real life from well-spread boards to death-beds, and from mourning weeds to holiday garments ..." (OT, xvii, 118). And it should be emphasised that the perception of incongruous urban relationships in these novels also provides a number of rich satiric themes.[6] Using the ancient handy-dandy methods of grotesque satire,[7] *Oliver Twist* (for instance) stresses the connections between criminals and upstanding members of the bourgeoisie, asking which are devils and which men, and whether the unofficial criminality of Fagin truly outstrips the official criminality of Fang. With Ralph Nickleby as its skeleton cynic, *Nicholas Nickleby* develops the ironic parallels between the city jungle of predators and dupes and the discontinuous series of tragicomic encounters between satirist and victim in The Dance of Death.

Yet whilst it is appropriate to emphasise that in these early novels the grotesque is already no mere effect of local gargoyles and freaks, it should also be made clear that there is a tendency to concentrate on particular individual characters and their attributes. Fagin is unmistakeably one such case; Squeers, Gride, and Sliderskew, phonically related as well as in narrative and theme, a related minor trio; and Quilp perhaps the culmination of the sequence. In later novels individual grotesques, though still evident, may come to seem less important than the ironies they exemplify; Dickens's great grotesque characters generally belong to the earlier half of his career,[8] and require (in due course) separate and extended discussion.

'Twist' is the appropriate surname of the hero of a novel in which grotesque thieves regularly congregate at a pub named The Three Cripples. Denoting deviousness and slyness, it is a favourite word to indicate physical and moral distortion in Dickens's work. In *Bleak House*, Jarndyce and Jarndyce instils "an extra moral twist and shuffle" into the solicitors' boys who are concerned with the case (*BH*, i, 5); in *Little Dorrit* the Barnaclean world near Park Lane breeds "wicked little grooms in the tightest fitting garments, with twists in their legs answering to the twists in their minds" (*LD*, xxvii, 325); and in *David Copperfield* the serpentine Uriah Heep reveals the primitive perception of emblematic relation between human and animal form that sustains the figure: "He had a way of writhing when he wanted to express enthusiasm, which was very ugly; and which diverted my attention from the compliment he had paid my relations, to the snaky twistings of his throat and body." (*DC*, xvi, 235) *Oliver Twist* itself is full of similar movements: Noah Claypole, relating Oliver's rebellion, "writhed and twisted his body into an extensive variety of eel-like positions" (*OT*, vii, 44); and that classic grotesque gargoyle Grimwig exhibits an extraordinary face in which"... the variety of shapes into which his countenance was twisted, defy description". (xiv, 97)

Yet, at its first level of apprehension, the relationship between name and nature is apparent rather than real. Oliver gets his name by alphabetic accident - it happens that 'T' is the next letter to be allocated to a foundling infant when he's born, and Mr. Bumble claims the poetic inspiration that hit upon 'Twist' (ii, 8).[9] And for all that he is claimed as one "of these dreadful creaturs, that are born to be murderers and robbers from their very cradle" (vi, 42-3),[10] Oliver's criminal nature stubbornly refuses to declare itself in a novel where it is subject to the intensest provocations and encouragement. The evidence of physiognomy in fact proclaims Oliver as an innocent, as swells like Toby Crackit are not slow to appreciate: "His mug is a fortun' to him." (xxii, 159)

Yet appearances do in fact deceive; Oliver's name, of course, is not really Twist, and that principle of the truth of caricature, of the concordance of name and appearance and nature, is in fact pervasively adhered to. Something like a medieval humours psychology seems to be employed in cases like Bumble - "a fat man, and a choleric" (ii,

6), who indeed bumbles - and Fang, red-faced and intemperate, who "... might have brought an action against his countenance for libel ..." (xi, 71) if it does not accurately bespeak his habits and essential nature. Grimwig is the appropriate name of someone who repeats a desire to eat his own 'powdered' head; Sowerberry, of an undertaker who reaps a disgusting harvest of pauper corpses; and Noah Claypoll alias Morris Bolter is both "... a large-headed, small-eyed youth, of lumbering make and heavy countenance ..." (v, 31) to express the truth of his former name, and the devourer of "... a monstrous slice of bread" in "... a series of large bites ..." (xlv, 343) to convey the fitness of his latter pseudonym. In a novel with the fairy-tale structure of *Oliver Twist*, in which the un-masking of truth is of central importance, such grotesque characterizations, or caricatures, have a functional role to play.

Even so, dissembling is more characteristic of the society of the novel than honesty and openness. Clothes make people:[11] Bumble strides out "... in the full bloom and pride of beadlehood; his cocked hat and coat were dazzling in the morning; he clutched his cane with the vigorous tenacity of health and power" (xvii, 19); Toby Crackit stands "... a trifle above the middle size, and apparently rather weak in the legs; but this circumstance by no means detracted from his own admiration of his top-boots, which he contemplated, in their elevated situation, with lively satisfaction". (xxii, 159)[12] Here as elsewhere, the handy-dandy theme plays through the incongruous relationship of beadle and thief "... inasmuch as there are a great number of spirited young bloods upon town, who pay a much higher price than Mr. Chitling for being seen in good society: and a great number of fine gentlemen (composing the good society aforesaid) who establish their reputation upon very much the same footing as flash Toby Crackit". (xxxix, 293)

Oliver Twist picks up and sharpens the analysis of bourgeois hypocrisy and pretension already witnessed in *Sketches by Boz*. An undertaker with "... an ingenious little model of a patent coffin" for a snuff-box (iv, 22) and a similar artistic sense in employing Oliver as mute to attend children's funerals ("It would be very new to have a mute in proportion, my dear" (v, 33) - handy-dandy again, for Sowerberry, like Fagin and Toby Crackit, appreciates the commercial value of Oliver's appearance) is a splendidly wrought example of that petit-bourgeois class of materialistic, dilettantish, classicizing connoisseurs of the picturesque portrayed in *Sketches by Boz*. Once more, the bourgeois 'soul' is imprinted on the environment that surrounds and accompanies it:[13] Bumble has a "large leathern pocket-book" (v, 33), nerves "like washable beaver hats that improve with rain" (xxvii, 269) - compare Horatio Sparkins, whose countenance brightens up "like an old hat in a shower of rain" at the encouragement of Teresa Malderton (*SB*, 359) - and is discovered, after his disastrous marriage to Mrs. Corney, contemplating "a paper fly-cage [that] dangled from the ceiling".(xxxvii, 267) And a delicious vein of mock heroic is there in the representation of Bumble, who compares himself to Jesus Christ: "I sold myself ... for six teaspoons, a pair of sugar-tongs and a milk-pot ..." (268).

The petit-bourgeois figures are in addition a major focus of the discontinuities and grotesque juxtapositions that the novel employs.[14] "Drat that beadle!" declares Mrs. Mann on the occasion of an early morning visit from Bumble, but her modulation is swift: "'Lauk, Mr. Bumble, only think of it being you! Well, dear me, it *is* a pleasure, this is! Come into the parlour, sir, please.'" (xvii, 119) The bacon is equally streaky when Mrs. Corney is in a dratting mood: "Drat the pot! ... a little stupid thing, that only holds a couple of cups!" (xxiii, 166) But she is impartial in her curses, conferring them equally on things and people, her tea-ceremony being shortly interrupted by a "soft tap" that she takes to be token of further impertinence: "'Oh, come in with you! ... Some of the old women, dying, I suppose. They always die when I'm at meals ... Dear me!' exclaimed the matron, in a much sweeter tone, 'is that Mr. Bumble?'" (166) A further interruption shortly ensues, and this time the transition is more lurid:

> It was no unfit messenger of death, who had disturbed the quiet of the matron's room. Her body was bent by age; her limbs trembled with palsy; her face, distorted into a mumbling leer, resembled more the grotesque shaping of some wild pencil, than the work of Nature's hand. (xxiv, 172)

Our sense of reality is disturbed again: the apparition is declared a fantastic monstrosity, 'grotesque' in the derogatory, classicist sense in which the representation of grotesques was the

imitation of chimerae of the artist's brain.[15]   Yet
this is of course an ironic 'fantastic paradox' -
'nature', in the shape of the Poor Law and its
administrators, has created monsters to outstrip any
diseased freak of the imagination.   In the handy-
dandy world of *Oliver Twist* it is Mrs. Corney who
makes these grotesques who so inconvenience her, and
who perhaps therefore is one.

The great grotesque figure of Fagin is thus
played into a pattern of ironies and paradoxes that
befit the world of the city he inhabits.   In a novel
where such registrations are clearly significant,
his name obviously associates him with 'feigning'
and 'faking' - and not merely that of swindlers and
thieves (Mr. Brownlow assures Oliver that 'We won't
make an author of you, while there's an honest trade
to be learned, or brickmaking to turn to" - xiv,95).
The pantomimic gestures with which he greets new-
comers to the city - the "low obeisance to Oliver",
(viii, 57)- the bow of "grotesque politeness" with
which he greets Noah and Charlotte (xlii, 326), as
Quilp will later welcome the single gentleman (*OCS*,
xlviii, 355) - cast him as its *eiron*, commenting
through parody on the vices and foibles of its
citizens.   At the same time, through his association
with diabolical evil and the supernatural, Fagin
manages to express the "inverse sublimity" that was
the hallmark of the romantic grotesque.

Still, the first thing to observe about Fagin
is that,like all good grotesques, he makes you
laugh.   On Oliver's first encounter with him he
laughs unrestrainedly at the Grimaldian pantomime
of theft, in which Fagin "... would look constantly
round him, for fear of thieves, and would keep
slapping all his pockets in turn, to see that he
hadn't lost anything, in such a very funny and
natural manner, that Oliver laughed till the tears
ran down his face".   (ix, 62)   It is the first time
that anyone has tried to entertain Oliver, and his
natural instinct for laughter asserts itself, as he
begins to feel at home with his 'new family'.   The
second occasion is less deceptive: Oliver has been
recaptured and can have no further illusions about
the 'merry old gentleman'; and yet, when "... the old
man would tell them stories of robberies he had
committed in his younger days, mixed up with so much
that was droll and curious, ... Oliver could not
help laughing heartily, and showing that he was
amused in spite of all his better feelings" (xviii,
134), the "attraction of repulsion" a powerful magnet
again.

As a mime artist, Fagin speaks a language of gestures, of bows, shrugs and grins, obviously connected with his mode of economic activity. He communicates with Barney in eye-signals, the latter "... exchanging a remarkable look with Fagin, who raised his eyes for an instant, as if in expectation of it, and shook his head in reply; so slightly that the action would have been almost imperceptible to an observant third person". (xv, 105) A little later the narrator speculates ironically "... whether a peculiar contraction of the Jew's red eyebrows, and a half-closing of his deeply-set eyes, warned Miss Nancy that she was disposed to be too communicative" (106); the colours and shapes of his appearance - "bright dark" (ix, 59) eyes that are "deeply-set", "shaggy" (xvi, 113) red eyebrows - obviously facilitate the transmission of signals. Moreover Fagin has the art of stealth, the ability to make sudden entrances without being heard, that belongs equally to his counterpart Quilp and their mutual ancestor Harlequin: "Sneaking in and out, so nobody hears how you come and go!" complains Sikes. (xv, 104)

With such histrionic skills he is able thus to parody the 'straight' bourgeois society of the novel he inhabits, and of which his own criminal world is an ironic mirror image. We first encounter Fagin cooking sausages, with a toasting-fork in his hands; he presents an image of domesticity, dispensing food and drink with a generosity unseen in the workhouse. Oliver is given gin, and feels sleepy - he feels himself 'gently' lifted to a sack where he can sleep, and again the gestures contrast with any he has known. Next morning Fagin makes coffee in a saucepan (not gruel in a copper), whistling softly to himself.

He is a kind of ironic Jewish patriarch[16] presiding over a family idyll which inverts familiar bourgeois values. The work of the family community is mock-work; the education it provides is a mock-education ("Fagin took the opportunity of reading Oliver a long lecture on the crying sin of ingratitude" - xviii, 127) whose graduates are mock-professionals ("see what a pride they take in their profession, my dear" - xliii, 330). A topsy-turvy morality prevails - "you've been brought up bad", the Dodger informs Oliver (xviii, 132); and Fagin curses Nancy's sentimental conscience until his cynic philosophy rescues him: "The worst of these women is, that a very little serves to call up some long-forgotten feeling; and the best of them is, that it never lasts." (xix, 143) Yet the community of thieves can at moments suggest a kind of inverse utopia - as when Charlie Bates unveils his swag, and declares it a grotesque cannibal Land of Cockaigne ("Sitch a rabbit pie, Bill ... sitch delicate creeturs, with sitch tender limbs, Bill, that the wery bones melt in your mouth, and there's no occasion to pick 'em" - xxxix, 289) - no less credible than the bourgeois paradise envisaged by Mr. Bumble together with Mrs. Corney ("What an opportunity for a jining of hearts and housekeeping!" - xxvii, 199), nor even, perhaps, than the promised land of the Maylies.

The grotesque is thus a mode of indirection, designed to elicit fresh perception and evaluation of the 'normal' world and its values. Fagin's appearance is constantly compared to animals, in the manner of physiognomy and caricature: he has fangs to eat with "as should have been a dog's or rat's" (xlvii, 356), lynx eyes (xxix, 296) and, in prison, "a countenance more like that of a snared beast than the face of a man".(lii, 409) Yet again he has no monopoly of relation to a lower level of creation - some pillars of society in the novel imitate him: the magistrate before whom Oliver appears is one entire Fang, and Mrs. Sowerberry has a "vixenish countenance".(iv, 27) In more general terms, the law, according to Bumble, if it supposes him to control his wife 'is a ass',[17] and in society at large "there are a good many ladies and gentle-men, claiming to be out-and-out Christians, between whom, and Mr. Sikes's dog, there exist strong and singular points of resemblance".(xviii, 130)

Yet in one passage at least Fagin's relation to the animal world takes on additional dimensions: "As he glided stealthily along, creeping beneath the shelter of the walls and doorways, the hideous old man seemed like some loathsome reptile, engendered in the slime and darkness through which he moved: crawling forth, by night, in search of some rich offal for a meal." (xix, 135) Here the beast in question is mythical as much as zoological, some primeval offspring of the first matter of this new urban creation,[18] whose deformities express the moral world that has been engendered with it. Elsewhere Fagin is unequivocally supernatural - listening to Noah Claypole "... with a subtle and eager look upon his face, that might have appertained to some old goblin" (xlii, 321), or broading over Nancy's betrayal of the criminals "... with face so distorted and pale, and eyes so red and bloodshot, that he looked less like a man, than like some hideous phantom, moist from the grave, and worried by an evil spirit".(xlvii, 356)

The passage suggests the range of effects created by the grotesque - alongside its gothic elements it contains a psychological dimension as it expresses Fagin's constant anxiety and inner torment (compare the paleness that afflicts him when he explains to Oliver why he has jewels (ix, 60) or the biting of his pale lip in suppressed hatred of Bill Sikes - xii, 87). Fagin is a thoroughly mixed creation - pantomimic buffoon, horrific sadist, mythic demon and, at the last, terrified victim. Sikes's phrases best seem to capture this conglomerate - "... you're fit for nothing but keeping as a curiosity of ugliness in a glass bottle, and I suppose they don't blow glass bottles large enough." (xii, 86) is one assay, but he seems compelled to return for others: "It's enough to turn a man ill, to see his lean old carcase shivering in that way, like a ugly ghost just rose from the grave." (xix, 136)

Yet however powerful and comprehensive Fagin may be as an individual expression of inverse sublimity, one may ultimately seek the source of this effect in the 'slime and darkness' of the city that engenders him. A perpetual oppressive atmosphere of cloud, fog and mist envelops London, stemming first from the mud that carpets it, as at Smithfield: "The ground was covered, nearly ankle-deep, with filth and mire; a thick steam, perpetually rising from the reeking bodies of the cattle, and mingling with the fog, which seemed to rest upon the chimney-tops, hung heavily above."[19] (xxi, 153) The vapour seems to have moral significance, like Nancy's murder ("Of all the horrors that rose with an ill scent upon the morning air, that was the foulest and most cruel" - xlviii, 363), for it appears that all crime leaves its material trace: "Oh! if when we oppress and grind our fellow-creatures, we bestowed but one thought on the dark evidences of human error, which, like dense and heavy clouds, are rising, slowly it is true, but not less surely, to Heaven, to pour their after-vengeance on our heads." (xxx, 219) The morality is a primitive, pre-Carlylean reckoning of cause-and-effect, stemming perhaps from Dickens's early 'sensational' reading;[20] but its main significance is that it feeds a coherent myth, worked out across polarities like mud and vapour, height and depth, with a cyclical sense of rising evil and falling vengeance: "The clouds, which had been threatening all day, spread out in a dense and sluggish mass of vapour, already yielded large drops of rain, and seemed to presage a violent thunderstorm ..." (xxxviii, 277).

The myth of a city enveloped in the mist and fog and steam of its own evil was to prove serviceable throughout Dickens's career, and capable of adaptation to a variety of themes: Chartism, the law, bureaucracy, industrial callousness, and all manner of public and private crimes. Its teasing, vaporous insubstantiality, seemingly combining matter and spirit, or mediating between them, was also to be a fertile source of grotesque modes of suggesting sublimity. With such resonances at stake, then, it is not surprising that Oliver, an innocent in the city alone at night in Smithfield with a "heavy mist, which thicked every moment and shrouded the streets and houses in gloom" (xvi, 109), should be overwhelmed with confusion and terror.

Nicholas Nickleby contains the same atmospherics: as Nicholas and Smike leave London by the Portsmouth Road "... a dense vapour still enveloped the city they had left, as if the very breath of its busy people hung over their schemes of gain and profit and found greater attraction there than in the quiet region above ..." (*NN*, xxii, 274). But it is their return from Portsmouth that brings the central, organising vision of the city:

> As they dashed by the quickly-changing and
> ever-varying objects, it was curious to observe
> in what a strange procession they passed
> before the eye. Emporiums of splendid dresses,
> the materials brought from every quarter of the
> world; tempting stores of everything to
> stimulate and pamper the sated appetite and
> give new relish to the oft-repeated feast;
> vessels of burnished gold and silver, wrought
> into every exquisite form of vase, and dish,
> and goblet; guns, swords, pistols, and patent
> engines of destruction; screws and irons for
> the crooked, clothes for the newly-born, drugs
> for the sick, coffins for the dead, churchyards

for the buried - all these jumbled each with
the other and flocking side by side, seemed to
flit by in motley dance like the fantastic
groups of the old Dutch painter, and with the
same stern moral for the unheeding, restless
crowd. (xxxii, 408-9)

The master-image is of the city as a dance of
death. It has a serial structure, like the set of
Holbein's prints, consisting of a succession of
separate scenes linked only by the skeleton who
lurks in each. It is perceived here, as it were,
in a rapid flicker of the pages, the speed of the
coach in which Nicholas and Smike are travelling
creating the 'making strange' effect, as earlier in
the description of the Saracen's Head coach "...
like some grim apparition, rushing each day with
mysterious and ghost-like punctuality". (iv, 29)
Yet the modern experience of speed is itself understood as subordinate to the city's function as a
giant market, where a concentration of population
produces all kinds of cravings that the economy
seeks to satisfy.[21] It operates as an enormous
magnet, drawing in rich and poor, predators and
victims and placing them side by side in a confused
jumble.

Hence, once more, the streaky bacon of *Nicholas
Nickleby*, its constant exploration and exploitation
of surprise collisions, contiguities, and above all,
contrasts. "I don't believe now," says Tom
Linkinwater, "that there's such a place in all the
world for coincidences as London is!" (xliii, 561)
Arthur Gride believes it too - which is why he wants
to wear a bottle-green suit on his wedding-day:
"The very day I put it on first, old Lord Mallowford
was burnt to death in his bed, and all the post-
obits fell in." (li, 668) The characters also
perceive such juxtapositions as a phenomenon of
language - "Old Arthur Gride and matrimony is a most
anomalous conjunction of words," remarks Ralph
Nickleby (xlvii, 614); but it is characteristic of a
society ruled by money that Rowlandsonian grotesque
contrasts between monstrous old lovers and beautiful
brides should habitually be countenanced. Dickens's
grotesque associations of ideas are the counterpart
of these contrasts, and they express the life of the
city - its way of throwing the most heterogenous
things and persons together, in pursuit of money.

Speculation is the activity to which London is
dedicated. It of course is eminently productive of
contrast between winners and losers, for "specalation

is a round game" (i, 5); the contrast between Ralph and his relatives is that they stand on opposite sides of the speculative merry-go-round: "A mania prevailed, a bubble burst, four stockbrokers took villa residences at Florence, four hundred nobodies were ruined, and among them Mr. Nickleby." (i, 5) The contrast of somebodies and nobodies[22] is made apparent early on in the confrontation of Ralph and Nicholas - "the old man's eye was keen with the twinklings of avarice and cunning; the young man's bright with the light of intelligence and spirit" (iii, 24) - and in it is to be contained the novel's dynamic examination of the possibilities of revolt in England in the late 1830's.

Ralph Nickleby is obviously the major predator portrayed in this novel (again the animal metaphors are extensive and deliberate), a cynic with a pessimist, materialist vision of the vanity of things. He shares the narrator's perception of life as a dance of death: "I am not a man to be moved by a pretty face," he asserts in soliloquy; "There is a grinning skull beneath it, and men like me who look and work below the surface see that, and not its delicate covering." (xxxi, 400) Later, when Arthur Gride is to marry Madeline Bray, he sneers about the "ripe lips, and clustering hair, and what not" (xlvii, 618) that the old man is about to acquire. The appetites of men and women are what he feeds on, and he understands them as essentially ephemeral, productive of city fashions; or, if they last, like Mrs. Mantalini's love for her husband, it is a case of vanity, equally to be exploited: "... all love is fleeting enough; though that which has its sole root in the admiration of a whiskered face like that of yonder baboon, perhaps lasts the longest, as it originates in the greater blindness and is fed by vanity. Meantime the fools bring grist to my mill, so let them live out their day, and the longer it is, the better." (xxxiv, 431) Ralph is the equivalent of the ironic skeleton, leading the dance, and deciding when it shall end.

Ralph's cynicism is parallel in the novel, as an essential trait, to Squeers's hypocrisy. Squeers as a hypocrite is a crude forerunner of Pecksniff: "Squeers covered his rascality, even at home, with a spice of his habitual deceit; as if he really had a notion of some day or another being able to take himself in, and persuade his own mind that he was a very good fellow." (viii, 87) His name - "queer", looking forward to Quilp, perhaps - and appearance are markedly grotesque:

He had but one eye, and the popular prejudice
runs in favour of two. The eye he had was
unquestionably useful, but decidedly not
ornamental: being of a greenish grey, and in
shape resembling the fanlight of a street door.
The blank side of his face was much wrinkled
and puckered up, which gave him a very sinister
appearance, especially when he smiled, at which
times his expression bordered closely on the
villainous.

The smile or leer that is suggested in his name
is characteristic of Dickens's grotesques,[23] never
more terrifying than when they are attempting to be
affable. The oddity of his appearance extends to
his clothes - he is described as "a one-eyed man
grotesquely habited, either for lack of better
garments or for purposes of disguise, in a loose
great-coat with arms half as long as his own" (lvii,
747) during his scheming with Peg Sliderskew - and
these seem to allegorise a moral disorder: "he
appeared ill at ease in his clothes, and as if he
were in a perpetual state of astonishment at finding
himself so respectable." (iv, 31) While Ralph
appears to stand outside the system of desires and
pretensions that he manipulates, Squeers is part of
it, and his grotesqueness an expression of its
twists and contortions.

The third major manipulative character in the
novel, Arthur Gride, is also markedly grotesque
("much bent, and slightly twisted"):

> His nose and chin were sharp and prominent, his
> jaw had fallen inwards from loss of teeth, his
> face was shrivelled and yellow, save where the
> cheeks were streaked with the colour of a dry
> winter apple; and where his beard had been,
> there lingered yet a few grey tufts which
> seemed, like the ragged eyebrows, to denote the
> badness of the soil from which they sprung.
> The whole air and attitude of the form, was one
> of stealthy cat-like obsequiousness; the whole
> expression of the face was concentrated in a
> wrinkled leer, compounded of cunning, lecher-
> ousness, slyness, and avarice. (xlvii, 610)

Together with his housekeeper Peg Sliderskew, her
name a kind of amalgam of "Gride" and "Squeers",
who looks "like an uncouth figure in some monstrous
piece of carving"[24] and is capable of "wrinkling her
cadaverous face into so many and such complicated

forms of ugliness, as awakened the unbounded astonishment and disgust even of Mr. Squeers" (lvii, 753), Gride represents as crudely robust an example of the grotesque in early Dickens as the detractors of this aspect of his art could hope to find.

Yet Gride is artistically redeemed, perhaps, by his function as a sexual predator in a novel where sexual themes stand, for Dickens, in comparatively sharp relief, with some allusions of considerable point, so to speak (like Nicholas's inquiry during Fanny Squeers's head-set at him: "Shall it be a hard or a soft nib?" - ix, 102). London is portrayed as an emporium for various sexual tastes, like Mantalini's vision of paradise ("... twenty thousand hemispheres populated with - with - with little ballet-dancers" - x, 125) or, more especially, the fantasies of elderly roués like the counterpart of Gride who arrives at Madame Mantalini's millinery shop, about to be married, and bestows "a grotesque leer" upon Kate.(xviii, 226)   The Dance of Death looms large: "It was a satisfactory thing to hear that the old gentleman was going to lead a new life, for it was pretty evident that his old one would not last him much longer." (225) [26]

It is a world in which people in general, and women in particular, are bought and sold (like Madeline Bray), or grovel before the power of money ("'Marleena Kenwigs', cried her mother, in a torrent of affection. 'Go down upon your knees to your dear uncle, and beg him to love you all his life through, for he's more an angel than a man, and I've always said so'" - xv, 179). It is a world dependent on advertisement, confidence and appearance - Squeers doesn't want Nicholas and Smike to escape because he'll get adverse publicity.(xiii, 148)   At Crummles's, where relatively innocent manipulation is practised, everything and everyone is put to use and placed on show - Smike's ghastly appearance, for instance (like Oliver the mute); one speciality is grotesque combat between disproportionate opponents ("'Size! ... Why it's the essence of the combat that there should be a foot or two between them.'" - xxii, 279). The more sensation, the more attention you get: "Notoriety, notoriety, is the thing" for Mr. Folair. "All the town would have come to see the actor who nearly killed a man by mistake; I shouldn't wonder if it had got him an engagement in London." (xxix, 378)   London is a place of appearances, proliferating multiple levels of reality, and generating confusion.

This confusion is mirrored in internal psychology. *Nicholas Nickleby* is a novel with considerable interest in mistaken notions of the world and their origins in verbal mistakes, the association of ideas according to private and eccentric systems. And the social milieu of the city is again understood to have a determining effect, as (though not for the first time) Dickens explores the theme of the paradoxical isolation experienced by many inhabitants of great cities.[27] "This wilderness of London" is Nicholas's phrase when he first meets Charles Cheeryble, who emphatically agrees: "Wilderness! Yes it is, it is ... It was a wilderness to me once. I came here barefoot." (xxxv, 450); and Miss La Creevy is described as "One of the many to whom, from straitened circumstances, a consequent inability to form the associations they would wish, and a disinclination to mix with the society they could obtain, London is as complete a solitude as the plains of Syria ..." (xx, 246) "Most men live in a world of their own," the narrator reflects *à propos* of Sir Mulberry Hawke and his circle (xxviii, 357); when Kate refers to them as Ralph Nickleby's friends, she gets a sharp retort: "'friends! ... *I* have no friends, girl!'" - 369), which provides exemplification of the narrator's reflection on the novel's first page; "It is extraordinary how long a man may look among the crowd without discovering the face of a friend, but it is no less true." (i, 1) Isolation and the practice of mystification in the city world foster worlds of private misunderstanding, that confused jumble of impressions in which grotesques are generated.

Mrs. Nickleby is the foremost example in the novel of such mental operations. The phrase most commonly used to describe them is "association of ideas",[28] and its meaning and essential relationship to London are suggested by an early instance of how false impressions may be obtained from names, in this case of the Saracen's Head Coach from Snow Hill, "... picturing to us by a double association of ideas something stern and rugged". (iv, 29) For her, a driver with a green *shade* over his left eye suggests a post-*chaise*; an Italian image boy (selling statues of famous people) induces a dream about Shakespeare (xxvii, 353);[29] and "a fine warm summer's *day* like this with the birds singing in every direction, always puts me in mind of roast pig, with *sage* and onion sauce, and *made gravy*" (xli, 529) - which in turn puts her in mind of *babies*. Such associations produce manifest grotesques: "'... the Prince Regent was proud of his legs, and so was Daniel Lambert, who was also a fat man; *he* was proud of his legs. So was Miss Biffin; she was - no,' added Mrs. Nickleby, correcting herself, 'I think she had only toes, but the principle is the same.'" (xxxvii, 481);[30] "'... of course I mean that his glazed hat looks like a gentleman's servant, and not the wart upon his nose; though even that is not so ridiculous as it may seem to you, for we had a foot-boy once, who had not only a wart, but a wen also, and a very large wen too, and he demanded to have his wages raised in consequence, because he found it came very expensive." (xlv, 583)   In Mrs.Nickleby's speech one thing leads to another by a curious sequential logic essentially parallel to the strange transitions and juxtapositions of the city environment.

Her mental habits are pushed to extreme limits by her lover and neighbour, the mad gentleman who throws cucumbers at her. This pleasantly obscene gesture is another illustration of the sexual energy exhibited in the novel; his determination to get at Mrs. Nickleby extends to a determination to descend her chimney ("Nothing will prevent him making love," declares his keeper - xli, 539). His appearance marks him as a grotesque, the relative of the novel's pantaloons: "a very large head, and an old face in which were a pair of most extraordinary grey eyes: very wild, very wide open, and rolling in their sockets, with a dull languishing leering look, most ugly to behold." (533) He is a London madman, his disordered speech full of the London streets in which confusion also reigns, as when he muses on the cause of Mrs. Nickleby's inadequate responses to his wooing: "is it ... in consequence of the statue at Charing Cross having been lately seen on the Stock Exchange, at midnight, walking arm-in-arm with the Pump from Aldgate, in a riding-habit?" (534)   His categories - calls for "bottled lightning", "a thunder sandwich" and "a fricassee of boot-tops and goldfish sauce" (xlix, 648) - are another way of making familiar things strange, analogous to Dickens's own habits of associative metaphor.

And - allowing for the possibility of some personal malice in the portrayal of Mrs. Nickleby[31] - there is ideological significance in these wayward verbal habits. "Die Gedanken sind frei" was one of Brecht's favourite mottos, and he receives unlikely corroboration from Mrs. Nickleby, responding sympathetically to one of Newman Nogg's cryptic protests against Ralph Nickleby: "O yes, I understand you, Mr. Noggs, Our thoughts are free, of course. Everybody's thoughts are their own, clearly." (xi, 130) The free uninstitutionalised mental life that characterises Mrs. Nickleby and the cucumber man in the novel are, so to speak, the raw material of the energies of the oppressed, and in characters like Newman Noggs, "ruminating ... upon a *vast* number of possibilities and impossibilities which crowded upon his brain", (xxxi, 407) we have the beginnings of a translation of these thoughts into violent action against his predatory employer: "I shall do it some day in that little back-parlour, I know I shall. I should have done it before now, if I hadn't been afraid of making bad worse. I shall double-lock myself in with him and have it out with him before I die, I'm quite certain of it." (xxxi, 405) In this grotesque Leporello with "two goggle-eyes, whereof one was a fixture, a rubicund nose, a cadaverous face" (ii, 8), the forerunner of Pancks and Wemmick, are felt the grotesque rudiments of a "new man".

But of course it is in the Nickleby family that the latent violence of protest against oppression is most strongly felt. Nicholas, a "ruthless and ardent mind", (liii, 692) is full of the energies of Chartism: "If you do raise the devil in me, the consequences shall fall heavily upon your own head" (xiii, 155), he warns Squeers, echoing on the personal plane the Carlylean doctrine of historic responsibility (you reap what you sow).[32] Kate shares that temper (and so too does Oliver, in his workhouse protest, or his outburst against Noah Claypole); her protest against the predations of Sir Mulberry Hawk and his gang draws from Ralph a suit-able compliment: "There is some of that boy's blood in you, I see." (xxviii, 370) Though the Cheerybles provide false solutions, in this novel, to the problems raised and discussed, and seriously compromise its integrity in its latter half, a revolutionary energy, more clearly reflected in the novels that follow, is unmistakeably felt.

And that energy has its counterpart in the workings of the imagination, its grotesque metamor-phosis of objects into one another through metaphor reflecting the movement of historical change. And it is able, at one moment in the novel to suggest, with a sublimity that is hardly just 'inverse', an epiphany of the city transformed and released from its vapours of unreality:

The ticket porter leans idly against the post

as the corner, comfortably warm, but not hot,
although the day is broiling. His white apron
flaps languidly in the air, his head gradually
droops upon his breast, he takes very long
winks with both eyes at once; even he is unable
to withstand the soporific influence of the
place, and is gradually falling asleep. But
now, he starts into full wakefulness, recoils
a step or two, and gazes out before him with
eager wildness in his eye. Is it a job, or a
boy at marbles? Does he see a ghost, or hear
an organ? No; sight more unwanted still -
there is a butterfly in the square - a real,
live butterfly! astray from flowers and sweets,
and fluttering among the iron heads of the
dusty area railings. (xxxvii, 469)

NOTES

1. The phrase is from Fanger, *op.cit.*, p.
129. Dostoevsky thought of St. Petersburg as the
'most fantastic' of all cities - see Fanger, p.105.
2. So unknown, in fact, that in 1850 Sir
Peter Laurie asserted that it "only existed in a
work of fiction, written by Mr. Charles Dickens ten
years ago." (see Philip Collins, *Dickens and
Crime*, second edition (London, Macmillan, 1964),
p.185; Dickens retaliated by questioning the
reality of Sir Peter Laurie). The exchange is an
interesting, if crude example of how terms like
'real' and 'fantastic' form part of social polemics
in Victorian England.
3. Quotation from Philip Collins, 'Dickens
and London', in *The Victorian City: Images and
Realities*, ed. H.J. Dyos and Michael Wolff (London,
Routledge Kegan Paul, 1973), p.541. It is
interesting to compare this with Gutzkow's view,
expressed in 1850, that the new novel of the 19th
century was the 'Roman des Nebeneinanders' (novel
of juxtapositions), exploring the contrasts and
contiguities of the city (see Karl Riha, *Die
Beschreibung der Grossen Stadt : Zur Entstehung des
Grosstadtmotivs in der deutschen Literatur ca.
1750-1850* (Bad Homburg, Gehlen Verlag, 1970), p.74.
4. See 'A Visit to Newgate', *SB*, 201-14,
and 'Night Walks', *UT*, 130, and, for a discussion
of these papers, M. Hollington, 'Dickens and
Flâneur', *The Dickensian LXXVII* (Summer, 1981), 81.
5. cf. Nemo's burial-place in *Bleak House*,
as described by Jo: "He was put there ... Over
yinder. Among them piles of bones, and close to

that there kitchin winder! They put him wery nigh
the top. They was obliged to stamp upon it to git
it in." (*BH*, xvi, 225).

6. Alexander Welsh's *The City of Dickens*
(Oxford, O.U.P., 1971), especially chapter one,
"The City of Satire", provides a useful and
stimulating discussion of the traditions of satiric
representations of the city.

7. cf. Shakespeare, *King Lear*, IV, vi, 152-
156: "Look with thine ears: see how yond justice
rails upon yond simple thief. Hark, in thine ear:
change places, and, handy-dandy, which is the
justice, which is the thief?" (handy-dandy is the
children's game which asks in which hand an object
is concealed). For the satiric principle, see Ian
Donaldson, *The World Upside Down: Comedy from
Jonson to Fielding* (Oxford, O.U.P., 1970).

8. For some this has meant that the
grotesque is principally a feature of an early,
inferior Dickens - e.g. Michael Steig in "Dickens,
Hablot Browne, and the Tradition of English
Caricatures", *Criticism* XI (1969), 219-234, and
Dickens and Phiz (Bloomington, Indiana University
Press, 1978). For a divergent view, see chapter 9
below.

9. "Well, you're quite a literary character,
sir!" exclaims Mrs. Mann in compliment to Bumble's
invention. (ii, 8) He is a relative of a class of
literary impostors in Dickens's novels, many of
whom refer obliquely to the Warrens experience; Mr.
Slum in *The Old Curiosity Shop*, for instance, is
the author of advertising jingles ("Ask the
perfumers, ask the blacking-makers, ask the
hatters, ask the old lottery-office keepers - ask
any man among 'em what my poetry has done for him,
and mark my words, he blesses the name of Slum."
- *OCS*, xxviii, 213).

10. The notion of an innate criminal nature,
evidenced in a distinctive phrenology or physiognomy,
was prevalent in the 19th century, and its
detection (in work like Lombroso's) a distinctive
preoccupation of criminologists. Lavater himself,
in fact, in founding the science of physiognomy,
thought it could become "the terror of vice",
through its capacity to read villainy in the face,
but Goethe argued against this crudely deterministic
approach (see José Lopez-Rey, "Goya's Caprichos:
Beauty, Reason, and Caricature" in Fred Licht, ed.,
Goya in Perspective (Englewood Cliffs, N.J.,
Prentice-Hall, 1973), p.117).

11. Whether or not he had yet read Carlyle's

Sartor Researtus (1831), Dickens began at an early point in his career to mock dandyism and the "philosophy of clothes" - (something to which he himself as a young man was not unsusceptible). The seminal text is "Meditations in Monmouth-Street" of 1836 (*SB*, 74-80; the subject of a stimulating analysis in J. Hillis Miller, "The Fiction of Realism; *Sketches by Boz, Oliver Twist*, and Cruickshank's Illustrations", *Charles Dickens and George Cruickshank. Papers Read at a Clark Library Seminar on May 9, 1970* (Los Angeles: William Andrews Clark Memorial Library, University of California, 1971), pp.1-69).

12. Even Oliver, to look his real bourgeois self again, must be dressed for the part: "How well he looks, and how like a gentleman's son he is dressed again", (*OT*, xli, 313) exclaims Mrs. Bedwin on his return to the Brownlow fold.

13. A characteristic, too, of similar figures in Balzac's work; see for instance Fraisier the lawyer in *Cousin Pons*, who imprints his nature on his office: "Le cabinet sentait si bien son Fraisier, qu'on devait croire que l'air y était pestilentiel" (Folio edition, Gallimard, Paris, 1973, p.207).

14. One manifestation of these juxtapositions is the habit of zeugma and oxymoron in the novel. For an example of the former, there is Mr.Bumble's exclamation to Mrs. Corney - "What an opportunity for a jining of hearts and housekeeping!" (xxvii, 199) - of the latter the account of Oliver's undertaking work: "it was a nice sickly season just at this time." (vi, 39). That these figures are intrinsically related to the 'streaky-bacon' principle is evidenced by their marked presence in the passage describing it ("it is the custom on the stage, in all good murderous melodramas, to present the tragic and the comic scenes, in a regular alteration, as the layers of red and white in a side of streaky bacon" - xvii, 118).

15. cf. Hollington, "Dickens's Conception of the Grotesque", 92.

16. Caricatures of Jews have of course an ancient and problematic history. Thomas Wright in fact claims that the first English caricature is a representation of a Jew - see Wright, *op. cit.*, p. 75.

17. Likewise grotesque caricatural representations of humans as donkeys. As often Goya's - influenced by English caricature - are amongst the most powerful and memorable - see e.g. Caprichos

39, "Asta su abuelo".

18. Monsters generated out of mud were to fascinate Dickens throughout his life - cf. (e.g.) the Megalosaurus in *Bleak House* (*BH*, i, 1) and the dinosaurs in *U7*, 347; *Household Words* has a number of articles on myths and legends concerning sea monsters. The reference is a distinctive and highly characteristic instance of that cross-fertilizing of everyday mundanity (the mud of the streets) and a mythic imagination.

19. Fog and mist are amongst the hallmarks of the Dickensian 'making strange'. The atmospheric light effects of the Romney Marshes seems to have made a powerful impression upon Dickens, and become an important theme in *Great Expectations* (see chapter 11 below). Right from the start, though, their presence in the city is exulted in - see 'The Streets-Night' in *Sketches by Boz*, for instance: "But the streets of London, to be beheld in the very height of their glory should be seen on a dark, dull, murky winter's night, when there is just enough damp gently stealing down to make the pavement greasy, without cleaning it of any of its impurities; and when the heavy, lazy mist, which hangs over every object, makes the gas-lamps look brighter, and the brilliantly-lighted shops more splendid, from the contrast they present to the darkness around." (*SB*, 53). The dominant image ('poeticising' the streets) is maritime - from the "thousand misty eddies" (*07*, xxiii, 165) of *Oliver Twist* to the "circling eddies of fog" (*OMF*, III, i, 420) of *Our Mutual Friend*, where buildings are engaged in a "struggle to get their heads above the foggy sea."

20. For instance, *The Terrific Register, or, Record of Crimes, Judgments, Providences and Calamities* of 1825, which Dickens imbibed avidly in his adolescence - whose frontispiece, a book open at the words, "God's Revenge Against Murder", indicates what lies in store. A monotonous and disingenuous catalogue of crimes and horrors is paraded; in all of them the villain is found out by the operation of a super-natural revenge working through natural or inanimate objects that rebel in protest against sin.

21. Balzac's writing frequently makes a very similar point about Paris as a place where the variety of human types points to the multiplicity of impulses and desires, that seek and find gratification there.

22. cf. Fielding's definition of 'nobody' in

his 'Modern Glossary': "All the people in Great
Britain, except about 1200" (quoted from Charles
Mitchell's introduction to *Hogarth's Peregrination*
(Oxford, 1952), xxx). 'Nobody' is one of Dickens's
favourite jokes - besides the original title of
Little Dorrit (*Nobody's Fault*) see (e.g.) 'Nobody's
Story' in *Christmas Stories* (*CS*, 59-66).

23. Two amongst many of Dickens's 'leering'
grotesques are Bagstock in *Dombey and Son* ("whose
eye had often wandered from his newspaper to leer
at the prospect" - *DS*, xx, 283) and, in the same
novel, Carker, "like a leering face on an old
water-spout" (*DS*, xlii, 597).

24. Thus she prefigures Dickens's very last
grotesque, the Princess Puffer, "as ugly and
withered as one of the fantastic carrings on the
under brackets of the stall seats" (xxiii, 278) as
she stands listening to Jasper's music-making on
the last page of *Edwin Drood*.

25. And again, like the bourgeois characters
of *Oliver Twist*, Arthur Gride imprints his nature
upon his surroundings, so that they become a kind
of shell or casing: "In an old house, dismal, dark
and dusty, which seemed to have withered, like
himself, and to have grown yellow and shrivelled in
hoarding him from the light of day, as he had, in
hoarding his money, lived Arthur Gride" (*NN*, li,
667).

26. The Rowlandson illustration of the old
roué getting into bed in expectation of his young
lover seems very pertinent to this episode - see
Hollington, "The Dance of Death", 66.

27. A distinct topos for 19th century
writers - cf. Baudelaire ("Multitude, solitude:
termes égaux et convertibles pour le poète actif et
fécond"), and a probable common ancestor, de
Quincey: "No man ever was left to himself for the
first time in the streets, as yet unknown, of
London, but he must have been saddened and
mortified, perhaps terrified, by the sense of
desertion, and utter loneliness, which belongs to
his situation". (*Autobiography* in *Collected
Writings* ed. David Masson (Edinburgh, 1889; 14
vols.), I, 182).

28. A phrase and concept - derived from
Locke via Sterne - to which Dickens appears to have
been particularly attached. It is used, not only
in the case of Mrs. Nickleby, but in that of Flora
Finching in *Little Dorrit* and Miss Tox in *Dombey
and Son* (among others). Dickensian humour seems to
owe a lot to it - at least according to the author's

own testimony ("Nothing in Flora made me laugh so much as the confusion of ideas between gout flying upwards, and its soaring with Mr. F-- to another sphere" (Forster, II, 183).

29. cf. *OCS*, lxxiii, 549, where Tom Scott assumes the name "of an Italian image lad".

30. Miss Biffin was a famous early nineteenth century 'freak', exhibited at circuses and fairs because of her deformities, and her ability to write with her toes. Dickens's many references to her - for instance, in *Martin Chuzzlewit* a drunk Viscount laments the absence of 'leg' in Shakespeare's heroines ("Why in that respect they're all Miss Biffins to the audience, Pip" - *MC*, xxviii, 454), and in *Little Dorrit* Mr. Merdle's habit of withdrawing his hands up his sleeves makes him seem "the twin brother of Miss Biffin" (*LD*, II, xviii, 631 - testify to his responsiveness to such versions of the grotesque.

31. It is often assumed that Mrs. Nickleby is a portrait of Dickens's mother, its decidedly unflattering edges a kind of revenge for Mrs. Dickens's enthusiasm that her son should work at Warrens'. See Letters I, 15n for some of the evidence for and against this view.

32. This is an early instance of the influence of Carlyle's concept of historical determinism, which is to become very marked in novels like *Hard Times*, with its tripartite division of sections ('Sowing', 'Reaping', 'Garnering'), or *A Tale of Two Cities*, where the organic linking of the revolution with what precedes it expresses a faith in the inevitable 'natural' consequences of historic misdeeds.

Chapter Four

THE OLD CURIOSITY SHOP AND THE NEW CURIOSITY SHOP

In any account of the grotesque in Dickens, *The Old Curiosity Shop* must have a significant place, in view of its author's assertion, in the preface to the 1848 edition, that "... in writing this book, I had it always in my fancy to surround the lonely figure of the child with grotesque and wild, but not impossible companions." (*OCS*, xii) Admittedly, this statement should not necessarily be taken to mean that Dickens had the grotesque in mind from the start, for in a letter of March 1840 to Samuel Williams, written when only the early chapters had been written, there is very similar phrasing, but a significant absence of the word 'grotesque': "... the object being to shew the child in the midst of a crowd of uncongenial and ancient things."[1] What does seem likely, though, is that during the writing of *The Old Curiosity Shop* Dickens's consciousness of himself as a grotesque writer had been appreciably raised, in particular by Thomas Hood's *Athenaeum* review of November,1840, written while the novel was still unfinished, which Dickens acknowledged as "... so earnestly, so eloquently, and tenderly appreciative of her [Nell], and of all her shadowy kith and kin, that it would have been insensibility in me, if I could have read it without an unusual glow of pleasure and encouragement."[2] In it Hood had emphasised the grotesque and picturesque in the novel, claiming he was unable to think of any fiction "... with a more striking and picturesque combination of images than is presented by the simple childish figure of little Nell amidst a chaos of such obsolete, grotesque, old-world commodities as form the stock-in-trade of the 'Old Curiosity Shop'" and praising the artist's representation of the child "asleep in her little bed, surrounded, or rather mobbed, by ancient armour and arms, antique furniture, and relics sacred and profane, hideous or grotesque."[3] Consciously, or unconsciously, Dickens may have borrowed that 'surrounded' for the 1848 preface, as he may have borrowed the significantly located emphasis on the grotesque with which the first chapter of the novel in its final form ends. It entered the work only in the first single volume issue of 1841 - after the Hood review:

> 'It would be a curious speculation,' said I, after some restless turns across and across the room, 'to imagine her in her future life, holding her solitary way among a crowd of wild grotesque companions; the only pure, fresh, youthful object in the throng...' (i, 13)[4]

Like *Nicholas Nickleby*, then, with its pattern of contrasts between old lechers and youthful victims, the novel makes the grotesque part of a central structural principle. This is a process that involves the collapsing of distinctions between characters and objects, human and inanimate matter - the contrast between Nell and the curios of the curiosity shop is later expanded into the contrast between Nell and Quilp or between Nell and the companions who surround her during her wanderings: Codlin and Short, Mrs. Jarley, and the band of itinerants travelling from fair to fair. Characters appear combined or set against the grotesque objects - Quilp sits among the bric-à-brac when he comes to take over the shop, and appears suddenly in a statue niche at Oxford, like one of the curios returned to its place of origin. In Little Nell's mind, the waxworks at Mrs. Jarley's associate with the other figures that surround her, coalescing with them in such a way that they are no longer easily separable. And at Wolverhampton, confronted with the new industrial environment for the first time, Nell meets the grotesque transposed onto another plane, in which dream and fantasy are merged with the frightening realities of modern society.

To understand why this pattern of contrasts should be so prominent it is necessary to gauge the impact on Dickens's mind of two important events that had occurred not long before the novel's inception. The first is a personal tragedy, the death of Mary Hogarth, who has obvious relation to Little Nell in the novel. *The Old Curiosity Shop* can be thought of as a memorial to Mary Hogarth, and the artistic consequence of this is an emphasis, stronger than anywhere else in Dickens, perhaps,

upon the kind of 'classic' realist doctrine of the
significance of mundane, everyday lives, as it is
formulated (for instance) in *Adam Bede*.[5] The novel
carries a number of reminders of the opportunities
for heroism in obscure lives. "Have I yet to learn"
the schoolmaster asks rhetorically, when he hears
the story of Little Nell's adventures and tribulat-
ions, "that the hardest and best-borne trials are
those which are never chronicled in any earthly
record, and are suffered every day!" (xlvi, 344),
and the manuscript continues at this point with what
looks like a reference to Mary Hogarth's death: "How
many thousands with no other motive to exertion or
endurance, and with no other reward, live unregarded,
and die unnoticed and unknown! What humble churchyard, but has many such heroes mingling with its
dust!"[6] Later he attempts to console Nell in her
gloomy conviction that the obscure dead are
forgotten by claiming that their influence lives on
in numerous deeds that are dedicated to them: "Do
you think there are no deeds far away from here, in
which these dead may be best remembered? Nell,
Nell, there may be people busy in the world at this
instant, in whose good actions and good thoughts
these very graves - neglected as they look to us -
are the chief instruments." (lv, 406)

Such an emphasis, chiming as it did both with
an emergent aesthetic and the dominant intellectual
influence of Carlyle,[7] made a strong appeal to the
novel's first readers; Caroline Fox, for instance,
writing in 1882 in *Memories of Old Friends*, but
remembering that period, praises Dickens because he
"forces the sympathies of all into unwonted channels,
and teaches us that Punch and Judy men, beggar
children, and daft old men are also of our species,
and are not, more than ourselves, removed from the
sphere of the heroic".[8] Little Nell's Pilgrim's
Progress[9] through the grotesque sloughs of despair,
monsters, giants and demons of early Victorian
England inhabits a sphere of heroism open to all the
talents.

The second and this time public phenomenon
whose shadow clearly hangs over *The Old Curiosity
Shop* is Chartist unrest in the late 1830's. Again
Carlyle is an important parallel for an influence
upon the way Chartism is reflected in this novel,
for manifestly the matrices of Dickens's analysis of
the social evils that produce unrest are to be found
in his writing ("That man is carrying out Carlyle's
work more emphatically than any", wrote Caroline
Fox in response to Dickens's novel).[10] In

particular it is evident that Dickens constantly reflected upon, whilst partially transforming, Carlyle's Romantic, organicist stress upon an ideal notion of nature (and within it human nature) in its pristine splendour, before distortion by the operation of culture in the industrial age of machine production, which produces unnatural monstrosities. The kind of ideas in Dickens's mind at this time, and their obvious relation to the grotesque in the novels of this period (*Oliver Twist* and *Nicholas Nickleby* as well as *The Old Curiosity Shop*) can be illustrated by a letter of January 1841, written just after the novel's completion:

> What do you think of the book in serious earnest - a true strong, sledge-hammer book about the children of the people, as much beaten out of Nature by iron necessity as the children of the nobility are, by luxury and pride? It would be a good thing to have the two extremes - Fairlie and Fielding - Hogarth and Chalon - the Princess Royal whom the nurse daren't kiss - and the baby on the step of a door whose mother tried to strangle it.[11]

Such responses to chartism - the emphasis upon how industrial civilization ("iron necessity") has produced a distortion of rich and poor alike, in themselves and in their relation to each other - are also to figure prominently in a number of the works that follow. *The Old Curiosity Shop* can be seen as the first of Dickens's novels in which the discussion of what has happened to 'nature' in contemporary society involves also the examination of the likelihood and desirability of revolution.

However, the first significant discussion of 'nature' in Dickens's work had already taken place in *Nicholas Nickleby*, in a passage where Charles Cheeryble corrects Nicholas's astonishment at Smike's "unnatural" fear and hatred of his father:

> My dear sir ... you fall into the very common mistake, of charging upon Nature, matters with which she has not the smallest connexion, and for which she is in no way responsible. Men talk of nature as an abstract thing, and lose sight of what is natural while they do so. Here is a poor lad who has never felt a parent's care, who has scarcely known anything all his life but suffering and sorrow, presented to a man who he is told is his

father, and whose first act is to signify his intention of putting an end to his short term of happiness, of consigning him to his old fate, and taking him from the only friend he has ever had - which is yourself. If Nature, in such a case, put into that lad's breast but one secret prompting which urged him towards his father and away from you, she would be a liar and an idiot. (*NN*, xlvi, 595)

This is far from any naive or sentimentalising attitude towards 'nature', or any nostalgic lament for the loss of the sphere of the 'natural'. And in an even more significant passage in *Martin Chuzzlewit*, directed perhaps partly against contemporary outrage at the 'unnaturalness' of Chartism, Dickens shows a firm understanding of how much of 'nature' is indeed culture:

Oh, moralists, who treat of happiness and self-respect, innate in every sphere of life, and shedding light on every grain of dust in God's highway, so smooth below your carriage-wheels, so rough beneath the tread of naked feet, bethink yourselves in looking on the swift descent of men who have lived in their own esteem, that there are scores of thousands breathing now, and breathing thick with painful toil, who in that high respect have never lived at all, nor had a chance of life! Go ye, who rest so placidly upon the sacred Bard who had been young, and when he strung his harp was old, and had never seen the righteous forsaken, or his seed begging their bread; go, Teachers of content and honest pride, into the mine, the mill, the forge, the squalid depths of deepest ignorance, and uttermost abyss of man's neglect, and say can any hopeful plant spring up in air so foul that it extinguishes the soul's bright torch as fast as it is kindled! And oh! ye Pharisees of the nineteen hundredth year of Christian Knowledge, who soundingly appeal to human nature, see first that it be human. Take heed it has not been transformed, during your slumber, and the sleep of generations, into the nature of Beasts. (*MC*, xiii, 224)

The essential point here is that in contemporary society the bestial and monstrous have become domesticated, and can't be dismissed as "unnatural" and thereby 'nobody's fault': emphasis is laid upon the necessity of responsibility for the human consequences of the industrial revolution. Sir Thomas Browne's assertion, that there are "no grotesques in nature",[12] receives thorough, ironical undermining in *The Old Curiosity Shop* (and the novels that succeed it).

Its central figure, Quilp, provides ample evidence of what has happened to 'human nature' in this society. His name already associates him with animals (Quilp suggests 'whelp' - as well as 'whip' and 'queer'), and very soon a range of bestial references are established. To begin with he is compared to the canine order of creation, with attention paid to his way of shaking himself "in a very dog-like manner" (*OCS*, v, 40) and in particular to his "dog-like smile" (iv, 37):

> But what added most to the grotesque expression on his face, was a ghastly smile, which appearing to be the mere result of habit and to have no connection with any mirthful or complacent feeling, constantly revealed the few discoloured fangs that were yet scattered in his mouth, and gave him the aspect of a panting dog. (iii, 22)

Other more and less grotesque creatures are soon invoked: Quilp is "as sharp as a ferret, and as cunning as a weasel", has a "hawk's eye" (v, 38) and "as watchful as a lynx" (xlviii, 360), screws his head up on one side like the ravens who are shortly to form a constant reference-point for Dickens's perception of the grotesque (iv, 36),[13] and makes "... every monstrous grimace of which men or monkeys are capable".(xlviii, 358)   These comparisons suggest once more the techniques of caricature, the perception of relationships between human and animal physiognomies, as in *Oliver Twist*; and the points of comparison between Quilp and the characters of that earlier novel, Fagin in particular, are really quite numerous - the fangs, the lynx eyes, the habit of "bowing with grotesque politeness" (xlviii, 355), and the Harlequin antics involving stealth, agility and the mastery of techniques of surprise ("I'll be a Will o' the Wisp, now here, now there, dancing about you always, starting up when you least expect me, and keeping you in a constant state of restlessness and irritation" - 1,377). But perhaps the later novel offers a slightly more generalised representation of a bestialised society - Quilp is not only compared to a dog but treats others as dogs as well (it's his constant name for Tom Scott, for instance).[14]

This is one sense, then, in which those who frequent Quilp's company, like his wife and Mrs. Jiniwin, tend to "doubt if he were really a human creature." (v, 40) But it isn't merely the case that Quilp appears as a sub-human animal; "... that taste for doing something fantastic and monkey-like, which on all occasions had strong possession of him" (ix, 72) has its 'fantastic', supernatural dimensions as well, the doubt about what he really is ("a constant state of restlessness and irritation") a part of the effect of the grotesque. The idea of demonic possession, of an evil spirit inhabiting Quilp and giving him quasi-mythical powers, like his apparent capacity to breath and drink fire ("He's a Salamander,you know, that's what he is" affirms Dick Swiveller at xxiii, 173; and see also lxii, 463), is strong in the novel, and his characteristic grotesque leer is frequently seen as something diabolical (contemplating his sadistic violence towards Mrs. Quilp he is described "... grinning like a devil as he rubbed his dirty hands together" - iii, 25) He appears amongst the curios at Nell's home (ix, 72) or as a statue in a niche at Oxford (xxvii, 207), like the product of an imagination haunted by demons (his grimaces are such as "... none but himself and nightmares had the power of assuming" - iv, 36).

Quilp is thus an essentially ambiguous figure inhabiting the borderline of fantasy and 'reality', "grotesque and wild, but not impossible". It is an ambiguity that has something to do with the fact that he is (in Kit Nubbles's words, relayed by Tom Scott) "a uglier dwarf than can be seen anywhere for a penny" (vi, 47); dwarfs, with the stature of children and an intelligence sharpened by the struggle to survive, are traditionally licensed to break conventions and comment ironically upon them.[15] Quilp is a parody of a child, "... rubbing his hands so hard that he seemed to be engaged in manufacturing, of the dirt with which they were encrusted, little charges for popguns" (iv, 34), his 'childishness' full of sinister edges (he sleeps in Nell's bed, for instance, because it fits him, but also because he has a partiality for young girls - xi, 86). And of course like Fagin he is a performer, a fairground creature capable of spinning that web of magic and strangeness that makes the "attraction of repulsion" that is once more so evident. Mrs. Quilp's marriage to him is "one of those strange infatuations of which examples are by no means scarce" (iv, 30); of

Tom Scott's relationship to him it is emphasised
that "... between this boy and the dwarf there
existed a strange kind of mutual liking" (v, 42);
and Nell herself, like Oliver in Fagin's lair,
feels "... much inclined to laugh at his uncouth
appearance and grotesque attitude". (vi, 44)
    In this relation of Quilp the dwarf to fair-
ground exhibits[16] the controlling idea of *The Old
Curiosity Shop* is to be discovered. The curios of
the antique shop modulate, as the novel progresses,
into these figures on display in the marketplace, in
a demonstration of the new curiosity shop that
Victorian England had become. The shop at the
beginning, "one of those receptacles for old and
curious things", hides its "musty treasures from the
public eye in jealousy and distrust" (i, 4); these
flaunt and exploit them. The past of grotesque art,
"fantastic carvings brought from monkish cloisters;
rusty weapons of various kinds; distorted figures in
china,[17] and wood, and iron, and ivory; tapestry,
and strange furniture that might have been designed
in dreams" (5), has become the present of Nell's
grotesque and wild companions, a living Quilp made
out of dreams, wooden, distorted creatures on
display in public places - "the faces all awry,
grinning from wood and stone" (14) leap as demons
and skeletons on to the page. Nell's death is felt
as inevitable at an early stage, as her project, to
escape from the grotesque into nature - to find "...
a relief from the gloomy solitude in which she had
lived, an escape from the heartless people by whom
she had been surrounded in her late time of trial,
the restoration of the old man's health and peace,
and a life of tranquil happiness" (xii, 94) - is
shown up as hopeless by the 'grotesques in nature'
she meets wherever she goes.
    Thus ominously at the outset of her travels
Nell meets Mr. Punch in a churchyard, "... perched
cross-legged upon a tombstone ..." (xvi, 122).
Giants appear next - or so the stilt-walkers seem
as they throw their "monstrous shadows" (xvii, 133),
transformed by the child's imagination into fabulous
beings. Yet side-by-side with this mythical heightening the fairground exhibits are also presented
very prosaically as mere property, commodities to
be managed carefully because of fluctuations in the
capitalist economy. Mr. Vuffin, "... the proprietor
of a giant, and a little lady without legs or arms
..." (xix, 143, the latter evidently a relative of
Miss Biffin) knows the laws of supply and demand on
which this economy operates: "... if you was to

86

advertise Shakspeare played entirely by wooden legs,
it's my belief you wouldn't draw a sixpence", and
likewise, "Once make a giant common and giants will
never draw again". (143) For want of such knowledge
Mrs. Jarley's waxworks falls on hard times, because
of "... the depressed state of the classical market
..." (xxxii, 243). One's employment prospects in
this world depend on one's commodity value - for
instance, dwarfs are more valuable than giants
because they get uglier as they age, whilst aged
giants get weak at the knees, and are reduced to
waiting on the dwarfs at dinner.(144)

However, these realities are manifestly not yet
contemplated with an unalloyed despair, or the dire
prophetic strains of Carlyle. The grotesque in *The
Old Curiosity Shop* still displays a 'joyful and
triumphant hilarity', an excitement of discovery,
even when what is discovered are relationships
between systems of evil. Kit Nubbles, entering the
novel with "... certainly the most comical expression of face I ever saw ..." and "... the most extraordinary leer I ever beheld ..." (i, 7), re-asserts
Thomas Wright's conviction of the naturalness of
laughter when he hears of his mother's conversion to
calvinist gloom: "Just hear this! Ha ha ha! An't
that as nat'ral as the sheep's bleating, or a pig's
grunting, or a horse's neighing, or a bird's singing?" (xxii, 167) The 'grotesques in nature'
exhibited in this novel perform a positive function
as they serve a 'natural' appetite for diversion, a
love of the curious belonging, according to Romantic
ideology, to children and unfallen adults, in which
the mingling of the horrifying and the ludicrous,
the supernatural and the mundane is of compelling
attraction.

The novel explores and proliferates connections
between its heterogenous assembly of grotesques as it
continues. Quilp becomes intermingled in Nell's
mind with the other companions who surround her:
"she could get none but broken sleep by fits and
starts at night, for fear of Quilp, who throughout
her uneasy dreams was somehow connected with the
wax-work, or was wax-work himself, or was Mrs.
Jarley, wax-work, and a barrel-organ all in one, and
yet not exactly any of them either." (xxvii, 209)
In dream these relationships form and dissolve, in
that fleeting unstable manner in which forms metamorphose into one another in grotesque art. Having
left behind the curios, Nell (not unlike Oliver
Twist among the coffins of Mr.Sowerberry's) sleeps
in the company of waxworks and Quilp, and levels of

reality are blurred:

> Quilp indeed was a perpetual nightmare to the
> child, who was constantly haunted by a vision
> of his ugly face and stunted figure. She slept,
> for their better security, in the room where
> the wax-work figures were, and she never
> retired to this place at night but she tortured
> herself - she could not help it - with imagin-
> ing a resemblance, in some one or other of
> their death-like faces, to the dwarf, and this
> fancy would sometimes so gain upon her that she
> would almost believe he had removed the figure
> and stood within the clothes. Then there were
> so many of them with their great glassy eyes -
> and, as they stood one behind the other all
> about her bed, they looked so like living
> creatures, and yet so unlike in their grim
> stillness and silence, that she had a kind of
> terror of them for their own sakes, and would
> often lie watching their dusky figures, until
> she was obliged to rise and light a candle, or
> go and sit at the open window and feel a
> companionship in the bright stars. (xxix, 217)

At this stage in the novel the theme darkens,
for Nell's grandfather succumbs to his mania for
gambling and goes off with the card-sharpers, stealing from Nell's room at night. This moral metamorphosis surpasses all these imaginary horrors:
"The terror she had lately felt was nothing compared
with that which now oppressed her." (xxxi, 230) He
becomes "... like another creature in his shape, a
monstrous distortion of his image ..." (230) as the
rhetoric of the 'romance of real life' establishes
itself once more.
This rhetorical pattern reaches its climax in
the descriptions of Wolverhampton:

> ... in this gloomy place, moving like demons
> among the flames and smoke, dimly and fitfully
> seen, flushed and tormented by the burning
> fires, and wielding great weapons, a faulty
> blow from any one of which must have crushed
> some workman's skull, a number of men laboured
> like giants. (xliv, 330)

Work, work, work: Miss Monflathers's project for the
children of the poor is here realised as a living
nightmare for their parents.[18] Fairground giants
and demons are here transformed into industrial

workers; the personal theme of Nell is subsumed into a larger portrayal of Hell, of what has happened to human nature in the emergent industrial order. For what makes its amalgam of reality and fantasy so terrifying is the solid consistency and schematic coherence of its organisation:

> On every side, and as far as the eye could see into the heavy distance, tall chimneys, crowding on each other, and presenting that endless repetition of the same, dull, ugly form, which is the horror of oppressive dreams, poured out their plague of smoke, obscured the light, and made foul the melancholy air. (xlv, 335)

Although this scene, from which all 'joyful and triumphant hilarity' is banished, dissipates in favour of the simpler and here more sentimentalised themes of pastoral in the latter stages of *The Old Curiosity Shop*, it has a more sharp-focussed relation to a unified theme of reality and fantasy than is commonly supposed.[19] In the world of this novel everyday things, objects, people contain vertiginous horrors; their capacity of metamorphosis implies a propensity to frighten, excite or amuse in bewildering alternations of sequence. Installed in the firm of Sampson Brass, Dick Swiveller is shown staring at Sally Brass "in a state of stupid perplexity, wondering how he got into the company of that strange monster, and whether it was a dream and he would ever wake" (xxxiii, 251); removed from the same employment, and succumbing to an illness that its strange consequences (combined with alcohol) induce, he wakes to find his surroundings transformed: "If this is not a dream, I have woke up, by mistake, in an Arabian Night, instead of a London one." (lxiv, 475) London, characteristically for Dickens, is particularly productive of such effects - Nell sits looking out of the windows of the curiosity shop onto its streets and houses "... fancying ugly faces that were frowning over at her and trying to peer into the room ..." (ix, 69). And inversely Kit, placed under arrest, the victim of a cruel theatre concocted by Quilp, sits gazing out of the window "... almost hoping to see some monstrous phenomenon in the streets which might give him reason to believe he was in a dream".(lx, 446)

Naturally the world of fairground exhibits is another sphere where the demarcation lines of illusion and reality are habitually blurred. Nell, working for Mrs. Jarley as a guide to the waxworks, is thought to be "... an important item of the curiosities ..." by children who are also "... fully impressed that her grandfather was a cunning device in wax ..." (xxviii, 211). Conversely, amongst the waxwork figures are those who appear remarkably like characters in the novel - Mr. Jacob Packlemerton, for instance, "... who courted and married fourteen wives and destroyed them all, by tickling the soles of their feet when they were sleeping in the consciousness of innocence and virtue ..." (214) seems remarkably like Quilp. Contrivance creates the 'delusion', as Mr. Short calls it, at the same time referring it back once more to the realm of society's own theatre: "Would you care a ha'penny for the Lord Chancellor if you know's him in private and without his wig? - certainly not." (xvi, 123)

But any account of the grotesque in *The Old Curiosity Shop* must return finally to Quilp. Quilp feeds on the socially-induced psychological confusion of the novel, inserting himself, "like a head in a phantasmagoria" (xlviii, 362), into other people's fantasies. "Such an amazing power of taking people by surprise" is Sampson Brass's embarrassed tribute, when Quilp is resurrected from the dead "like the Ghost of Hamlet's father". (xlix, 368) Travelling with Mrs. Nubbles alone in a stagecoach he is delighted "... inasmuch as her solitary condition enabled him to terrify her with many extraordinary annoyances", which include "... staring with his great goggle eyes, which seemed in here the more horrible from his face being upside down", Quilp adapts himself to her own imaginings of hell: "... she was quite unable for the time to resist the belief that Mr.Quilp did in his own person represent and embody that Evil Power, who was so vigorously attacked at Little Bethel." (xlviii, 361)

And this constitutes the power of the conception of Quilp, and is the basis of the fascination he exerts. The grotesque, officially dismissed as outside nature, repellent and obscene, is shown in the centre of psychic and material reality. Quilp's savagery (he is compared to an African chief (xiii, 103), and at the end of the novel is described eating a beefsteak "... which he cooked himself in somewhat of a savage and cannibal-like manner" (lxvii, 504)) is the ironic expression of Victorian savagery, those primitive levels of social justice achieved in a society dedicated to progress; Quilp's cannibalism ("I don't eat babies; I don't like 'em" - xxi, 160) the satiric, handy-dandy reflection of

the domestic violence latent in ladies like Mrs.
Jiniwin ("'When my poor husband, her dear father,
was alive, if he had ever ventur'd a cross word to
me, I'd have -', the good lady did not finish the
sentence, but she twisted off the head of a shrimp
with a vindictiveness which seemed to imply that the
action was in some degree a substitute for words."
(iv, 31)) Blazing away all night (Quilp shares a
supernatural wakefulness with later Dickensian
monstrosities[20]) he parallels the Wolverhampton
factories.

"In these real times, when all the Fairies are
dead and buried ..." (*BR*, xxxi, 237) - so begins
Dickens's ironic commentary in *Barnaby Rudge* on the
Victorian commonplace of the death of the fairies
in an unromantic age.[21] From *The Old Curiosity
Shop* onwards it would be his aim to show how these
fairies had survived as the grotesques of an
industrial, mercantile, urban society. And Quilp
is the ironic fairy who comments on this fact,
again (like Ralph Nickleby) the skeleton joker in a
dance of death. For dancing is a major mode of
mockery with him: "I'll be a Will o' the Wisp, now
here, now there, dancing about you always ..." (1,
377). As Tom Scott and Kit Nubbles fight, Quilp
careers about "... in a kind of frenzy" (vi, 46);
celebrating the putative engagement of Sophy
Wackles to Dick Swiveller, he "... flourishes his
arms and legs about" (xxi, 163) in a mode of
celebration which eventually turns into "... a kind
of demon-dance round the kennel, just without the
limits of the chain, driving the dog quite wild".
(165) [22] His dancing style is clearly not the
fairies' 'light fantastic' of *A Midsummer Night's
Dream* but something markedly grotesque, "... a sort
of skip, which, what with the crookedness of his
legs, the ugliness of his face, and the mockery of
his manner, was perfectly goblin-like".(iv, 36)

"Well, I like a little wildness," he confesses
to Nell's 'bad' brother; "I was wild myself once."
(xxiii, 175) The irony asks us to consider in what
sense Quilp is no longer 'wild', and what this
implies about a society in which a 'tame' Quilp can
be produced and accommodated. In the novel which he
so dominates, the curious names of Daniel Quilp and
Sampson and Sally Brass[23] are inscribed as the
legend on the façade of the new curiosity shop that
is England in the age of the new charter.

NOTES

1. See Letters, II, 49.
2. Letters, II, 149. For details of the
exchange of letters between Hood and Dickens, see
Collins, *Dickens: The Critical Heritage* (London.
Routledge and Kegan Paul, 1971), pp.94-5, and Alvin
Whitley, 'Hood and Dickens: some new letters',
Huntington Library Quarterly XIV (1951), 392-3.
3. Quoted from Tom Hood, ed., *The Works of
Thomas Hood* (London, 1862; 7 vols.), V, 356.
4. For Hood's influence on the text of
chapter one of *The Old Curiosity Shop*, see John
Harvey, *Victorian Novelists and their Illustrators*
(London, Sidgwich and Jackson, 1970).
5. In chapter 17, pp.129-32 of the Random
House edition of *The Best-Known Novels of George
Eliot* (New York, n.d.), as reprinted in *Documents
of Modern Literary Realism*, ed. George J. Becker
(Princeton, N.J., Princeton University Press, 1963),
112-116. E.g. on Dutch genre paintings: "I find a
source of delicious sympathy in these faithful
pictures of a monotonous homely existence, which
has been the fate of so many more among my fellow-
mortals than a life of pomp or of absolute
indigence, of tragic suffering or of world-stirring
actions". (p.114)
6. See the footnotes to chapter 46 in Angus
Easson's Penguin English Library Edition of *The Old
Curiosity Shop* (Harmondsworth, 1972), p.707.
7. The simultaneity of *The Old Curiosity
Shop* (April 1840-February 1841) and *On Heroes, Hero-
Worship and the Heroic in History* (delivered in
lecture form in May 1840, and published in 1841) is
remarkable. *Chartism*, published December 1839 and
also significantly concerned with ideas of heroism,
clearly influenced the writing of *The Old Curiosity
Shop* as well.
8. Quoted by Philip Collins in his
introduction to *Dickens: The Critical Heritage*,
pp.6-7.
9. It is interesting and instructive to
connect Dickens's obvious indebtedness to Bunyan in
The Old Curiosity Shop and elsewhere with the wider
impact of that book in England in the early 19th
century. "*Pilgrim's Progress* is, with *Rights of
Man*, one of the two foundation texts of the English
working-class movement," writes E.P. Thompson,
citing Q.D. Leavis to support his assertion that
"many thousands of youths found in *Pilgrim's
Progress* their first adventure story, and would

have agreed with Thomas Cooper, the Chartist, that it was their 'book of books'", (see *The Making of the English Working Class* (Harmondsworth, Penguin Books, 1968), p.34, and elsewhere).

    10. See Collins, *op. cit.*, p.6.

    11. Letters, II, 201 (to Mrs. Gore, 31/1/41).

    12. *Religio Medici*, I, 15; see Arthur Clayborough, *The Grotesque in English Literature* (Oxford, O.U.P., 1965), p.3.

    13. Dickens owned a raven as early as February 1840, when he was working on *The Old Curiosity Shop* (see Letters II, 28). It is clear that he observed these birds closely, and made them the basis of a number of character-sketches in his writings. The most obvious case is that of Tackleton in *The Cricket on the Hearth*: "He didn't look much like a bridegroom, as he stood in the Carrier's kitchen, with a twist in his dry face, and a screw in his body, and his hat jerked over the bridge of his nose, and his hands tucked down into the bottoms of his pockets, and his whole sarcastic ill-conditioned self peering out of one little corner of one little eye, like the concentrated essence of any number of ravens." (*CB*, 175) But the echoes of ravens are recurrent, particularly whenever words like 'screw' or 'twist' are evident - Miss Tox has "a kind of screw in her face and carriage", and "her head had quite settled on one side", in *Dombey and Son* (*DS*, i, 5, 6) and Flintwinch in *Little Dorrit* has a head that's "awry" and a neck that is "twisted" (*LD*, I, iii, 377) just like a raven's.

    14. Phiz's illustration to chapter LX, "Quilp's Grotesque Politeness" which appears opposite page 447 of the Oxford Illustrated Dickens edition, gives a lot of visual clues as to how to read Quilp. In it, Quilp is leaning through a window, hat in head, bowing obsequiously and grinning; on a poster to his left, a notice with the words 'MAN' and 'BEAST' in large capitals can be made out.

    15. The related example here is of course Miss Mowcher in *David Copperfield*, commenting ironically on appearances and realities from her privileged vantage-point as beautician/manicurist. The ambiguous child/dwarf Oskar Matzerath in Günter Grass's *The Tin Drum* is a major modern instance of a similar critical perspective.

    16. For copious documentation of the exhibits at fairgrounds in Victorian England see Richard D. Altick, *The Shows of London* (Cambridge,

Mass.,Harvard University Press, 1978).

17. Figures on china patterns were commonly regarded as 'grotesques' in the early nineteenth century; see especially Charles Lamb's essay "Old China": "I had no repugnance then - why should I now have? - to those little, lawless, azure-tinctured grotesques, that under the notion of men and women, float about, uncircumscribed by any element in the world before perspective - a china tea-cup." (*The Complete Works and Letters of Charles Lamb*, New York, Random House, 1935, p.217). Dickens regularly associates China with the grotesque - see e.g. the letter about a visit to a Chinese junk, "so narrow, so long, so grotesque", quoted in Forster's biography (Forster, ed. cit., II, 37).

18. Miss Monflathers's poetic effusion in *The Old Curiosity Shop*:

> In work, work, work. In work alway
> let my first years be past,
> That I may give for ev'ry day
> Some good account at last. (*OCS*, xxxi,
> 236)

ironically anticipates Hood's 'The Song of the Shirt' (published December 1843):

> - work - work - work
> Till the brain begins to swim,
>   Work - work - work
> Till the eyes are heavy and dim, etc.
> (Quoted from *The Oxford Book of Victorian Verse*, 1968 reprinting, p.50).

19. F.S. Schwarzbach in *Dickens and the City* (London, The Athlone Press, 1979) is among those who take the view that "the ineffective [sic], hallucinatory episode set in an industrial town ... bears as little relation to the actual experience of factory life as Nell herself does to flesh and blood." (pp.72-3). It is clear that the criteria of ineffectiveness here are naively realist (the scene seems to be "ineffective" *because* hallucinatory), and can't do justice to the subtler strategies of Dickens's grotesque art.

20. Uriah Heep is the most striking of the figures associated with sleeplessness in later Dickens, his eyes "so unsheltered and unshaded, that I remember wondering how he went to sleep". (*DC*, xv, 219).

21. Cf. Jane Eyre, replying to Rochester's

suspicion that she is of fairy origin: "The men in green all forsook England a hundred years ago ... I don't think either summer, or harvest, or winter moon, will ever shine on their revels more." (*Jane Eyre*, Oxford, O.U.P., 1973, p.123).

22. That Quilp was associated in Dickens's mind with grotesque dancing can be inferred from a passage in a letter of 1842 concerning U.S. newspapers: "All manner of lies get there, and occasionally a truth so twisted and distorted that it has as much resemblance to the real fact as Quilp's leg to Taglioni's" (Letters, III, 72; Taglioni was a famous ballerina of the time).

23. The physiognomy of Sampson and Sally Brass (the singular is appropriate) illustrates clearly enough how systematic and recurrent are the facial attributes of Dickens's grotesques. Sampson Brass, "with a nose like a wen , a protruding forehead, retreating eyes, and hair of a deep red," (xi, 84), anticipates Gradgrind, with his "square wall of a forehead, which had his eyebrows for its base, while his eyes found commodious cellarage in two dark caves, overshadowed by the wall" (*HT*, I, i, 1); and Sally, with "reddish demonstrations" on her upper lip, "in all probability nothing more than eyelashes in a wrong place, as the eyes of Miss Brass were quite free from any such natural impertinences" (*OCS*, xxxiii, 245), clearly has a family resemblance to the red-headed Uriah Heep, "who had hardly any eyebrows, and no eyelashes" (*DC*, xv, 219).

Chapter Five

THE GROTESQUE IN HISTORY:
BARNABY RUDGE AND *A TALE OF TWO CITIES*

Dickens's conception of history is notorious for its
extreme, one might say its grotesque crudity. Since
Humphrey House, the seven fictitious volumes that
adorned the study at Gad's Hill Place ("The Wisdom
of our Ancestors - I. Ignorance. II. Superstition.
III. The Block. IV. The Stake. V. The Rack.
VI. Dirt. VII. Disease."[1]) have served as a paradigm of Dickens's attitude towards the past and
those who revere it. "When he writes of the Middle
Ages, or even of the late eighteenth century, he
does so with an amused contempt for their standards
of life ...", says House; and Angus Wilson
elaborates with reference to Dickens's dealings with
contemporary manifestations of nostalgia like the
Oxford Movement and Young England Toryism: "...
Dickens was always suspicious of reverence for the
past; but his distaste for such reverence grew
greatly in the forties and fifties when he was
confronted with many movements in England that
seemed to him reactionary and obscurantist."[2] His
contemporaries frequently deplored this position -
the most vivid and vehement amongst them perhaps
Ruskin: "Dickens was a pure modernist - a leader
of the steam-and-whistle party *par excellence* - and
he had no understanding of any power of antiquity
except a sort of jackdaw sentiment for cathedral
towers."[3] Of *A Child's History of England* Swinburne
wrote that its "cheapjack radicalism" made it the
"only one book which I cannot but regret that
Dickens should have written", and George Bernard
Shaw that it "had not even the excuse of being
childish".[4]
     Yet although there have been understandably few
attempts to rehabilitate that particular work, the
stock of Dickens's two historical novels *Barnaby
Rudge* and *A Tale of Two Cities* has risen since the

publication in 1962 of the English translation of
Lukacs's *The Historical Novel*, with its criticism of
their "petty bourgeois humanism and idealism".[5]
Jack Lindsay praises them as "contributions to the
historical genre itself, adding a symbolic interplay
and an enrichment of aesthetic elements to the
methods developed by Scott"; and Avrom Fleishman
describes them as "complex visions of social
permanence and change, of the persistence of the
past and the inevitable transition beyond it".[6]
But, since so much writing on the historical novel
takes the aesthetics of 'classic realism' as its
yardstick, assessing the merit of historical fictions
according to the degree of fidelity they display to
the historical events they describe, and frequently
using the criteria of a naive empiricism, it is rare
for the contribution of the grotesque in Dickens's
historical novels to receive much consideration.
Even valuable exceptions like Harry Stone's
discussion of fantastic elements in *Barnaby Rudge*
seems to see these as excrescences, and to accept
that "there is often a jarring dislocation between
the fanciful and the real".[7] We must ask here
whether, even in the case of these works, the
'classic realist' approach is adequate to Dickens's
methods, or whether the grotesque is in fact a
distinctive feature of the version of history they
offer.
        Two features of Dickens's historical writing
must be noted immediately. The first of these is
that for better or worse there is a marked tendency
to present historical figures and events in a
manner quite specifically reminiscent of caricature,
that may directly reflect Dickens's exposure to that
art as a young man. Certainly in reading a letter
concerning the inherent problems of American
democracy - "the Republic had its growth - not in
liberal principles, but in the wrongest-headed
Toryism and the obstinacy of that swine-headed
anointed of the Lord - his Majesty King George The
Third" - reminders of Gillray's representations of
Farmer George are likely;[8] and similar physiognomic
methods of seizing upon a telling feature mark that
monarch's appearance in *A Tale of Two Cities*:
"There were a king with a large jaw and a queen with
a plain face, on the throne of England; there were a
king with a large jaw and a queen with a fair face
on the throne of France." (*TOTC*, I, i, 1) And in
A Child's History of England most of the kings and
queens (except for King Alfred) are seen from the
perspective of a bourgeois radical mechanically

reproducing the techniques of a caricaturist
observing animal resemblances - James I is "his
Sowship", Henry VIII 'a frightened cur' and 'a
Royal Pig'.[9] Destitute of Dickens's customary
imaginative vitality as these examples may be, they
represent a habit of synecdoche that is part of
Dickens's attempt to provide a "popular and picturesque" realisation of history.

Secondly it should be stressed that Dickens's
sense of history is frequently shot through with a
sense of irony, not all of it crude, that bears
considerable similarities to some themes of
grotesque satire. The passage just quoted from *A
Tale of Two Cities* is a simple example, expressing
as it does through the stylistic device of repetition the handy-dandy irony of the identity of *soi-
disant* 'liberal' England and *ancien régime* autocratic France. But another passage in *A Child's
History of England*, ridiculing the Druids of Ancient
Britain for their attachment to magic and cultic
practices, exemplifies an even more characteristic
irony:

> But it is pleasant to think that there are no
> Druids, *now*, who go in that way, and pretend
> to carry Enchanters' Wands and Serpents' Eggs
> - and of course there is nothing of the kind
> anywhere. (*CHE*, 132-3)

But of course *Bleak House*, the novel that
Dickens was then in the process of writing shows how
many Druids are operating *now*, in the legal and
political spheres, for instance, and how many magic
circles they describe, so that the streets of London
offer "a shameful testimony to future ages, how
civilization and barbarism walked this boastful
island together". (*BH*, xi, 151) Living in a society
with so much interest in the progress it had made
and would make, sharing himself to a very large
extent these same beliefs and aspirations, Dickens
was nevertheless highly conscious of the difficulty
of real change or progress in history; and his
consistent and undoubtedly crude conception of the
unenlightened, savage past served as a never-failing
source of ironic emphases on the failures of modern
'civilization'. The Sunday closure of museums and
entertainments ("all *taboo* with that enlightened
strictness that the ugly South sea gods in the
British Museum might have supposed themselves at
home again" - *LD*, I, iii, 28) and the pompous
wedding rituals of rich British boors like the

Merdles and the Dorrits in Rome ("the murderous-headed statues of the wicked Emperors of the Soldiery, whom sculptors had not been able to flatter out of their villainous hideousness, might have come off their pedestals to run away with the Bride" - II, xv, 609) both reveal their barbarism through association with the practices of the "good old days"; and in *The Uncommercial Traveller* the state of progress in nineteenth century Britain is gauged by the free admission of "no-go areas" in London: "To tell us in open court, until it has become as trite a feature of news as the great gooseberry, that a costly police-system such as was never before heard of, has left in London, in the days of steam and gas and photographs of thieves and electric telegraphs, the sanctuaries and stews of the Stuarts! Why, a parity of practice, in all departments, would bring back the Plague in two summers, and the Druids in a century!" ("On An Amateur Beat", *U7*, 346).

The preoccupation enclosed in this irony - how to achieve genuine and not illusory progress, at the personal as well as the historical level[10] - is the essential subject of both Dickens's historical novels. It runs for instance through their handling of revolution, where what is expressed is that however justified and deep-seated the causes of revolutionary violence may be, it merely seems to result in the reinstatement of old injustices in new forms (and in *Barnaby Rudge* the revolution that threatens in the first half of the novel isn't in the end a real revolution at all, but - as Fleishman points out[11] - merely a pogrom). It is conveyed in their constant binary, comparative structure - the old and the new, before and after, then and now, England and France, London and Paris, Carton and Darnay - which tends to operate less commonly as a progressive dialectic with thesis and antithesis leading to synthesis than as a Carlylean analysis of the circularity of history, opposites revealing their similarity to express the truth that there is nothing new under the sun. Dickens's views on temperance in a letter of 1842 certainly seem to express this historical principle:

> I am a great friend to Temperance, and a great foe to Abstinence. The more stoutly that Abstinence is insisted upon now, the more clearly I can foresee, I think, that the next age will run riot in Drunkenness. For all history and experience warn us that of one

violent extreme, its opposite has always sprung.[12]

And the grotesque in the historical novels functions as a means of giving vivid expression to such problems. Perceived first as an aspect of the 'old' order of things, a mode as it were of caricaturing 'them' and marking them off from 'us', it nevertheless persists, in however modified a form, into the 'new'. In doing this it challenges any comfortable sense of the past as superseded, and asks that we assume full responsibility for history. Making the past appear strange, it shows us how that past strangeness lingers on, and thus aims to make us see the present afresh.

————————

The opening pages of *Barnaby Rudge*, written in 1839, before *The Old Curiosity Shop*, construct a picture of 'Merrie Old England' before the industrial revolution, initially without apparent ironic comment. The pub, The Maypole, its name referring to ancient national customs and rituals of a popular kind, is a kind of 'old curiosity shop' in itself - its chimneys producing smoke that comes "in more than naturally fantastic shapes", its porch "quaintly and grotesquely carved". (*BR*, i, 1, 2) Its illustrator was Cattermole, the specialist in 'picturesque' reproduction of Gothic architecture whom Dickens also employed for the architectural illustrations of *The Old Curiosity Shop*.[13] With its anthropomorphic bricks, "yellow and discolored like an old man's skin", and its ivy "like a warm garment to comfort it in its age" (2) it seems to embody tradition and resistance to change.

Yet almost immediately there are hints of suppressed energies rebelling against the static order implied by the house, waiting for their chance of insubordination. We learn that Queen Elizabeth is supposed to have slept here, and that she "boxed and cuffed an unlucky page for some neglect of duty" (1); the reference is not complimentary to Queen Elizabeth or to her class (and in *The Old Curiosity Shop* the bachelor is to "deny the glory of Queen Bess, and assert the immeasurably greater glory of the meanest woman in her realm, who had a merciful and tender heart". (*OCS*, liv, 401)) Objects and inanimate forces again seem to carry much of this energy - the flame in the hearth, for instance, which as the pub regulars tell their stories, "struggling from under a great faggot, whose weight almost crushed it for the time, shot upward with a strong and sudden glare" (*BR*, i, 11) as if deliberately to illuminate the face of Rudge sr, the initial perpetrator of the crimes of the novel. But the same forces flare up quickly in the relation between the father and son of The Maypole, Joe Willett suddenly protesting that "he cannot bear the contempt that your treating me in the way you do, brings upon me from others every day. Look at other young men of my age. Have they no liberty, no will, no right to speak?" (iii, 24) This is the age, not only of the Gordon riots, but of the 'glorious' American revolution (Dickens's illusions about that country have not yet been shattered), and its rhetoric is reflected in the private conflict of father and son which seems to carry, in miniature, the theme of the violent overthrow of an established social order.

Still, for the time being at least, the old order holds sway, its associations of rural harmony dominant; The Maypole seems to stand for an idealised conception of nature as a source of bounty, fertility and a cyclical order of time: "the wheeling and circling flights of runts, fantails, tumblers, and pouters, were perhaps not quite consistent with the grave and sober character of the building, but the monotonous cooing, which never ceased to be raised by some among them all day long suited it exactly, and seemed to lull it to rest." (1, 2) "The Maypole's was the very snuggest, cosiest and completest bar, that ever the wit of man devised," it appears later, a cornucopian paradise of food and drink, "crammed to the throat with eatables, drinkables, or savoury condiments". (xix, 151) And for the purposes of emphatic contrast the entire myth is summed up immediately prior to the ransacking of The Maypole by the rioters at a time when the "birds were at roost, the daisies on the green had closed their fairy hoods, the honeysuckle twining round the porch exhaled its perfume in a twofold degree, as though it lost its coyness at that silent time and loved to shed its fragrance on the night; the ivy scarcely stirred its deep green leaves. How tranquil and how beautiful it was!" (liv, 412)

The version of the grotesque that is associated with The Maypole in the novel's opening stage forms part of this atmosphere. It seems to fall into a category that Dickens would later characterise as "innocent grotesqueness" (*OMF*, II, ix, 330), and is here not wholly separable from the picturesque[14] -- something pleasantly amusing in its strangeness: John Willett (a reflection of Gillray's John Bull[15]) sits in the "ancient porch, quaintly and grotesquely carved" (i, 2) "like a monstrous carbuncle in a fairy tale" (liv, 410), and the figures in the best apartment of the Maypole are "grinning and grotesque" (x, 78) adornments like those that fringe the frontispieces of these early novels.[16] Even at night when in this room "chairs and tables, which by day were as honest cripples as need be, assumed a doubtful and mysterious character" (xxxi, 232), the transmutation of objects into fanciful quirks of the imagination occurs benignly, in a manner reminiscent of the inset stories of *Pickwick Papers*: "a queer, old, grey-eyed general, in an oval frame - seemed to wink and doze as the light decayed, and at length, when the last faint glimmering speck of day went out, to shut its eyes in good earnest and fall fast asleep." (232)

But with the transition from the country to the city, and the emergence of the novel's central grotesque characters - Barnaby and his raven - effects that are rather less tame begin to appear. Barnaby is introduced by torchlight with "an expression quite unearthly", his clothes a collection of motley scraps that "by a grotesque contrast set off and heightened the more impressive wildness of his face" (iii, 28); his pet raven Grip makes Gabriel Varden start "as if he had seen some supernatural agent" (vi, 50) and shortly makes comic assertion of diabolical powers: "I'm a devil, I'm a devil, I'm a devil. Hurrah!" (29) Both of them thus inhabit borderline categories - Barnaby straddling childishness and maturity, idiocy and insight, natural and supernatural levels of reality since infancy, when (anticipating Paul Dombey) he lay in his cradle "old and elfin-like in face, but ever dear to her, gazing at her with a wild and vacant eye, and crooning some uncouth song as she sat by and rocked him" (xxv, 189); and Grip combining animal and human, comic and horrific, diabolical and benign modes of existence in habits like his propensity to inspect tombstones and their epitaphs, "strop his beak upon the grave to which it referred, and cry in his hoarse tones, 'I'm a devil, I'm a devil, I'm a devil!'" (xxv, 195)

Yet even more importantly perhaps, Barnaby and Grip are not only central grotesques but also central truth-tellers in the novel, the possessors

of a fractured visionary authority that is
vindicated and realised by the historical events
they obscurely foretell. We may deal first with
Grip, the simpler case, of whose intelligence
Dickens wrote to Cattermole in January 1841
("Barnaby being an idiot my notion is to have him
in company with a pet raven who is immeasurably more
knowing than himself"[17]). He serves as an ironic
mimic and commentator on the events of the novel,
in a manner that bears some relation to earlier
eirons like Fagin and Quilp - the human with bestial
propensities here transposed into the beast with
human faculties - but more to the parrot that
functions as a savage chorus to Mrs. Merdle's
hypocritical disquisitions in *Little Dorrit.* When
Rudge sr   returns to haunt his family, the raven
comments with "Never say die!" and "Polly put the
kettle on", "muttered in a sepulchral voice" (xvii,
135); in the churchyard at Chigwell he is described
"walking up and down when he had dined, with an air
of elderly complacency which was strongly suggestive
of his having his hands under his coat-tails; and
appearing to read the tombstones with a very
critical taste".(xxiv, 195)   Like Quilp he is a
master of surprise appearances and interventions
(see for instance vi, 50 and xvii, 136) and an
amateur of satiric, diabolical (or druidical?)
dancing in the school of Holbein, as at Barnaby's
reunion with his father in prison: "Grip croaked
loudly, and hopped about them, round and round, as
if enclosing them in a magic circle, and invoking
all the powers of mischief." (lxii, 478)
    But most importantly, Grip comments on the
prospects of revolutionary violence - most obviously
on an occasion where Barnaby and his mother meet on
their travels (like Nell and her grandfather) a
monstrous 'fine old country gentleman' for whom
"Grip drew fifty corks at least, and then began to
dance; at the same time eyeing the gentleman with
surprising insolence of manner, and screwing his
head so much on one side that he appeared desirous
of screwing it off upon the spot" (xlvii, 356),[18]
and most constantly in his habit of drawing off
corks. The corking up of fermenting liquids is a
favourite Dickensian image for the repression of
political and other energy,[19] and in this novel it
is closely connected with the signs of revolution.
Sim Tappertit is like "certain liquors, confined in
casks too cramped in their dimensions ... (that)
ferment and fret, and chafe in their imprisonment"
in such a manner that "the spiritual essence or soul

of Mr. Tappertit would sometimes fume within that
precious cask, his body, until with great foam and
froth and splutter, it would force a vent". (iv,
34)[20] And when John Willett uses it to patronise
Hugh ("he has all his faculties about him, some-
wheres or another, bottled up and corked down" - xi,
86) it is evident that it provides an ironic link
between the staid old Maypole, and its landlord's way
of conducting his trade and his life, and the
revolutionary processes at work in *Barnaby Rudge.*

Barnaby also sees signs of approaching revolution - in clothes on the line for instance: "Look
down there ... do you mark how they whisper in each
other's ears; then dance and leap, to make believe
they are in sport? Do you see how they stop for a
moment, when they think there is no one looking,
and mutter among themselves again; and then how
they roll and gambol, delighted with the mischief
they've been plotting? Look at 'em now. See how
they whirl and plunge. And now they stop again,
and whisper, cautiously together - little thinking,
mind, how often I have lain upon the grass and
watched them. I say - what is it that they plot and
hatch?" (x, 81) It is telling that Chester should
see nothing in them ("they are only clothes ...
such as we wear; hanging on those lines to dry, and
fluttering in the wind") in an ironic exchange that
reflects and comments upon Carlyle's philosophy of
clothes: whereas Barnaby (whose motley scraps are
"fluttered and confused" - iii, 28) perceives the
relationship between clothes and men, Chester (for
whom appearance is so important) is devoid of
imaginative understanding.

The first point of significance here is that
(as Harry Stone notes)[21] Barnaby's mental operations, like Mrs. Nickleby's and her mad lover's, are
not dissimilar to Dickens's own: it was he who, in
'Meditations in Monmouth Street', had brought alive
whole shopfuls of second clothes. They form part of
a serious deliberation, in the novel, on the
workings of associative logic and the grotesque
images and truths it permits glimpses of. The
consideration of Gabriel Varden's half-awake
impressions as he enters London at night first
displays this preoccupation:

> A man may be very sober - or at least firmly
> set upon his legs on that neutral ground which
> lies between the confines of perfect sobriety
> and slight tipsiness - and yet feel a strong
> tendency to mingle up present circumstances

with others which have no manner of connection
with them; to confound all consideration of
persons, things, times, and places; and to
jumble his disjointed thoughts together in a
kind of mental kaleidoscope, producing
compositions as unexpected as they are
transitory. (iii, 26)

The notion of the kaleidoscope and its association
with the city (it had first appeared in 'Omnibusses'
in *Sketches by Boz*[22]) is a precise image for the
momentary constellations of fragmentary, visionary
perception that figure so importantly in this novel
- above all in the description of the riots.
    Moreover, what in Varden is a fleeting state
of mind is in Barnaby a permanent condition.
Seeing clothes, he links them with plotters; gazing
at stars (and *Barnaby Rudge* is perhaps the first of
Dickens's novels in which this activity becomes a
focus for thoughts about human destiny)[23] he
interprets them as someone's eyes (iii, 28); and
watching the fire (like Lizzie Hexam, who is to be
addicted to staring into the fire and seeing
portents there) he perceives a whole landscape of
"rivers, hills and dells, in the deep, red sunset,
and the wild faces". (xvii, 133) These habits
make him the precise obverse of John Willett,
"looking steadily at the boiler for ten minutes by
the clock" (x, 80), the loss of which during the
riots delivers him over to "a perfect bog of
uncertainty and mental confusion" (lxxii, 554) -
notwithstanding Willett's complacent view that Hugh
"has no more imagination than Barnaby has". (xi,
86) For Barnaby "images were often presented to
his thoughts by outward objects quite as remote and
distant" (xlvii, 361) as the golden clouds that
suggest money; for Dickens "it is my infirmity to
fancy or perceive relations in things which are not
apparent generally".
    This pattern of relationships between Barnaby
and the 'normal' characters of the novel - Willett
and Chester, for example - introduces the theme of
handy-dandy in the novel, in which Barnaby's role
is again prominent. At a number of points the novel
asks which is the idiot and which the wise philosopher - the child of nature or the cynic, the
visionary half-wit or the blank meditator of the
fireside? But the theme surfaces most markedly in
the relation between Barnaby and Lord George Gordon,
connected on his first appearance with the grotesque
as a kind of Don Quixote: "a more grotesque or more

ungainly figure can hardly be conceived." (xxxvii,
280) "My Lord's half off his head," (xxxv, 271)
worries Grueby, expressing the link between the two
innocents of the novel, which achieves its full
resonance at the time of their first meeting:

> 'He has surely no appearance,' said Lord
> George, glancing at Barnaby, and whispering in
> his secretary's ear, 'of being deranged? And
> even if he had, we must not construe any
> trifling peculiarity into madness. Which of
> us' - and here he turned red again - 'would be
> safe, if that were made the law!' (xlviii,366)

On another plane where civilization and
barbarism are the operative terms, the theme of
handy-dandy operates in the relationship of Mr.
Chester and Hugh. Chester is an eighteenth century
'gentleman' representing culture against nature -
he thinks of Haredale as a species of animal ("A
rough brute. Quite a human badger!" (xii, 95),
calls his son (like Quilp) a dog (xv, 114) and is
fond of quoting the fairytale of Valentine and
Orson to express his sense of shocked distance from
the rude, unpolished naturals with whom he is
compelled to have contact (e.g. at xv, 116). The
contrast is at its sharpest when Chester meets Hugh
and forms their alliance - though here, significantly
it is expressed through Hugh's consciousness: "his
own rough speech, contrasted with the soft persuas-
ive accents of the other; his rude bearing and Mr.
Chester's polished manner; the disorder and
negligence of his ragged dress, and the elegant
attire he saw before him ... quelled Hugh completely."
(xxii, 176)

But Hugh is as devoid of physiognomic insight
as he is of status and possessions. In a brilliant
passage of 'The Paris of the Second Empire in
Baudelaire' Walter Benjamin remarks that "it is not
strange that resistance to controls, something that
becomes second nature to asocial persons, returns in
the propertied bourgeoisie";[24] beneath the surface
contrast, the novel explores this ironic relationship between Hugh and Chester. Hugh represents the
classless *Lumpenproletariat*,[25] so far removed from
the nexus of ownership and power that he calls out
"No Property" when the other rioters yell "No
Popery". The ideological issues of the Gordon riots
mean nothing to him - it's the frisson of violent
excitement that draws him to them as indifferently
as to Chester's scheme for suppressing his son and

the Haredales: "... what do *I* risk! What do I
stand a chance of losing, master? Friends, home?
A fig for 'em all: I have none; they are nothing
to me. Give me a good scuffle; let me pay off old
scores in a bold riot where there are men to stand
by me; and then use me as you like - it don't
matter much to what the end is!" (xl, 305) This
amoralism returns in the pseudo-sophisticated
rationalisations of Chester's 'enlightened' cynic
libertinism: "The world is a lively place enough,
in which we must accommodate ourselves to circumstances, sail with the stream as glibly as we can,
be content to take froth for substance, the surface
for depth, the counterfeit for the real coin."
(xii, 91) This kind of barbarism - "Chicane in
furs, and Casuistry in lawn" - thus finds itself
quite naturally in league with Hugh's during the
novel.

Yet there is one particular passage where the
handy-dandy theme is evident in which the links
that relate it to issues of violent protest against
social injustice are particularly interesting.
This is where Barnaby perceives billows of smoke
going up the Maypole chimney and interprets their
significance in a characteristic way: "Why do they
tread so closely on each other's heels, and why are
they always in a hurry - which is what you blame me
for, when I only take pattern by these busy folk
about me. More of 'em! catching to each other's
skirts; and as fast as they go, others come! What
a merry dance it is! I would that Grip and I could
frisk like that!" (x, 84) 'There's no smoke
without fire' is the cliché that hovers hereabouts,
the fire in question being a symbol for revolution
(Mr. Chester, interviewing Haredale, restores some
"errant faggots to their places in the grate with
the toe of his boot" - xii, 94) and the clouds of
smoke the gathering mob who will later dance the
'No Popery' jig. The swiftness of Barnaby's
associations is not merely the ironic reflection
of the bustle of city life that the novel emphasises: it also, as we shall see, anticipates the
welter of the rioting mob.

For the patterns of injustice seen in the first
half of the novel - the suppression of sons by
fathers, the exclusion of all but a few 'somebodies'
from property rights, the urban conditions that
create homelessness and vagrancy - lead 'naturally'
to the expression of revolutionary energy implied
and contained in the Gordon riots, through imagery
that clearly reflects Carlyle's organicism. "More

seed, more seed," says Gashford, looking out on the gathering Protestants: "When will the harvest come!" (xxxvi, 276) Even at the stake at the end, the differing attitudes of Hugh and Dennis are the consequence of a process understood in organicist terms: "Such was the wholesale growth of the seed sown by the law, that this kind of harvest was usually looked for, as a matter of course." (lxxvi, 586)

But Dickens's irony is that the kind of 'natural' outcome that is to ensue, in the latter half of the novel, is a very different thing from anything that might be predicated by the picture of the stable, static Maypole at the beginning of the novel. What takes its place is a disturbing new world in which things are turned upside down, and dreams and nightmares become realities, their monstrosity a consequence of the veiled monstrosity of the 'normal' world now left behind. The riots throw up characters like Dennis, a grotesque in the school of Quilp ("... in his grimy hands he held a knotted stick, the knob of which was carved into a rough likeness of his own vile face" - xxxvii, 283), odd relationships and alliances like that between Hugh and Sim Tappertit ("this giant and the dwarf struck up a friendship which bade fair to be of long continuance" - xxxix, 296), and extraordinary leaders: a half-wit, a savage, a hangman.

But the most important focus of the grotesque in the novel's latter half is the mob itself. Its associations with Barnaby and his visions are multiple, and they include the persistent theme of madness: "The mob raged and roared, like a *mad* monster as it was, unceasingly, and each new outrage served to swell its fury." (xlix, 375; my italics). Later, in another version of the rhetoric of the 'fantastic paradox' in Dickens, we learn that it really outstrips ordinary madness: "If Bedlam gates had been flung open wide, there would not have issued such maniacs as the frenzy of that night had made." (lv, 423) And in a third instance the emphasis has shifted slightly, perhaps, to a perspective upon what makes people regard madmen in general - and Barnaby in particular - as objects of loathing and terror:

It was said that they meant to throw the gates of Bedlam open, and let all the madmen loose. This suggested such dreadful images to the people's minds, and was indeed an act so fraught with new and unimaginable horrors in

the contemplation, that it beset them more
than any loss or cruelty of which they could
foresee the worst, and drove many sane men
nearly mad themselves. (lxvii, 514)

Moreover, the mob is presented in a manner that
authenticates Barnaby's fragmentary visions. Some
of the best prose of *Barnaby Rudge* goes into the
description of it:

> The more the fire crackled and raged, the
> wilder and more cruel the men grew; as though
> moving in that element they became fiends, and
> changed their earthly nature for the qualities
> that give delight in hell. (lv, 422)

> ... a vision of coarse faces, with here and
> there a blot of flaring, smoky light; a dream
> of demon heads and savage eyes, and sticks and
> iron bars uplifted in the air, and whirled
> about; a bewildering horror, in which so much
> was seen, and yet so little, which seemed so
> long, and yet so short, in which there were so
> many phantoms, not to be forgotten all through
> life, and yet so many things that could not be
> observed in one distracting glimpse. (1, 386)

The private phantasmagoria of dreams becomes here a
public nightmare - this is Wolverhampton again, or
the kaleidoscopic city of *Sketches by Boz*.
And of course it arouses once more that
ambivalent "attraction of repulsion" that is the
hallmark of the Dickensian grotesque. News of the
disturbances in London doesn't arouse any simple
fear and trepidation throughout the length and
breadth of the land; instead it appears that "the
tidings were everywhere received with that appetite
for the marvellous and love of the terrible which
have probably been among the *natural* characteristics
of mankind since the creation of the world". (liv,
410; my italics) Again the word 'natural' is
prominent, and it is assembled here on the side of
a view of 'nature' that includes the monstrous and
fantastic in criticism of that narrow view of the
'natural' exemplified in the Maypole world. Here
too in the city uprisings human nature is authent-
ically expressed; revolutionary violence is not
some "horrible wonder apart" (to use the phrasing
of *Edwin Drood*[26]) but a possibility latent within
nature that is realised by the historical process.
And so it is that the new grotesque, the

historic consequence of the old that had been
embodied in The Maypole, descends like a nemesis
upon that shrine, "a mass of faces, some grinning,
some fierce, some lighted up by torches, some
indistinct, some dusty and shadowy" (liv, 413) -
the ironic live contemporary counterpart of those
carved figures, "grinning and grotesque" (x, 78),
that adorn the ghostly screen in one of its state-
rooms. But the irony perhaps betokens Dickens's
ambivalent attitude towards revolution. Understanding the forces that go to making it, and
depicting them clearly, he nevertheless stops short
of endorsing it. He shows how people manipulate
the revolution for private ends - in this novel,
Chester and Gashford, in *A Tale of Two Cities*, the
Defarges; the abuse of power, addiction to manipulation and autocratic styles of dealing with people
become just as much a part of the new movement as
of the old it had hated. The irony is that
'revolution' is not revolution - its victims are
once again the weak and the poor, like Barnaby,
those who can be labelled as grotesque and treated
as outcasts.

That this is true, not only of 1775 and 1780
but also of 1841 is suggested in an interesting
passage that comments on the fairytale strangeness
of everyday mundanities. Joe Willett, cast out by
his father,

> bought a roll and reduced his purse to the
> condition (with a difference) of that
> celebrated purse of Fortunatus, which, what-
> ever were its favoured owner's necessities,
> had one unvarying amount in it. In these real
> times, when all the Fairies are dead and
> buried, there are still a great many purses
> which possess that quality. The sum-total
> they contain is expressed in arithmetic by a
> circle, and whether it be added to or multi-
> plied by its own amount, the result of the
> problem is more easily stated than any known
> in figures. (xxxi, 237)[27]

"These real times" are our own, and the aim of
Barnaby Rudge is to get us to see that the history
we consume there is a continuing one whose outcome
only we may determine.[28]

"It has been one of my hopes to add something
to the popular and picturesque means of understanding that time." (707C, xiii) Any approach to the
grotesque in *A Tale of Two Cities* must begin with

this passage from Dickens's preface, applying it first, perhaps, to the tight, symmetrical binary structure of the novel. It is unlike any other by this author in its commitment to a simple pattern of London and Paris, the *ancien régime* and the revolution, Carton, Darnay, doubling within characters (Manette, Carton, Darnay). Within this structure, the role of the grotesque is perhaps to be found - first of all in a mode of representation. The caricature method of presenting characters by 'charging' a very limited number of characteristics with special significance - the hoarse voice and spiky hair of Jerry Cruncher, for instance (*TOTC*, I, ii, 7) - is reproduced in the handling of history through synecdoche and personification. Figures like "Monseigneur", "Vengeance", "La Guillotine", "Hunger", "St. Antoine", "The Sheep" are the principal protagonists in a novel which to some extent draws away from individualism. The narrative takes on some qualities of parable and allegory as it dramatises the fates of these abstractions - the omnipresence of 'Hunger' will be illustrated in the breaking open of a wine cask (signifying 'Blood') and its consumption by the starving people, the sadistic cruelty and indifference of 'Monseigneur' by the death of a child beneath the wheels of his carriage.

Thus the writing out of the old order of Society is presented as an inventory of the symptoms of a disease (it is no accident that Dr. Manette's profession is to administer to the sick, or that he should have been prevented from exercising it for so long). During this inventory, familiar ironies are evident - in the name of 'civilization', hideous barbarities have been sanctioned. In France, Christian teaching decrees idolatrous postures of genuflection and grovelling self-debasement, and tyrannically cruel punishments for those who refuse them: "Under the guidance of her Christian pastors, she (France) entertained herself, besides, with such humane achievements as sentencing a youth to have his hands cut off, his tongue torn out with pincers, and his body burned alive, because he had not kneeled down in the rain to do honour to a dirty procession of monks which passed within his view, at a distance of some fifty or sixty yards." (I, i, 2) In England, which prides itself on its advanced liberal institutions there were until recently "heads exposed on Temple Bar with an insensate brutality and ferocity worthy of Abyssinia or Ashantee". (II, i, 50) In both

countries the animism and fetishism of primitive
savages is practised in place of religion - in
England, where "the Cock-lane ghost had been laid
only a round dozen of years" (I, i, 1), and in
France, where Monseigneur constitutes "in his inner
room, his sanctuary of sanctuaries, the Holiest of
Holiests to the crowd of worshippers in the suite
of rooms without". (II, vii, 98) Here is the
fundamental symptom, the worship of false gods -
Carlylean terminology that is also apparent in the
analysis of the magic that sustains this corrupt,
hollow ordering of society: "Dress was the one
unfailing talisman and charm used for keeping all
things in their places." (II, vii, 101) It is a
Circean world in which people are "changed into wild
beasts, by terrible enchantment long persisted in".
(xxiv, 223)

This old order of things is responsible for
one version of the grotesque in the novel. Culture
moulds nature so that people and things become
almost unrecognisable, like the coins Mme. Defarge
takes from her customers, "as much defaced and
beaten out of their original impress as the small
coinage of humanity from whose ragged pockets they
had come". (II, xv, 157) These distortions surface
in the revolution: the diabolical dance of death
that is performed then shows, for instance "how
warped and perverted all things good by nature were
become."(III, v, 265) This is the Carlylean
language of Gabriel Vardon, most fully expressed in
the last chapter of the novel: "Crush humanity out
of shape once more, under similar hammers, and it
will twist itself into the same tortured forms."
(III,xv, 353)[29] It expresses an historical
determinism that governs the material and moral
conditions of the people - their art, for instance,
as manifest in a wayside crucifix ("studied ...
from the life - his own life, maybe - for it was
dreadfully spare and thin" - II, viii, 110) or the
shop signs of Paris ("The butcher and the porkman
painted up, only the leanest scrags of meat, the
baker, the coarsest of meagre loaves" - I, v, 29).

The "tortured forms" thrown up by the historical
process include the novel's central grotesque
character, Jerry Cruncher, and his resurrectionary
arts.[30] These are the consequence of the prejudices
of a not very 'enlightened' age - because medical
practitioners may not legally study anatomy from
human skeletons, these must be provided illegally.
A splendid grotesque humour is created - a new
'professional' eye that weighs up the skeletal

endowments of a condemned man ("you see that there
Cly that day, and you see with your own eye that he
was a young 'un and a straight made 'un" - II, xiv,
150). A comedy of materialist determinism[31]
generates his appearance - his hair, for instance,
"so like smith's work, so much more like the top of
a strongly spiked wall than a head of hair" (I, iii,
11), the apparent product of a milieu that includes
prison, Temple Bar and cemetery railings. In bed
his hair looks "as if it must tear the sheet to
ribbons" (II, i, 54) - Jerry Cruncher suggests a
comically grotesque kind of violence, savage, and
cannibalistic, conveyed in the "bone-crunching"
associations of his name, or his habit of taking
"quite a lunch of rust off his nails" (II, iii, 69)
in following the evidence at court.

But Jerry is only one individual manifestation
of a legal system which, both in Britain and France,
likes to see its victims "butchered and torn
asunder". (II, ii, 58) Flies cluster round the
court in London, as if expecting fresh meat from
the "human stew that had been boiling ... all day".
(II, iv, 74) In France aristocrats hunt peasants
like game, and gaze indifferently at one of them
"whose life was ebbing out as if he were a wounded
bird, or hare, or rabbit; not at all as if he were
a fellow-creature". (III, x, 307)

The revolution effects a defamiliarising of
these everyday monstrosities. As in *Barnaby Rudge*,
where during the Gordon riots "scores of objects,
never seen before, burst out upon the view, and
things the most familiar put on some new aspects"
(*BR*, lxiv, 492) so in *A Tale of Two Cities* Darnay
notes during his progress in captivity to Paris
"many wild changes observable on familiar things
which made this wild ride unreal". (III, i, 237)
Truths can be perceived only through the operation
of imaginative vision, as when Darnay connects the
gaoler of the conciergerie with the corpses of the
Paris Morgue to express the omnipresence of Death
during the terror: "a wandering fancy wandered
through the mind of the prisoner leaning against
the wall opposite to him, that this gaoler was so
unwholesomely bloated, both in face and person, as
to look like a man who had been drowned and filled
with water." (III, i. 244)

Thus the revolution is constantly connected
with dreams, phantoms, and psychological anomalies.
As in *Barnaby Rudge*, madness appears to govern the
passions of the crowd: "The mad joy over the
prisoners who were saved, had astounded him

scarcely less than the mad ferocity against those who were cut to pieces." (III, iv, 257) There is an absence of logical sequence or rational consistency in their behaviour: "With an inconsistency as monstrous as anything else in this awful nightmare, they had helped the healer, and tended the wounded man with the gentlest solicitude." (257) Dr. Manette, who is the perceiving subject of this irrationality on more than one occasion, offers through his own reactions to the sentence passed by the revolution on his son-in-law another instance of the dream-like volatility of these events and their consequences: "As if all that had happened since the garret time were a momentary fancy, or a dream, Mr. Lorry saw him shrink into the exact figure that Defarge had had in keeping." (III, xii, 325)

But it would be misleading to suggest that the revolution dissolves entirely into idealist insubstantiality.[32] In this novel Dickens holds to a Carlylean conception of "the real" - that which transcends the individual perception of a fragment of the whole process of history. Lucy, for Manette, is a touchstone of "the real": "she was the golden thread that united him to a Past beyond his misery, and to a Present beyond his misery." (II, iv, 74) The "leprosy of unreality" had been the disease of the pre-revolutionary, Monseigneur surrounded by mystificatory characters and amateurs "unconnected with anything that was real, or with lives passed in travelling by any straight road to any fine earthly end". (II, vii, 100) The reality of the revolution is established by its necessity, for it is portrayed as the essential historic consequence of causes that have overwhelming substance.

But its 'unreality' (and here the analysis begins to go beyond what *Barnaby Rudge* had achieved) consists in its inability to make progress towards the goals it sets itself, as it devours itself instead in a process of self-destruction that eventually involves regression to the stage it seeks to supersede. The idea emerges first at a psychological level: ontogeny and phylogeny frequently interact in this novel. People appear to die wilfully and willingly under the guillotine: "In seasons of pestilence, some of us will have a secret attraction to the disease - a terrible passing inclination to die of it." (III, vi, 268) Of this variation on the theme of the "attraction of repulsion" Sydney Carton is an obvious example, standing with his boot in the fire ("his indiffer-

ence to fire was sufficiently remarkable to elicit
a word of remonstrance from Mr. Lorry" - III, ix,
294). But it is quickly transferred to the
revolution itself in a passage that tries to
explain its relation to what precedes: "There
could have been no such Revolution, if all laws,
forms, and ceremonies, had not first been so
monstrously abused that the *suicidal* vengeance of
the Revolution was to scatter them all to the winds."
(III, ix, 300; my italics) In a kind of premonition
of Freud's theory of sado-masochism,[33] Dickens
portrays the violent energy that feeds the revolution as essentially (and paradoxically) self-directed;
and so we should understand Sydney Carton's impulses
"to strike the life out of him (the woodsawyer)"
(III, ix, 297) and to "seize that arm (of Mme.
Defarge), lift it, and strike under it sharp and
deep" (III, xii, 324) or the extroversion of the
self-sacrifice he has already determined upon. The
excrescent violence of the prose of the novel (e.g.
at II, xxi, 202) may perhaps be approached in the
same way.

One way of putting the problem of the revolution is that it displays the characteristics of what
Dickens had come to regard as bad art. It offers
itself as a kind of equivalent to the transformation
scene of fairytale and pantomime,[34] in which the
past is utterly abandoned and cast aside. "All
here is so unprecedented, so changed, so sudden and
unfair," declares Charles Darnay to Defarge,
registering his perception of the phenomenon (III,
i, 90); we now enter a utopian project for the
abolition of temporality ("there was no pause, no
pity, no peace, no interval of relenting rest, no
measurement of time" - III, iv, 259). The irony
once more is that the new regime merely recapitul-
ates the fantasies of the old, with its conviction
"that a system rooted in a frizzled hangman,
powdered, gold-laced, pumped, and white silk-
stockinged, would see the very stars out!" (II, vii,
102)

The novel unfolds an alternative way of
achieving progress. It is written into its
narrative technique - in describing the unfolding
of the story of Dr. Manette to Wilkie Collins, for
instance, Dickens had declared his belief that "the
business of art is to lay all that ground carefully
... only to *suggest*, until the fulfilment comes".[35]
The idea of carefully laying the ground becomes a
paradigm of the right mode of intervention in
history ("These are the ways of Providence, of which

all art is but a little imitation"). Significant
details in the novel are one way of indicating what
Dickens meant by it: Sydney Carton falls asleep in
a drunken stupor early in the novel next to a "long
winding-sheet in the candle dripping down upon him"
(II, iv, 79), and the sepulchral image anticipates
the mode of his resurrection. The sunset strikes
into the Marquis's coach so "that its occupant was
steeped in crimson" - "it will die out ...
directly" says the Marquis (II, viii, 107),
displaying a fundamental obtuseness about the
historical process now at work (the bursting of
the wine cask having 'laid the ground' for that
crimson). The figure of death appears next - "All
covered with dust, white as a spectre, tall as a
spectre!" (109) - yet the Marquis cannot or will
not read the signs. Barnaby's powers of prediction
reappear in this novel as a question of interpretative acumen in the act of reading.

Again this alternative way of thinking about
time and history links ontogeny and phylogeny. As
in *Little Dorrit* the righting of a wrong is an
important focus, and when Darnay receives Gabelle's
letter he suffers guilt that it has been done in a
partial, fragmentary way: "He knew very well, that
in his love for Lucie, his renunciation of his
social place, though by no means new to his own
mind, had been hurried and incomplete. He knew
that he ought to have systematically worked it out
and supervised it, and that he had meant to do it,
and that it had never been done." (II, xxiv, 230)
And on the novel's concluding pages Sydney Carton
prophecies the slow, systematic working out of the
accumulated wrongs of the past: "I see the evil of
this time, and of the previous time of which this
is the natural birth, gradually making expiation
for itself and wearing out." (III, xv, 357)

This view of time eschews eschatology, elsewhere prominent in this novel. It is announced on
the very first page, as the fallacy of sectarian
groups: "Mrs. Southcott had recently attained her
five-and-twentieth blessed birthday, of whom a
prophetic private in the Life Guards had heralded
the sublime appearance by announcing that arrangements were made for the swallowing up of London and
Westminster." (I, i, 1) 'Signs' of the end of the
world recur frequently in the novel, most
particularly in association with the revolution,
where the language of apocalypse, and its numerology,
describes the release of the prisoners in the
Bastille: "Seven faces of prisoners, suddenly

116

released by the storm that had burst their tomb,
were carried high overhead: all scared, all lost,
all wondering and amazed, as if the Last Day were
coming, and those who rejoiced around them were
lost spirits." (II, xxi, 209-10)

Yet there are no final revelations in Dickens.
History is a continuous process in which revelations are to be had at a number of points;[36] its
stages may exhaust themselves and require cancell-
ation (see xxiv, 226), but there is an underlying
teleology ("I tell thee it never retreats, and
never stops. I tell thee it is always advancing,"
insists Mme. Defarge of the revolution - II, xvi,
171). Jerry Cruncher's incomprehension ("Mr.
Cruncher himself always spoke of the year of our
Lord as Anna Dominoes: apparently under the
impression that the Christian era dated from the
invention of a popular game, by a lady who had
bestowed her name upon it" - II, i, 51) balances
Monseigneur's: "Strange that Creation, designed
expressly for Monseigneur, should be soon wrung dry
and squeezed out!" (II, xxiii, 216); only
imaginative projection beyond the here and now can
give an account of the entire Providential scheme.
In Dickens's sense of history the future is
essentially positive: "Troubled as the future was,
it was the unknown future, and in its obscurity
there was ignorant hope." (III, i, 241) This
carefully paradoxical sentence expresses the
necessary qualifications and uncertainties of
historical prediction where the past is a nightmare,
the future the only possible arena of hope for
change and development.[37]

It is the imagination that lodges alternatives
to illusions of transcendence and apocalypse. The
Lucy/Manette story defines its peculiar magic, as
Manette tells his grand-daughter of "a great and
powerful Fairy who had opened a prison-wall and let
out a captive who had once done the Fairy a service".
(III, vii, 277) It is the magic of the everyday,
of a continuous applied effort of work translated
into history through its gradual accumulations
("Only his daughter had the power of charming this
black brooding from his mind" - II, iv, 74). What
kind of metamorphoses time can and cannot effect is
expressed in the novel's final vision of the reality
of history:

> Six tumbrils roll along the streets. Change
> these back again to what they were, thou
> powerful enchanter, Time, and they shall be

seen to be the carriages of absolute monarchs,
the equipages of feudal nobles, the toilettes
of flaring Jezebels, the churches that are not
my father's houses but dens of thieves, the
huts of millions of starving peasants! No;
the great magician who majestically works out
the appointed order of the Creator, never
reverses his transformations. 'If thou be
changed into this shape by the will of God,'
say the seers to the enchanted, in the wise
Arabian stones, 'then remain so! But if thou
wear this form through mere passing conjurat-
ion, then resume thy former aspect!' Change-
less and hopeless the tumbrils roll along.
(III, xv, 353)

NOTES

1. See *The Dickens World*, second edition
(Oxford, O.U.P., 1942; Oxford Paperbacks, 1960),
p.35.
2. See House, p.34, and Wilson, *The World
of Charles Dickens* (Harmondsworth, Penguin Books,
1972), p.192.
3. From a letter to Charles Eliot Norton
of 19/6/70, quoted from Stephen Wall's Penguin
critical anthology *Charles Dickens* (Harmondsworth,
1970), 191.
4. For Swinburne's remark, see Derek
Hudson's Introduction to the Oxford Illustrated
Edition, x, and for Shaw's, see Wall, *op. cit.*,
p.291.
5. See Georg Lukács, *The Historical Novel*
(London, Merlin Press, 1962), transl. Hannah and
Stanley Mitchell, p.243.
6. In 'Barnaby Rudge', *Dickens and the
Twentieth Century*, eds. John Gross and Gabriel
Pearson (London, Routledge Kegan Paul, 1962), p.
105, and *The English Historical Novel: Walter
Scott to Virginia Woolf* (Baltimore and London,
Johns Hopkins Press, 1971), p.103, respectively.
Lindsay's essay is particularly stimulating.
7. See *Dickens and the Invisible World*
(London, Macmillan, 1980), p.90.
8. See Letters III, 434 (to Andrew Bell,
1/2/43). A good study of Gillray and his work is
Draper Hill, *Mr. Gillray the Satirist* (London,
Phaidon Press, 1965).
9. I owe several of these references to
Hesketh Pearson, *Dickens: His Character, Comedy
and Career* (London, Methuen, 1949), p.199. It is

interesting also to reflect that Dickens - of whose
first publication, *Sketches by Boz*, Sydney Smith
wrote that "the Soul of Hogarth has migrated into
the Body of Mr. Dickens" (see Letters, I, 431n) -
should have set both his historical novels in a
period in which Hogarth's influence upon English
caricature was beginning to be felt.

    10. Nicholas Rance, in *The Historical Novel
and Popular Politics in Nineteenth Century England*
(London, Vision Press, 1975), p.101, quotes
Carlyle's "Signs of the Times" ("to reform a world,
to reform a nation, no wise man will undertake; and
all but foolish men know that the only solid,
though a far slower reformation, is what each
begins and perfects on himself") to suggest the
ontogeny / phylogeny connection in Dickens's work,
and its essential Carlylean derivation.

    11. See Fleishman, p.105.

    12. Letters III, 403-4 (to Mrs. Lydia Mary
Child, 28/12/42).

    13. Dickens particularly chose Cattermole
for his special skill and renown as an illustrator
of Gothic and Elizabethan architecture for the
church designs of *The Old Curiosity Shop*; see
Letters II, 8.

    14. 'Picturesque' is undoubtedly a 'complex
word' in Dickens's vocabulary - at times opposed to
'grotesque', at others in close alignment with it.
That the word was on his mind during the writing of
Barnaby Rudge, in contexts that are by no means
entirely negative, may be suggested by two letters -
to Forster 5/7/41, describing Kate Dickens in
Scotland in the rain under an umbrella, "very
picturesque and uncomfortable" (Letters II, 322),
and to Cattermole about the illustration 'The
Turret' for chapter 56 of *Barnaby Rudge* in August
1841: "I think it will make a queer picturesque
thing in your hands." (Letters II, 352; 6/8/41).
For further discussion, see Nancy K. Hill, *A
Reformer's Art: Dickens's Picturesque and
Grotesque Imagery* (Athens, Ohio, Ohio University
Press, 1981), pp.12-43, and chapter 7 below.

    15. Cf. p. 14 above.

    16. E.g. *Pickwick Papers*, where goblins and
pantomime clowns are shown in the frontispiece,
raising the curtain on Mr.Pickwick and Sam Weller.

    17. Letters, II, 197. In the 1868 Preface
to *Barnaby Rudge*, Dickens stresses the "preter-
natural sagacity" of the two ravens he owned (see
BR, xxiii-xxiv).

    18. For the impact of this perception of

ravens, see fn. 13 to chapter 4 above.

19. Cf. for instance, *Edwin Drood*, where Mr. Grewgious goes to his cellar to fetch some bottles of wine: "Sparkling and tingling after so long a nap, they pushed at their corks to help the corkscrew (like prisoners helping rioters to force their gates), and danced out gaily." (*ED*, xi, 119).

20. The passage (with its pun on 'spirit' and mockery of religious cliché) is an excellent example of that habitual reduction of spirit to matter that Bergson sees as a quintessential feature of comedy, and that certainly seems to be an important principle of the Dickensian grotesque. For a stimulating discussion of comedy and materialism see Victor Sage, "Dickens and Beckett: two uses of materialism", *Journal of Beckett Studies* no. 2 (Summer, 1977), 15-39.

21. Stone, *op. cit.*, p.87, states that Barnaby's imagination "is Dickens' own imagination in its most fanciful and antic phase."

22. Cf. above, p. 39. For a study of *Barnaby Rudge* as a city novel, see Volker Klotz, *Erzählte Stadt* (Munich, 1969), pp.147-163.

23. For other passages where Barnaby communes with the stars, see lxxiii, 563 and lxxvii, 595. Miggs is also found stationed at the window of Varden's: "she gazed out pensively at the wild night sky ... perhaps marvelled how they [the stars] could gaze down on that perfidious creature, man, and not sicken and turn green as chemists' lamps." (ix, 69; see also xxix, 217 for the narrator's not dissimilar reflections). The passage looks forward to many others in later novels - *Little Dorrit, A Tale of Two Cities, Great Expectations*, etc., etc. - which see the stars gazing down from remote heights upon human passions and crimes. Cf. especially chapter 11 below.

24. See *Charles Baudelaire: A Lyric Poet in the Era of High Capitalism*, transl. Zohn (London, NLB, 1974), p.46.

25. See Fleishman, p.104, for emphasis on the rôle of this class in *Barnaby Rudge*.

26. *ED*, xx, 225.

27. The Fortunatus story is alluded to frequently at this stage of Dickens's career - e.g., twice in the next novel he would publish, *Martin Chuzzlewit* (Pecksniff has "a Fortunatus's purse of good sentiments in his inside" - *MC*, ii, 12; and Martin and Mark set out for America "quite as rich as if we had the purse of Fortunatus in our

baggage" - xiv, 243). The emphasis is laid upon the continuing ironic relevance of fairytales to prosaic times.

28. Cf. the emphasis at the end of *Hard Times*, directly appealing for a collaborative effort to ensure the continued survival of "imaginative graces and delights": "Dear reader! It rests with you and me, whether, in our two fields of action, similar things shall be or not." (*HT*, III, ix, 299)

29. Similar terminology, of course, pervades *Hard Times*. William Oddie sees that work, together with *A Tale of Two Cities*, as providing "the most detailed and satisfactory evidence of Carlyle's 'influence' over Dickens "(*Dickens and Carlyle: The Question of Influence*, London, The Centenary Press, 1972, p.41).

30. In the context of this book, it is perhaps worth remembering that Dickens seems to have been fond of drawing grotesque analogies between the resurrectionist's art and the comic writer's, and that in particular he once left a card for the editor of *Bell's Life in London* with the inscription "Charles Dickens, Resurrectionist, in search of a subject." (Letters, I, 77n). See also Andrew Sanders, *Charles Dickens: Resurrectionist* (London, Macmillan, 1982).

31. The essay by Victor Sage, "Dickens and Beckett: two uses of materialism" in *Journal of Beckett Studies* number 2 (Summer, 1977), pp.15-39, explores the extent to which Dickens anticipates Beckett's mockery of the principles of materialist logic. Cf. fn. 20 above.

32. As it tends to in Taylor Stoehr's influential discussion of the novel in *Dickens: the dreamer's stance* (Ithaca, N.Y., Cornell University Press, 1966).

33. This is not meant to imply any blanket approval of Freudian approaches to Dickens, which on the whole (with major exceptions, of course, like Edmund Wilson's essay "The Two Scrooges") have proved less than fully satisfying. However (though this may suggest that the novel is, after all, intimately concerned with individual psychologies) *A Tale of Two Cities* may be amongst those Dickensian novels that offer most to Freudian criticism.

34. *A Tale of Two Cities* is full of references to pantomime; a study of these, and their possible relation to the novel's structure, which seems to parallel or parody the two halves of a traditional pantomime, could be useful.

35. From to Wilkie Collins, 6/12/59 (Letters,

Nonesuch Edition, III, 125).

36. Cf. a letter to William de Cerjat, 21/5/63 (Letters, Nonesuch Edition, III, 352): "What these bishops and suchlike say about revelation, in assuming it to be finished and done with, I can't in the least understand. Nothing is discovered without God's intention and assistance, and I suppose every new knowledge of His works that is conceded to man to be distinctly a revelation by which men are to guide themselves."

37. Cf. Bertolt Brecht, "Der Radwechsel" ("Changing the Wheel") in *Poems 1913-1956*, eds. John Willett and Ralph Manheim (London, Eyre Methuen, 1976), p.439:

> I sit by the roadside
> The driver changes the wheel.
> I do not like the place I have come from.
> I do not like the place I am going to.
> Why with impatience do I
> Watch him changing the wheel?

Chapter Six

THE GROTESQUE IN AMERICA:
AMERICAN NOTES AND *MARTIN CHUZZLEWIT*

'I reckon,' his friend returned, 'that they
are made of pretty much the same stuff as
other folks, if they would but own it, and
not set up on false pretences.'
'In good faith, that's true,' said Martin.
'I dare say,' resumed his friend, 'you might
have such a scene as that in an English comedy,
and not detect any gross improbability or
anomaly in the matter of it?'
'Yes, indeed!'
'Doubtless it is more ridiculous here than
anywhere else,' said his companion; 'but our
professions are to blame for that ...'

(*MC*, xvii, 292)

As everyone knows, *Martin Chuzzlewit* marks an
important watershed in Dickens's career. After the
two novels which preceded it, written in weekly
instalments for the requirements of *Master
Humphrey's Clock*, Dickens felt the need for a rest
from writing. He wished to avoid the fate of Scott,
suffering continually declining sales because (he
felt) his novels followed each other without a
break; moreover, he wanted an opportunity to produce
more carefully considered and organised work.[1] At
the same time, during the election year of 1841, in
the summer of which the Tories were returned to
power, Dickens found his political attitudes harden-
ing into firm opposition to the British social
hierarchy as his preoccupations turned to increasing
sympathy for the Chartist cause and anxiety about
the possibility of revolution in England. "By Jove
how radical I am getting!" he wrote in August, and
a little later, concerning the conservatism of the
medical profession, "I grow so vicious that with

bearing hard upon my pen, I break the nib down."[2]
Earlier that summer he had read an impassioned
attack upon the factory system (*A Narrative of the
Experience and Suffering of William Dodd, a Factory
Cripple*), and commented: "I wish we were all in
Eden again - for the sake of these toiling
creatures."[3] The combination of these moods urged
him in late 1841 towards America, to study and
report back upon a post-revolutionary 'Eden' where
(he felt) principles of freedom, justice and
equality sorely wanting in Britain, might be seen
in action.

What happened of course is that his illusions
were rudely shattered. Some institutions and
individuals, like universities and their professors,
particularly in New England, the most 'civilized'
part of the country, met with his unqualified
admiration and approval. But the *idea* of America
as a whole that he had held, it now appeared, had
been a primitivistic myth: the reality, he
discovered, included a great deal of mindless
violence and lawlessness, cut-throat competitiveness,
and brutish indifference to the rights or needs of
fellow human beings. Henceforth Dickens was to be
wary throughout his life of euphoric or utopian
idealism in thought and language, and hostile to
the idea that the transformation of society that
was so urgently needed might be accomplished by
tearing down the old and making a radical new start
in imitation of the United States.

American Notes and *Martin Chuzzlewit* both
record this disillusionment, and in doing so
incurred for Dickens a temporary diminution of
popularity - particularly in North America, of
course - and an ironic decline in sales. In many
quarters it was felt that one of the main reasons
for this was that in these two books Dickens had
over-indulged his liking for grotesque exaggeration
and caricature. Ralph Waldo Emerson is typical of
many when he complains in his Journal of the
'monstrous exaggeration' of *American Notes*: "He
has picked up and noted with eagerness such odd
local phrases that he met with, and, when he had a
story to relate, has joined them together, so that
the result is the broadest caricature ...".[4] And
an anonymous reviewer in *Parker's London Magazine*
in 1845 dismisses all the characters of *Martin
Chuzzlewit*, with the exception of Sarah Gamp, as
'exaggerated caricatures'.[5]

What is of special interest here, however, is
Dickens's response to such criticism. He saw it as

the symptom of a special form of hypocritical
blindness which in turn, perhaps, led to a deepen-
ing of his understanding of the grotesque in
Victorian England. "I find that a great many people
(particularly those who might have sat for the
character) consider, even Mr. Pecksniff a grotesque
impossibility," he writes in a letter of January,
1844 to Richard Lane, and comments of a specific
person of their acquaintance: "... if I was to put
such a father as he into a book, all the fathers
going (and especially the bad ones) would hold up
their hands and protest against the unnatural
caricature." Likewise concerning the Americans'
response to his account of them he claimed in a
letter to Jane Carlyle of the same month that "it's
impossible to caricature Americans, they are already
walking caricatures".[6] The rhetoric here involves,
at its simplest level, an appeal to the aesthetics
of realism: grotesques are in nature and the artist
must reproduce them as they are. Beyond that,
however, Dickens appears to see denigration of the
grotesque as a mode of representation as a manifestation of an unwillingness to see things as they are
by those who themselves can be thought of as
'grotesque'. Setting themselves apart from the
'grotesque', they use the term as a means of
categorising otherness, when all the while the
grotesque is apparent here and now.
      It is the satirist's task to lay bare the gap
between pretension and reality; and in this respect
Dickens's experience of America was to prove fruit-
ful. It offered a particularly vivid case of self-
satisfaction based upon an illusory and mistaken
notion of what is serious and 'real' and what merely
'grotesque'. The issue of slavery, for instance,
seems to foster such confusion; even a pretty
abolitionist like Miss Norris instructs Martin "that
the negroes were such a funny people, so excessively
ludicrous in their manners and appearance, that it
was wholly impossible for those who knew them well,
to associate any serious ideas with such a very
absurd part of the creation", a view that the
narrator feels compelled to correct: "As if there
were nothing in suffering and slavery, grim enough
to cast a solemn air on any human animal; though it
were as ridiculous, physically, as the most
grotesque of apes, or morally, as the mildest
Nimrod among tuft-hunting republicans!" (*MC*, xvii,
287) And on another occasion the essentially
idealist nature of this mode of thinking is laid
bare in a passage where Dickens gets his own back

at Emerson (disguised as a Washington blue-stocking):

> 'Mind and matter,' said the lady in the wig,
> 'glide swift into the vortex of immensity.
> Howls the sublime, and softly sleeps the calm
> Ideal, in the whispering chambers of Imaginat-
> ion. To hear it, sweet it is. But then, out-
> laughs the stern philosopher, and saith to the
> Grotesque, "What ho! arrest for me that Agency.
> Go, bring it here!" And so the vision fadeth.'
> (xxxiv, 543)

There is an ironic precision about these
deliciously cloudy remarks, for the method of
American Notes and *Martin Chuzzlewit* is indeed a
humorous arrest of 'castles in the air'. Right at
the start of the former book the pattern establishes
itself when "Charles Dickens, Esquire, and Lady"
board the not-so-good ship *Britannia* at Liverpool.
Instead of the "small snug chamber of the imagination" that they have been anticipating for four
months previous, they find themselves installed in
a "state-room" that is in reality an "utterly
impracticable, thoroughly hopeless, and profoundly
preposterous box". (*AN*, i, 1-2) "The idea of
London!" is Mercy Pecksniff's outburst of fervent
anticipation when a visit is proposed, meriting
Pecksniff's splendidly inflated deflation: "And
yet there is a melancholy sweetness in these youthful hopes! It is pleasant to know that they never
can be realised. I remember thinking once myself,
in the days of my childhood, that pickled onions
grew on trees, and that every elephant was born
with an impregnable castle on his back." (*MC*, vi,
86) No Castles of Otranto, then, in a novel that
concerns itself with bogus architecture:[7] Martin's
'great expectations' before he leaves for America
("he never once doubted, one may almost say the
certainty of doing great things in the New World,
if he could only get there" - xiii, 225) attract
the narrator's authoritative commiseration as they
persist in the face of clear contrary signals:
"Poor Martin! For ever building castles in the air.
For ever, in his very selfishness, forgetful of all
but his own teeming hopes and sanguine plans."
(xxi, 352)

Elsewhere in *Martin Chuzzlewit* the establishing
of the utopian nature of such aims and visions is
done more skilfully, perhaps, through an ironic
undermining of their habitual rhetoric. General
Choke projects a myth of America as an unfallen

Eden as he 'opinionates' with the aid of platitude, cliché, and buttonholing address: "We are a new country, sir; man is in a more primeval state here, sir; we have not the excuse of having lapsed in the slow course of time into degenerate practices; we have no false gods; man, sir, here, is man in all his dignity." (xxi, 349) Elijah Pogram's encomium for Hannibal Chollop rests on a similar travesty of 'Nature', martyred in similes of ludicrous orotundity:

> "Our fellow-countryman is a model of a man, quite fresh from Nature's mould! ... He is a true-born child of this free hemisphere! Verdant as the mountains of our country; bright and flowing as our mineral licks; unspiled by withering conventionalities as air our broad and boundless Perearers!" (xxxiv, 534)

And 'Poetry' comes in for some inspired mauling at the hands of a correspondent to Martin who compares himself appropriately enough to an alligator - "I am young, and ardent. For there is a poetry in wildness, and every alligator basking in the slime is in himself an Epic, self-contained ..." (xxii, 364) - and signs himself, in further grotesque arrest, as "Putnam Smif".

'Slime' is in fact a focal deflationary image for what America in fact has to offer Martin. There is, for cisatlantic comparison at an earlier stage of his progress, the drunken 'natural genius' Chevy Slyme and his promoter Tigg, expressing the handy-dandy "high principle that Nature's Nobs felt with Nature's Nobs, and that true greatness of soul, all the world over" (vii, 106) when taking advantage of Tom Pinch's innocent good nature. Arriving at Eden, Martin finds an anticlimactic post-diluvian scene: "The waters of the Deluge might have left it but a week before: so choked with slime and matted growth was the hideous swamp which bore that name." (xxiii, 377) The nature that grows there is a tangle of wild vegetation, trees "forced into shapes of strange distortion" and an underfoot "jungle deep and dark, with neither earth nor water at its roots, but putrid matter, formed of the pulpy offal of the two, and of their own corruption". (381)

It is good soil for the grotesque. America is depicted as an ironic jungle paradise for predators - Jonsonian Volpones and Corvinos like Zephaniah

Scadder with his extraordinary mask:[8] "rumpled tufts were on the arches of his eyes, as if the crow whose foot was deeply printed in the corners had pecked and torn them in a savage recognition of his kindred nature." (xxi, 353) As in Brecht's *Threepenny Opera*, where bourgeois highwaymen practice more sophisticated savagery than sharks,[9] and animate clichés of human/animal comparisons, America outdoes any mundane version of cannibalism, as Mrs. Lupin suggests in her lament for Mark Tapley's disappearance: "How could he ever go to America! Why didn't he go to some of those countries where the savages eat each other fairly, and give an equal chance to every one!" (xliii, 657) It generates, not only monstrous people, but machines like the appropriately named boat on which Martin and Mark arrive - The Screw, "which with its machinery on deck, looked, as it worked its long slim legs, like some enormously magnified insect or antediluvian monster" (xv, 254) - spawned once more in its mud. And it makes demons, and people possessed by them, whose compulsive predation brings no satisfaction to themselves: "dyspeptic individuals bolted their food in wedges; feeding, not themselves, but broods of nightmares, who were standing at livery within them." (xvi, 271)

The combination of these realities and the utopian fictions of American propaganda create a society that is nothing if not pantomimic. In *American Notes* the appearance of Boston itself seems theatrical:

> When I got into the streets upon the Sunday morning, the air was so clear, the houses were so bright and gay; the signboards were painted in such gaudy colours; the gilded letters were so very golden; the bricks were so very red, the stone was so very white, the blinds and area railings were so very green, the knobs and plates upon the street doors so marvellously bright and twinkling; and all so slight and unsubstantial in appearance - that every thoroughfare in the city looked exactly like a scene in a pantomime. (*AN*, iii, 26)

At social gatherings a self-styled 'General' falls over, coming up "stiff and without a bend in him, like a dead clown" (xvii, 289), and a Mrs. Hominy appears "in a highly aristocratic and classical cap, meeting beneath her chin: a style of head-dress so admirably adapted to her countenance, that if the late Mr. Grimaldi had appeared in the lappets of Mrs. Siddons, a more complete effect could not have been produced.' (xxii, 369) And pantomimic gestures regularly support deceptions and self-deceptions like the conviction of Colonel Diver and Jefferson Brick of the fearsome impact of their journalism in Britain: "'The libation of freedom, Brick,' hinted the colonel. 'Must sometimes be quaffed in blood, colonel,' cried Brick. And when he said 'blood', he gave the great pair of scissors a sharp snap, as if *they* said blood too, and were quite of his opinion." (xvi, 262)

The pantomimic principle of the interchange-ability of human and inanimate matter also operates in a markedly satiric way in the representation of America. All mortals are reified - Queen Victoria is compared to a railway engine ("Well, sir, I tell you this - there ain't a en-gine with its biler bust, in God A'mighty's free U-nited States, so fixed, and nipped, and frizzled to a most e-tarnal smash, as that young critter, in her luxurious location in the Tower of London, will be, when she reads the next double-extra Watertoast Gazette" - xxi, 345), Zephaniah Scadder to the innards of a harpsichord ("... every time he spoke something was seen to twitch and jerk up in his throat, like the little hammers in a harpsichord when the notes are struck" - xxi, 353). It is a pattern of reference that puts the lie to the romantic fiction of America as an organic prelapsarian society - it appears in reality to be as mechanised and materialistic as the 'world's workshop' whose values it purports to oppose:

> Steel and iron are of infinitely greater account, in this commonwealth, than flesh and blood. If the cunning work of man be urged beyond its power of endurance, it has within it the elements of its own revenge; whereas the wretched mechanism of The Divine Hand is dangerous with no such property, but may be tampered with, and crushed, and broken, at the driver's pleasure. Look at that engine! it shall cost a man more dollars in the way of penalty and fine, and satisfaction of the out-raged law, to deface in wantonness that sense-less mass of metal, than to take the lives upon the bloody stripes; and Liberty pulls down her cap upon her eyes, and owns oppress-ion in its vilest aspect, for her sister. (xxi, 341)

So much, then, for the American alternative to
Europe. Just as in *Barnaby Rudge* and *A Tale of Two
Cities*, where historical separations between old
oppression and new liberation are constantly
breaking down, in *American Notes* and *Martin
Chuzzlewit* geographical distance seems to count for
nothing. And the grotesque is with us everywhere.
Above all it is slavery that makes this 'new world'
a very precise equivalent of Kafka's penal settlement:

> What! shall we declaim against the ignorant
> peasantry of Ireland, and mince the matter
> when these American taskmasters are in
> question? Shall we cry shame on the brutality
> of those who ham-string cattle: and spare the
> lights of Freedom upon earth who notch the
> ears of men and women, cut pleasant posies in
> the shrinking flesh, learn to write with pens
> of red-hot iron on the human face, rack their
> poetic fancies for liveries of mutilation
> which their slaves shall wear for life and
> carry to the grave ... (*AN*, xvii, 242-3)

Putnam Smif's poetic alligator clearly has a number
of human colleagues.[10] In the end all that appears
to remain of the ideal Dickens had come to seek is
Niagara Falls - and here it is found no longer in
temporal or spatial realities but in a transcendental vision of immortality:

> But always does the mighty stream appear to die
> as it comes down, and always from its
> unfathomable grave arises that tremendous
> ghost of spray and mist which is never laid:
> which has haunted this place with the same
> dread solemnity since Darkness brooded on the
> deep, and that first flood before the Deluge -
> Light - came rushing on Creation at the word
> of God.[11] (*AN*, xiv, 201)

But of course in *Martin Chuzzlewit* at least
America is only as it were a streak in the bacon.
The analogy is a close one, since the juxtaposition
of America and England (often criticised as an
aspect of the novel's looseness of structure) is
one way in which the novel generates ironies
similar to those of *Oliver Twist* - the chapter
following Martin's arrival in 'Eden', for instance,

130

transports us to Mr.Pecksniff at his country retreat
engaged in "an ancient pursuit, gardening ... I do
a little bit of Adam still." (xxiv, 384), and the
next opens in Mr. Mould's own tradesman's paradise
in the City of London,[12] where the sound of workmen
making coffins "puts one in mind of the sound of
animated nature in the agricultural districts. It's
exactly like the woodpecker tapping". (xxv, 402)
'Poetry', it is clear, thrives in England as well
as in America - above all perhaps in Montague Tigg,
who gives the Anglo-Bengalee Insurance Company
those special touches it needs for success ("But
the ornamental department, David; the inventive and
poetical department" - xxvii, 431) - and it broadens
into the theme of bad art and bogus professionalism
which is henceforth to concern Dickens in many
novels,[13] and which contains within it several
important aspects of the Dickensian grotesque.

Pecksniff and Gamp are clearly amongst the
major bearers of the theme in this novel. "He has
found I'm professional. He heard me inside just
now, I have no doubt" (ix, 139) is Pecksniff's
"soft cry" when he wants to gain admittance to the
house where Mary Pinch is working, arousing
attention and admiration with his praise of its
"cornice, which supports the roof", "the airiness
of its construction" and the "fluted pillars in the
portico". Mrs. Gamp, described as one of those
"persons who have attained to great eminence in
their profession" (xix, 313), bestows her eye for
the picturesque upon less classical sights, like
Lewsome in his delirium, "as a connoisseur might
gaze upon a doubtful work of art", deciding after
inspection that "he'd make a lovely corpse". (xxv,
412) Where Jonas Chuzzlewit and the Anglo-Bengalee
Insurance Company deal in 'lives' (xxvii, 440)
(synecdoche is again a feature of this novel - Mrs.
Gamp describes her deceased husband as "a wooden
leg gone likeways home to its account" (xl, 625)),
and Mr. Mould in deaths, Mrs. Gamp is indiscriminate
in her professionalism: "she went to a lying-in or
a laying-out with equal zest and relish." (xix,
313)

Against these multiple dilettantes and
charlatans the narrator sets himself up as a model
professional in his conduct of the novel's
organisation: "As the surgeon's first care after
amputating a limb is to take up the arteries the
cruel knife has severed, so it is the duty of this
history, which in its remorseless course has cut
from the Pecksniffian trunk its right arm, Mercy,

to look to the parent stem, and see how in all its
various ramifications it got on without her." (xxx,
470) Its structure is in part modelled on that of
earlier novels like *Nicholas Nickleby* and *The Old
Curiosity Shop* - the "Piljian's Projiss", as Mrs.
Gamp calls it (xxv, 404), with its hero's confrontation of a serial array of modern grotesques, here
in particular the "Giant Despair" of America.(xxiii,
377)[14] But another pattern emerges here, indirectly
derived from Gothic fiction, which is to be
important in later novels like *Little Dorrit* and
Bleak House - the 'mystery' structure in which
secrets are gradually uncovered. In the handling
of 'mysteries' and 'secrets' in *Martin Chuzzlewit*,
the contrast between real and fake professionalism
is explored.

"I don't particularly favour mysteries. I
would as soon, on a fair and clear explanation, be
judged by one class of man as another," (*LD*, II,
viii, 515) is Daniel Doyce's judgement on the matter
in *Little Dorrit*. It is not shared by many
characters in *Martin Chuzzlewit*. Montague Tigg is
introduced early on in a cravat "like one of those
mantles which hairdressers are accustomed to wrap
about their clients, during the progress of the
professional mysteries" (iv, 44), to indicate that
the kind of business in which he is to be involved
is likely to be shady. Pecksniff insists on
leaving young Martin the run of his house while he
is absent in London ("there is no mystery; all is
free and open" - vi, 87), but gets his pupil to
design a grammar school for him by emphasising the
importance of the professional mysteries, "the
magical effect of a few finishing touches from the
hand of a master". (88) Mrs. Gamp introduces
herself to her newlywed charge Mercy Chuzzlewit
"with innumerable leers, winks, coughs, nods, smiles
and curtseys all leading to the establishment of a
mysterious and confidential understanding between
herself and the bride". (xxvi, 425)

But *Martin Chuzzlewit* is an exact contemporary
of Eugene Sue's *Mysteries of Paris*,[15] and the theme
passes beyond the confines of the issue of
professionalism. In particular, it is closely
bound up in this novel with the presentation of the
city as a network of secrets that form the 'mystery'
of the evil at the heart of the social system. This
is first suggested on Tom Pinch's arrival in
Salisbury, where he sets forth "on a stroll about
the streets with a vague and not unpleasant idea
that they teemed with all kinds of mystery and

bedevilment". (v, 69) He is an appropriate focus
because, like little Nell in Wolverhampton, he is
an innocent confronting for the first time the
realities of the new urban industrial scene, feeling
its "attraction of repulsion": "Every morning when
he shut his door at Islington, he turned his face
towards an atmosphere of unaccountable fascination,
as surely as he turned it to the London smoke ..."
(xl, 618) And he also exemplifies the way in which
everyone is inevitably and often unconsciously
involved in its secrets, as he brushes against the
"man of mystery", Mr. Nadgett (xxxviii, 589), in
his progress through the city streets.

Once more, these contiguities express the link
between the city and processes of thought that
Dickens connects with madness. Strange juxtapositions are emphasised first in places removed from
London - like Pecksniff's house at night, which
"shuts in as many incoherent and incongruous
fancies as a madman's head" (v, 84), or the pub
where Martin and Mark celebrate their return from
America, "full of mad closets", with "more corners
in it than the brain of an obstinate man". (xxxv,
549) But the theme is highlighted when Pecksniff
and Chuzzlewit arrive in London in the early
morning: "There was a dense fog too: as if it
were a city in the clouds, which they had been
travelling to all night up a magic beanstalk; and
there was a thick crust upon the pavement like oil-
cake: which, one of the outsides (mad, no doubt)
said to another (His keeper, of course), was Snow."
(viii, 122)

Lewsome's delirium "dimly finding fear and
horror everywhere," (xxvi, 414) continue this
preoccupation - but the great thing now is the co-
presence of Mrs. Gamp. Her appearance at all
crises of life is the most brilliant expression, in
this novel, of grotesque juxtaposition. Lewsome
raves on about hallucinatory crowds of grotesque
figures, "five hundred and twenty-one men, all
dressed alike, and with the same distortion on
their faces, that have passed in at the window, and
out at the door", and Mrs. Gamp chimes in with her
own active, alcoholic fantasies: "Ah! _I_ see 'em
... all the whole kit of 'em numbered like hackney-
coaches, ain't they?" (xxv, 415) Jonas in the
grip of paranoid fantasy after the murder of Tigg
is dependent upon Mrs. Gamp to look after Chuffey,
but in an extraordinary tragicomic moment he has to
cope with the mythical Mrs. Harris as well,
nervously resurrected since her demolition by Betsy

Prig:

> '... I've brought another, which engages to
> give every satisfaction.'
> 'What is her name?' asked Jonas.
> Mrs. Gamp looked at him in an odd way without
> returning any answer, but appeared to under-
> stand the question too.
> 'What is her name?' repeated Jonas.
> 'Her name,' said Mrs. Gamp, 'is Harris.'
> It was extraordinary how much effort it cost
> Mrs. Gamp to pronounce the name she was
> commonly so ready with. (li, 778)

And at the grand dénouement scene, where Old Martin
unmasks the hypocrites and villains like the Duke
of Milan in *Measure for Measure*, Mrs.Harris has
undergone further resurrection to provide grotesque
flourishes to Mrs. Gamp's claim for a share of the
treasures dispensed:

> Mrs. Harris as has one sweet infant (though
> she *do* not wish it known) in her own family by
> the mother's side, kep in spirits in a bottle;
> and that sweet babe she see at Greenwich Fair,
> a-travelling in company with the pink-eyed
> lady, Prooshan dwarf, and livin' skelinton,
> which judge her feelins when the barrel-organ
> played, and she was showed her own dear
> sister's child, the same not bein' expected
> from the outside picter, where it was painted
> quite contrairy in a livin' state, a many
> sizes larger, and performing beautiful upon
> the Arp, which never did that dear child know
> or do: since breathe it never did, to speak
> on, in this wake! And Mrs. Harris, Mr.
> Chuzzlewit, has knowed me many year, and can
> give you information that the lady which is
> widdered can't do better and may do worse,
> than let me wait upon her, which I hope to do.
> (lii, 814)

A kind of summary of the novel's preoccupation
is available here. A falsifying, idealising art
depicts the child in angelic state, inhabiting a
fake paradise; whether it be rural Wiltshire or
the American Eden, this novel has abandoned such
fantasies, and the central figure has gained
greatly by his 'expectations well lost'. The
falsity is declared in part by the simultaneous
presence of monstrosities - albinos, dwarfs and

skeletons - that underscore the deformity of the
embryo itself,   and yet contain the irresistible,
magical "attraction of repulsion". The sublime is
displaced from the level of prelapsarian mirages to
reassert itself inversely in the grotesque.

Thus *Martin Chuzzlewit* is in essence about art
and truth. It wants to make us see that the truth
of art can only be indirect, through its capacity
for fictions like Mrs. Gamp and Mrs. Harris (it
calls itself at one point "this slight chronicle -
a dream within a dream ..." (xvii, 297)). It
cannot represent the unmediated vision of bliss
that the imagination had sought in America, and
miserably failed to find ("this is not the republic
of my imagination"); dwelling on the quite
unredeemed world of hopeless shams like Pecksniff
and Gamp, it discovers in the transforming power of
art a model of the metamorphosis of society.

NOTES

1. For Dickens's consciousness of Scott's
career as a cautionary precedent, see for instance
the letter to Thomas Mitton of 23/8/41: "Scott's
life warns me that let me write never so well, if I
keep on writing, without cessation, it is in the
very nature of things that the sale will be
unsteady, and the circulation will fall." (Letters,
II, 365). For evidence of a roughly contempor-
aneous preference for tight organisation, see a
letter earlier in the same year claiming *The Old
Curiosity Shop* as his best work, because "I never
had the design and purpose of a story so distinctly
marked in my mind, from its commencement." (II,
233).

2. Letters, II, 357 (13/8/41), and 368 (to
Macready, 23/8/41).

3. Letters, II, 346 (31/7/41).

4. Entry for 25 November 1842. Quoted from
Wall, *op. cit.*, p.62.

5. See Collins, *Dickens: The Critical
Heritage*, p.170.

6. Letters IV, 5 (2/1/44) and 33 (27/1/44).
See also the letter to Angela Burdett Coutts of
17/9/45 which comments on George Cruikshank in a
similar fashion: "I should promise that Cruikshank
is one of the best creatures in the World, in his
own odd way (he is a live Caricature himself)."

7. Architectural metaphor - in particular
the notion of 'castles in the air', false hopes and
ideals - is common in Dickens's work, culminating

perhaps in the two brilliant chapters of *Little Dorrit* ('A Castle in the Air' and 'The Storming of the Castle in the Air') where Mr.Dorrit's fantasies immediately prior to his death are explored.

8. The impact of Ben Jonson's art upon Dickens has been frequently noted and commented upon - e.g. in Evelyn M. Simpson's "Jonson and Dickens: A Study in the Comic Genius of London" (*Essays and Studies* XXIX (1943), 82-92) and William Axton, *op. cit.*, p.141. One's impression is that it deserves a new, systematic account.

9. See the first stanzas of 'The Ballad of Mac the Knife', in John Willett and Ralph Manheim's translation (*Bertolt Brecht: Collected Plays*, volume two, part two, London, Eyre Methuen Ltd., 1979, p.3):

> See the shark with teeth like razors.
> All can read his open face.
> And Macheath has got a knife, but
> Not in such an obvious place.
>
> See the shark, how red his fins are
> As he slashes at his prey.
> Mac the Knife wears white kid gloves which
> Give the minimum away.

10. 'Poetry' is the frequent focus of Dickensian satire. The alligator's habitat clearly link him with Chevy Slyme, and thence with Slum in *The Old Curiosity Shop* - which suggests the possible origin of these attitudes, in Dickens's experiences at Warren's Blacking. Forster recalls that "The poets in the house's regular employ he remembered, too, and made his first study from one of them for the poet of Mrs. Jarley's waxwork" (see "The Blacking Laureate: The Identity of Mr. Slum, A Pioneer in Publicity" by Wilfred Partington in *The Dickensian* XXXIV (Summer, 1938), 199).

11. During the 1867/8 visit to the U.S.A. Dickens again visited Niagara Falls, and rediscovered this sensation of translation to an immortal plane: "The majestic valley below the Falls, so seen through the vast cloud of spray, was made of rainbow. The high banks, the river rocks, the forests, the bridge, the buildings, the air, the sky, were all made of rainbow. Nothing in Turner's finest water-colour drawings, done in his greatest day, is so ethereal, so imaginative, so gorgeous in colour, as what I then beheld. I seemed to be lifted from the earth and to be looking into Heaven." (to Forster, 13/3/68; Letters, Nonesuch Edition, III, 633).

12. Dickens's London habitually contains hidden rural nooks where - suddenly, unexpectedly - a pastoral paradise is glimpsed in the midst of noise and confusion. The Temple, in *Barnaby Rudge*, is one such place, its motto, apparently, "'Who enters here leaves noise behind'" (*BR*, xv, 113) - as is Dr.Manette's corner of Soho, "a cool spot, staid but cheerful, a wonderful place for echoes, and a very harbour from the raging streets." (*TOTC* I, vi, 86).

13. It is hardly a coincidence that this preoccupation with artistic professionalism should deepen in what was Dickens's most carefully planned novel to date. Incidents like the visit to Abbotsford in July 1841 and the death of Theodore Hook in the same year (see Letters, III, 39n and 500) appear to have been influential in causing Dickens to think deeply about the purpose and meaning of the artistic vocation in the period just before the writing of *Martin Chuzzlewit*.

14. The structural similarities of some features of Dickens's novels to the Hogarthian 'Progresses' have recently been studied in Nancy K. Hill's *A Reformer's Art: Picturesque and Grotesque Images in Dickens's Novels* (Athens, Ohio, Ohio University Press, 1981).

15. During his tours of Italy Dickens was to discover coachmen reading Sue's novel, and was to meet Sue himself later in Paris (see Letters IV, 404 and 684).

Chapter Seven

THE NEW PICTURESQUE: *PICTURES FROM ITALY* AND
LITTLE DORRIT

"The condition of the common people here is abject
and shocking. I am afraid that the conventional idea
of the picturesque is associated with such misery and
degradation that a new picturesque will have to be
established as the world goes onwards."[1]
    The critical and economic axes running as they
do, a good deal more attention has been paid to
Dickens's two journeys to the United States than to
his more numerous visits to Europe. Yet it is
arguable that these latter are no less important
for his development as a writer, and in particular
that his relationship to Italy - where he lived for
a year between July 1844 and June 1845, and which
he revisited in the autumn of 1853 - can be usefully studied in a comparative manner as a
significant complement to his relationship to
America. Both experiences generate a travel book,
and later form the subject, in major novels, of
significant episodes meditating upon the possibilities of travel as a means of stimulating personal
growth and change. Both also emphasise political
issues, and reckon, with some keenness, national
prospects and destinies, noting not only the
evident contrasts (Italy clearly exciting no great
expectations, and offering no political pointers
for the establishment of an earthly paradise) but
also the unexpected similarities (America, in
institutions like slavery, uncannily resembling its
unliberated counterpart). These narratives of two
countries, it appears, bear a relationship that
anticipates the structure of *A Tale of Two Cities.*
    Yet in other respects the impact of Italy upon
Dickens's imagination is deeper and more lasting
than that of America. As the country of pantomime,
marionettes, Mr. Punch, the *commedia dell'arte*,
Italy is one of the main sources of the popular

138

theatrical tradition to which Dickens's art of the grotesque is so obviously indebted.[2] A youthful devotee of the clown Grimaldi, it is not perhaps surprising that Dickens should eventually be drawn to the country of his origin, confessing as he does in the introduction to *Pictures from Italy* that his imagination "had dwelt for years" (*PI*, 260) on Italian places. The Grimaldi family is in his mind in 1844, just prior to departure for Italy, as for instance in May when he mentions in a letter to Forster the death of Joseph Grimaldi in a pub in 1832 (from delirium tremens: the event is luridly recalled in 'The Stroller's Tale' in *Pickwick Papers*).[3] Soon after his arrival, in another letter to Forster of July, he comments upon "the Genoese manner, which is exceedingly animated and pantomimic"; and in *Pictures from Italy* the account of the Dickens family's arrival in Albaro (the suburb of Genoa where they spent their first months in Italy, in the 'Pink Jail') includes a reference to a lady whose carriage gets stuck in a narrow lane, and who is "hauled through one of the little front windows, like a harlequin". (*PI*, 285) But the association of Italy with the theatre had begun well prior to *Pictures from Italy*, and in a somewhat different mode. From Dickens's earliest works onwards, the novels and sketches contain characters with theatrical ambitions who provide themselves - more frequently in imitation of the then-fashionable opera stars than of Grimaldi[4] - with fine-sounding Italian names. In *Sketches by Boz* there is the singing-master Lobskini, and the dancing-master Billsmethi ("Sentiment", *SB*, 329, and "The Dancing Academy", *SB*, 256); in *Nicholas Nickleby* the actresses Snevellici, Belvawney, Bravassa, and Gazingi, and, in another sphere of sham, Mantalini ("originally Muntle, but it had been converted, by an easy transition into Mantalini: the lady rightly considering that an English appellation would be of serious injury to the business" - *NN*, x, 124). More Grimaldianly, in *The Old Curiosity Shop*, Tom Scott changes his name after the fall of the house of Quilp - more engagingly than Flintwinch, who resurfaces in Antwerp as 'Mynheer van Flyntevynge' after the Clennam crash - to Scotto, perhaps: "he assumed the name of an Italian image lad, with whom he had become acquainted; and afterwards tumbled with extraordinary success, and to overflowing audiences." (*OCS*, lxxiii, 549)

Perceiving the class-pretensions contained in some of these inventions, Dickens seems also to

have formed an early aversion to Italian 'high
culture', enshrined most particularly in Italian
opera. "I really cannot please myself with any of
the sketches I have made for an opera to which the
title of 'The Gondolier' would be applicable," he
writes to Hullah in 1835, expressing a preference
for "the popularity and beauty of many of the old
English operas".[5] Bellini's *Il Pirata*, seen in 1844
in Paris, comes close to being damned with faint
praise ("as good and great as it is possible for
anything Operatic to be"), and Verdi's *Il Trovatore*
is described in 1853 as "on the whole rubbish".[6]
Thus it is that in *Pictures from Italy* Verdi's
I Due Foscari performed in the San Carlo theatre is
contrasted most unfavourably with the pantomime
theatre next door, where a truly popular art of
grotesque realism is to be had: "But for astonishing truth and spirit in seizing and embodying the
real life about it,the shabby little San Carlino
Theatre - the rickety house one storey high, with a
staring picture outside: down among the drums and
trumpets, and the tumblers, and the lady conjurer -
is without a rival anywhere." (*PI*, 421)
     Yet whilst enthusiastically endorsing tradition-
al Italian popular culture, Dickens is careful to
refuse any merely aesthetic response to it. *Pictures
from Italy* is one of the central places where
Dickens's critique of conventional ideas of the
'picturesque', and the bogus art connoisseurship
associated with them, is mounted. And in this
interrogation the word 'grotesque' has a dialectical
function, undermining the 'picturesque' and replac-
ing it with something less comfortable, more
ambiguous and challenging as a response to Italy in
modern times.
     Essentially, to write a book with the title
Pictures from Italy in the mid-nineteenth century
was to engage with the term 'picturesque' - 'capable
of making good pictures'[7] - in the country with
which it had hitherto had its strongest associations
("Italy has been made to supply so much of the easy
picturesqueness, the crude local colour of poetry
and the drama," wrote Henry James in 1875[8]).
Inevitably, then, *Pictures from Italy* is full of
the word: in Genoa, for instance, there are "bold
and picturesque rocks on the sea shore" (*PI*, 284,
286), and to circle the city walls is to encounter
"in not the least picturesque part of this ride ...
a fair specimen of a real Genoese tavern". (291)
Verona has a market-place that is "fanciful, quaint,
and picturesque" (337), and a "picturesque old

bridge" (338); Carrara is "very picturesque and bold" (356), and the Campagna full of ruins "broken aquaducts, left in the most picturesque and beautiful clusters of arches" (367); and the 'aspect' of Ferrara at dawn "was as picturesque as it seemed unreal and spectral". (326)

But to see *only* such effects is to be taken in, as Pip is to be by "Miss Havisham and Estella and the strange house and the strange life [which] appeared to have something to do with everything that was picturesque". (*GE*, xv, 103) The letters from Italy prepare this theme - they comment disparagingly on artists who come to Italy, hire themselves models who "dispose themselves in conventionally picturesque attitudes" and "go on copying these people elaborately time after time out of mind, and find nothing fresh or suggestive in the actual world about them".[9] And in *Pictures from Italy*, in Naples (where this critique comes to its climax), there is a direct appeal to the tourist to look for something other than the picturesque façade:

> But, lovers and hunters of the picturesque, let us not keep too studiously out of view the miserable depravity, degradation, and wretchedness, with which this gay Neapolitan life is inseparably associated. It is not well to find Saint Giles's so repulsive, and the Porta Capuana so attractive. A pair of naked legs and a ragged red scarf, do not make *all* the difference between what is interesting and what is coarse and odious? Painting and poetising for ever, if you will, the beauties of this most beautiful and lovely spot of earth, let us, as our duty, try to associate a new picturesque with some faint recognition of man's destiny and capabilities; more hopeful, I believe, among the ice and snow of the North Pole, than in the sun and bloom of Naples. (413)[10]

To get beyond the 'conventionally picturesque' apprehension requires a kind of double-take adumbrated first, perhaps, in 'The Mudfog and Other Sketches' of 1837 ("The town of Mudfog is extremely picturesque. Limehouse and Ratcliff Highway are both something like it ..." - *SB*, 608). As the traveller approaches Italian towns, "in every case each little group of houses presents in the distance, some enchanting confusion of picturesque and fanciful shapes" - but once entered, they appear rather

141

'grotesque' than 'picturesque': "the streets are
narrow, dark, and dirty; the inhabitants lean and
squalid; and the withered old women ... are like a
population of Witches."(*PI*, 313, 312)

In fact, the 'grotesque' is omnipresent in
Pictures from Italy: no book by Dickens uses the
word so frequently. Even en route, French towns
contain "little towers at the angles, like grotesque
faces, as if the walls had put a mask on, and were
staring down into the moat", and as the Alps are
approached horses wear strange, excessive harness,
"with a pair of grotesque horns growing out of the
collar". (*PI*, 264) Votive offerings in the chapels
of the cathedral at Lyons are quaint and primitive
products of popular tradition: "in a grotesque
squareness of outline, an impossibility of perspective, they are not unlike the woodcuts in old books."
(273)

Then, in Italy, the references multiply. First
in Genoa, there is a church that contains a painting
of a sinner in hell, "a most grotesque and hideously
comic old soul, for ever blistering in the red sun,
and melting in the mimic fire, for the gratification
and improvement (and the contributions) of the poor
Genoese". (298-9) In Parma the cathedral,
baptistery and campanile are "ancient buildings of
a sombre brown, embellished with innumerable
grotesque monsters" (318); in Venice, there are yet
more churches, and vast palaces through which
Dickens wanders, with rooms "where the furniture,
half awful, half grotesque, was mouldering away".
(335) And at Mantua Dickens confronts the great
grotesque *jeux d'esprits* of Mannerists like Giulio
Romano in the Palazzo del Té, including above all
the Sala dei Giganti, where he remarks on "the
unaccountable nightmares with which its interior has
been decorated (among other subjects of more
delicate execution), by Giulio Romano. There is a
leering Giant over a certain chimney piece, and
there are dozens of Giants (Titans warring with
Jove) on the walls of another room, so inconceivably
ugly and grotesque that it is marvellous how any man
can have imagined such creatures". (343)

Yet the grotesque in *Pictures from Italy* not
only deflates conventional expectations of beauty:
it proposes others. The marionettes of Genoa, for
example, like the *commedia dell'arte* of Naples,
stand for a "new picturesque"; what Dickens praises
in them is the essential realism of their effects.

"The Theatre of Puppets, or Marionetti - a
famous company from Milan - is without any exception,

142

the drollest exhibition I ever beheld in my life.
I never saw anything so exquisitely ridiculous.
They *look* between four and five feet high, but are
really much smaller; for when a musician in the
orchestra happens to put his hat on the stage, it
becomes alarmingly gigantic, and almost blots out
an actor. They usually play a comedy, and a ballet.
The comic man in the comedy I saw one summer night,
is a waiter in a hotel. There never was such a
locomotive actor, since the world began. Great
pains are taken with him. He has extra joints in
his legs: and a practical eye, with which he winks
at the pit, in a manner that is absolutely
insupportable to a stranger, but which the uninitia-
ted audience, mainly composed of the common people,
receive (as they do everything else) quite as a
matter of course, and as if he were a man. His
spirits are prodigious. He continually shakes his
legs, and winks his eye. And there is a heavy
father with grey hair, who sits down on the regular
conventional stage-bank, and blesses his daughter in
the regular conventional way, who is tremendous. No
one would suppose it possible that anything short of
a real man could be so tedious. It is the triumph
of art." (303-4)

Like *Martin Chuzzlewit*,[11] the passage contemplates
the relations between art and reality. On the one
hand it praises grotesque art - a realist art
depending not on lavish detail but on psychological
penetration, seizing upon a few sketches and strokes
that can be interpreted and made into a reality,
capturing and delighting the popular audience. On
the other hand, this enthralment is also negative,
for it seems to exemplify the hold of fraudulent
men and their practices on the lives of ordinary
people in Italian society. The "attraction of
repulsion", returning to the country that first
conceptualised it ("quell'orror bello che
attristando piace"[12]), is a major feature of the
grotesque in *Pictures from Italy*.

Thus there is continuous emphasis on the
ubiquity of contrast in Italian life - the kinds of
contrasts that habitually mingle the 'attractive'
and the 'repulsive'. Genoa itself is one instance
- and Dickens describes how he grew to love its
variety: "it abounds in the strangest contrasts:
things that are picturesque, ugly, mean, magnificent,
delightful, and offensive, break upon the view at
every turn." (291) On its streets, even the most
unpleasant faces - those of monks and priests -
offer some pleasure to the physiognomical observer

because of the multiple chicaneries they bear
witness to: "I have no knowledge, elsewhere, of
more repulsive countenances, than are to be found
among these gentry. If Nature's handwriting be at
all legible, greater varieties of sloth, deceit, and
intellectual torpor could hardly be observed among
any class of men in the world." (296) Even the
fetish-worship that Dickens so fiercely deplores as
an aspect of catholicism has its comic side in
Pictures from Italy, as when the monks of Santa
Maria in Aracoeli in Rome unveil an icon of the
Infant Jesus, "a little wooden doll, in face very
like General Tom Thumb, the American Dwarf". (381)
    Such are the fresh and suggestive 'new
pictures' that the practised eye, turning aside from
the conventional picturesque, can take in. Dickens
seeks to avoid idealisation in his portrayal of
Italy, to confront its hopelessness and backwardness
squarely, as in a letter to D'Orsay: "It seemed as
if one had reached the end of all things - as if
there were no more progress,motion, advancement, or
improvements of any kind beyond, but here the whole
scheme had stopped centuries ago, never to move on
any more, but just lying down in the sun to bask
there 'till the day of Judgement'."[13] At the same
time the energising of such a world through moments
of active perception - seeing monks at a funeral,
for instance, "as if they were Ghoules or Demons,
bearing off the body for themselves" (302) -
suggests that it may after all be subject to change.
    For, after all, what *Pictures from Italy*
emphasises - again like *American Notes* - is not the
solidity and permanence of the world it represents,
but its dreamlike insubstantiality. This is true,
first, of the images or 'pictures' themselves -
"faint reflections - mere shadows in the water",
the preface calls them. (260) The idea spreads
from these representations to envelop also what they
represent - the Palazzi of Genoa, for instance, full
of "dreary, dreaming, echoing vaulted chambers"
(292), or its streets, "a bewildering phantasmagoria,
with all the inconsistency of a dream, and all the
pain and pleasure of an extravagant reality". (293)
Not only is sightseeing like dreaming - "the rapid
and unbroken succession of novelties that had passed
before me, came back like half-formed dreams" (329)
- the sights themselves appear as dreams. Venice is
the most vivid of all, surpassing anything one might
imagine, even in opium dreams: "The gorgeous and
wonderful reality of Venice is beyond the fancy of
the wildest dreamer. Opium couldn't build such a

place, and enchantment couldn't shadow it forth in a vision." And so the experience of it is depicted as the entering into a new state - "a new sensation, a new memory, a new mind came upon me".[14] The manner in which, in Italy, everyday reality can become strange and fantastical, suggests that the apparently hopeless fixity of its political condition may yet offer possibilities of trans-formation.

And with all their faults, the Italian people are described in *Pictures from Italy* in terms that markedly contrast with those of *American Notes*. Again the contemporary letters capture the spirit of Dickens's unequivocally sympathetic response to Italian manners: "Without being obsequious or servile, which is not at all the characteristic of the people in the North of Italy, the waiters are so amiably disposed to invent little attentions which they suppose to be English, and are so lighthearted and goodnatured that it is a pleasure to have to do with them. But so it is with all the people."[15] England and Englishmen were not the enemies they had been seen as in America - Dickens heard the Marchese di Negro describe his country as "Dear England, merry England, the young and joyous, home of the Fancy, free as the air, playful as the child".[16] The compliment was returned: writing from Switzerland in the summer of 1845, Dickens looked back fondly to "the beautiful Italian manners, the sweet language, the quick recognition of a pleasant look or cheerful word; the captivating expression of a desire to oblige in everything ... left behind the alps. Remembering them, I sigh for the dirt again." And back in London in the spring of 1846, "I talk to all the Italian Boys who go about the streets with Organs and white mice, and give them mints of money *per l'amore della bell' Italia*".[17]

Little Dorrit is obviously about a good deal more than Italy. But since holistic readings of this text not infrequently neglect or underestimate its Italian dimension, it may be useful for once to give this concentrated attention. It may be that in fact the grotesque is again an important emphasis in the representation of Italy, and that it is once more connected with themes of personal and historical change.

To begin with, it appears that the portrait of Italy in this novel is structured around the contrast between two alternative ways of looking at and responding to the experience of Italian travel. The one is Mrs. General's, and it is essentially

classical: a tour of the ruins, which are to be
looked at with an antiquary's eye, that kind of automatic reverence for Greco-Roman tradition that had
been superseded during the Romantic period.[18] Yet
it is allied with a very unclassical prudery, an
emphasis on genteel and proper sights - "nothing
disagreeable should ever be looked at" (*LD*, II, v,
477) - that expresses the narrowest, most frigid
mid-Victorian middle-class taste. Anticipating
Podsnappery, it is jingoistic and philistine, and
quite unable to discriminate in matters of aesthetic
quality: "Mr. Eustace, the classical tourist did
not think much of it [Venice]; and ... he compared
the Rialto Bridge, greatly to its disadvantage, with
Westminster and Blackfriars Bridges." (II, v, 475)
The Meagles's collection of touristic kitsch -
"antiquities from Central Italy, made by the best
modern houses in that department of industry; ...
morsels of tesselated pavement from Herculaneum
and Pompeii, like petrified mince veal; ashes out
of tombs, and lava out of Vesuvius" (I, xvi, 192-3)
- betrays their enslavement to such a mode of
seeing. Blinded by a reverence for high culture,
they are duped into purchasing lifeless academic
paintings with "such coats of varnish that every
holy personage served for a fly-trap, and became
what is now called in the vulgar tongue a Catch-em-
alive-O". (193)

The other view of Italy clusters around the
word 'grotesque' and - with the special 'new'
Dickensian connotations - its analogue 'picturesque'.
In the novel's first chapter John Baptist Cavaletto
is introduced, "a sunburnt, quick, lithe, little
man, though rather thick-set. Earrings in his
brown ears, white teeth lighting up his grotesque
brown face ..." (I, i, 4), patiently pacing out his
prison "at a grotesque kind of jog-trot pace". (12)
He belongs to a class of grotesques that includes
Mr. Dick ("a pleasant-looking gentleman, with a gray
head, who shut up one eye in a grotesque manner" -
DC, xiii, 190) and Phil Squod ("a little grotesque
man, with a large head" - *BH*, xxi, 303), but is
also essentially a pantomimic Genovese, named after
the city's patron saint. In *Pictures from Italy*
Dickens had remarked how "great numbers of the
common people are christened Giovanni Baptista,
which latter name is pronounced in the Genoese
patois 'Batcheetcha', like a sneeze" - (*PI*, 287).

Thus he exemplifies the 'vulgar' side of Italy,
representing social and political realities that the
classical tourist ignores. His patience expresses

146

the acquired habit of a class that has grown inured
to the deferment of political hopes: "it is
necessary, as they say in Italy (and as they know,
poor people) to have patience." (II, xxviii, 743)
At the same time, his small stature goes with an
essential speed and agility of gesture, "a swiftness
incredible to one who has not watched an Italian
peasant". (II, xxii, 676) The combination of
patience and swiftness - descending as it does from
a classical maxim (*festina lente* - 'making haste
slowly') that has embedded in Italian social life at
levels beyond the reach of Mr. Eustace - is of
considerable significance in *Little Dorrit*.

A second important grotesque figure in the
novel is Flora Finching, associated more strongly
with Italy than is immediately apparent. Her name,
first, brings her into contact with the classical
gods worshipped by Mrs. General ('the realms of
Flora and old Pan'); and her gestures are pantomimic
in the classical Roman style, including "tossing her
head with a caricature of her girlish manner, such
as a mummer might have presented at her own funeral,
if she had lived and died in classical antiquity".
(I, xiii, 150) It is this self-mimicry that makes
her, in Arthur Clennam's eyes, grotesque - "all
this grotesque revival of what he remembered as
having once been prettily natural to her". (155)

For all that, Flora's image of Italy goes
beyond Mr.Eustace's. Her grammatically incoherent
monologue, markedly anticipating Molly Bloom's,
contains a fractured vision of a dynamic, exploding
Italy whose authenticity is secured in the way it
manifestly reworks Dickens's own response to Italian
organ boys and white mice: "In Italy is she really?
with the grapes and figs growing everywhere and lava
necklaces and bracelets too that land of poetry with
burning mountains picturesque beyond belief though
if the organ-boys come away from the neighbourhood
not to be scorched nobody can wonder being so young
and bringing their white mice with them most humane."
(II, ix, 539)

Flora's response to Italy ("picturesque beyond
belief"), containing as it does a realisation of how
the conditions of life affect ordinary people, may
be thought of, perhaps, as containing elements of
the 'new picturesque'. If so, there is clearly
another kind of contrast in the novel, between this
notion of the 'picturesque' and Rigaud's: "I love
and study the picturesque in all its varieties. I
have been called picturesque myself. It is no merit
to be picturesque - I have greater merits, perhaps -

but I may be, by an accident." (I, xxx, 358)[19]
Here we are back with the 'old picturesque', a kind
of commodity purchased by gentleman artists in Rome
and elsewhere; Gowan uses him as a model because of
it, and recognises Rigaud's commodity value: "the
picturesque ease of Blandois would be cheaply
purchased (if it were not a gift and unpurchasable)
for a hundred thousand francs," he claims.(II, vi,
489) Chasing this kind of 'picturesque', Gowan
reveals himself as the occupant of the category of
'bad artist' in the novel, physiognomically obtuse,[20]
taken in by surface, cynical, bored, and gaining
nothing from his stay in Italy.

In *Little Dorrit*, the 'new picturesque' of
Italy is felt in the ferment of social life -
"beggars of every sort everywhere: pitiful,
picturesque, hungry, merry". (II, iii, 465) Its
chief observer and recording consciousness is Little
Dorrit herself, standing in Rome, as she had done as
a child in the Marshalsea, at the "window projecting
over the street and commanding all the picturesque life and variety of the Corso both up and down"
(II, xiv, 594), seeking contact with the 'real',
plural world outside herself. The letters she writes
to Clennam are *her* 'Pictures from Italy', expressing
her sense of the dreamlike ephemerality of the
substantial world ("it seemed to her as if those
visions of mountains and picturesque countries might
melt away at any moment, and the carriage, turning
some abrupt corner, bring up with a jolt at the old
Marshalsea gate" - II, iii, 463).

With this illusionistic capacity for metamorphosis, Italy is the appropriate yet highly problematical theatre of attempts at growth and change. It
is, first,the place where William,Edward and Fanny
Dorrit are to attempt to shake off the prison-taint
of the Marshalsea. Yet their progress through Italy
is an exemplum of how *not* to succeed in breaking
with the past. Attempting to avoid all contact with
anything that will remind them of the past - all
'lowness', in fact - the past continually reasserts
itself, and the real world becomes, in paranoid
fashion, a threatening intrusion. William Dorrit's
Italy is a 'castle in the air', as chapter eighteen
of book two is entitled; it can be traced back to
the Gothic Italy of Walpole and Mrs. Radcliffe,[21]
'picturesque' in the old sense, but with a thin
rooting in reality. Fanny Dorrit's marriage to
Sparkler places her in a classical chariot and is to
take her from Rome to Florence, but "after rolling
for a few minutes smoothly over a fair pavement, had

begun to jolt through a Slough of Despond, and through a long, long avenue of wrack and ruin". (II, xiv, 610) The Pilgrim's Progress, it seems, is as powerful an idea for Dickens in Italy as it is elsewhere.[22]

By contrast, Amy and Fred Dorrit do manage to make progress in Italy. Amy learns the language, while Fanny continues to use English everywhere; and she changes colour. That "pale transparent face, quick in expression, though not beautiful in feature, its soft hazel eyes excepted" (I, v, 53), seems to blossom in Italy: "she looked something more womanly than when she had gone away, and the ripening touch of the Italian sun was visible upon her face" (II, xxix, 757); the latent similarities with John Baptist Cavaletto (both of them essentially 'little' and 'quick') are realised.

Yet the main thrust of the portrayal of Italy in *Little Dorrit* is to show how inextricably political and personal change are linked. Ossified in an antiquated social and political system, this is no transalpine Eldorado: in it the horrors of England are recapitulated and intensified. The metaphoric priesthood surrounding Merdle is replaced by an actual order of religious oppressors. The patience practised by the Italian people is in fact a waiting and longing for the fall of rotten institutions, as in Venice where "troops of idle soldiers" are observed "leaning out of the state windows, where their accoutrements hung drying on the marble architecture, and showing to the mind like hosts of rats who were (happily) eating away the props of the edifices that supported them, and must soon, with them, be smashed on the heads of the other swarms of soldiers, and the swarms of priests, and the swarms of spies, who were all the ill-looking population left to be ruined, in the streets below". (II, iii, 465-66)

But the house it appears (like that other picturesque edifice, the House of Clennam) *will* eventually fall. Like the political exiles in London whom Dickens befriended and championed,[23] John Baptist sits in the Little Dorrit position at the top of the steps in Bleeding Heart Yard, on the lookout: "some of us thinks he's peeping out towards where his own country is." (I, xxvi, 305) Not without hope, perhaps, for even on the novel's opening page, with the oppressive state of the sun beating down everywhere, the only relief comes from Italy: "Towards the distant line of Italian coast, indeed, it was a little relieved by light clouds of mist, slowly rising from the evaporation of the sea, but it softened nowhere else."

NOTES

1. See Letters, IV, 266 (to Forster, 11/2/45).
2. Cf. above, p.9.
3. Letters, IV, 129 (15/5/44).
4. For the vogue of Italian opera in early nineteenth century England, see C.P. Brand, *Italy and the English Romantics* (Cambridge, Cambridge University Press, 1957), pp.174-184.
5. Letters, I, 113 (29/12/35).
6. See Letters, IV, 239 (to Forster, 13/12/44) and Letters, Nonesuch Edition, II, 513 (to Georgina Hogarth, 13/11/53). But these negative responses should perhaps be balanced against Dickens's apparent passion for opera-going - he saw *Il Trovatore* twice, in Milan and Naples, in the space of a fortnight in 1853 - and such responses as that to Gounod's *Faust* in 1863: "it affected me so, and sounded in my ears so like a mournful echo of things that lie in my own heart" (see Edgar Johnson, *Charles Dickens: His Tragedy and Triumph* (London, Allen Lane, 1977; abridged version), p.502.
7. For a useful study of the picturesque, see Christopher Hussey, *The Picturesque: Studies in a Point of View* (London, Frank Cass and Co., 1967; new edition).
8. See Kenneth Churchill, *Italy and English Literature* (London, Macmillan, 1980), p.140.
9. Letters, IV, 281 (to Miss Burdett Coutts, 18/3/45).
10. It is interesting to compare Dickens's critique of tourists of poverty with that of the Fourierist Cantagrel commenting on sightseers in the Palais Royal: "il y a des gens qui ont l'audace de trouver cela beau, de trouver cela pittoresque! Pittoresque! la boue, les ordures, le laid! ..." (*Le Fou des Palais-Royal*, 1841, p.234; quoted in Pierre Citron, *La Poésie de Paris dans La Littérature française de Rousseau à Baudelaire* (Paris, les Editions de Minuit, 1961; 2 vols.), II, 156n.).
11. Cf. above, p. 135.
12. I.e., it's clear that this favourite phrase of Dickens has a connection with the aesthetics of Gothic fiction. For Ippolito Pindemonte's phrase, and a splendid analysis of

Gothic aesthetics, see Mario Praz's Introductory
Essay to *Three Gothic Novels*, ed. Peter Fairclough
(Harmondsworth, Penguin Books, 1968).

13. Letters, IV, 169 (7/8/44). The passage
goes straight into *PI*, 317.

14. For a history of representations of
Venice, and an account of the influence of Byron
and Turner upon such perceptions of the city as
Dickens's, see Churchill, *op. cit.*

15. Letters, IV, 222 (to Forster, 17 and
18/11/44).

16. See Letters, IV, 181n, for this passage
from Dickens's article "New Year's Day" (*Household
Words*, 1 January 1859).

17. Letters, IV, 321-2 (to Forster, 15/6/45)
and 535 (to Mrs. de la Rue, 17/4/46).

18. Yet J.C. Eustace's *Classical Tour*, which
is Mrs. General's bible in *Little Dorrit*, was the
most popular guide to Italy in the early nineteenth
century. Written, as C.P. Brand informs us, "from
the viewpoint of the classical 1841"(see Brand, *op.
cit.*, pp.16, 159, 162).

19. The accidental, unpremeditated, and
'spontaneous' were important aspects of the
picturesque aesthetic, sought after by its devotees.

20. Possibly the most interesting of Dickens's
criticisms of art and artists in his time is "The
Ghost of Art" (*RP*, 438-444), in which the narrator
is haunted by an artist's model he has seen used in
innumerable pictures for miscellaneous, heterogenous
historical and fictional subjects. The point of the
piece is that artists who use such models for such
a variety of subjects have no feeling for the truth
of physiognomy, in which character is expressed in
physical appearance. Gowan is one such, employing
Rigaud to stand as a Doge.

21. Clearly in Dickens's mind when he
describes himself, in March 1844, building "Italian
Castles, bright in sunny days, and pale in moonlight
nights." (Letters, IV, 70; to T.J. Thompson,
11/3/44). In *Pictures from Italy* the debt becomes
apparent when he describes the courtyard of the
Palazzo Vecchio as "worthy of the Castle of Otranto
in its ponderous gloom" (*PI*, 430).

22. For the enormous popularity of *The
Pilgrim's Progress*, obviously reflected in Dickens's
frequent allusions and indebtedness to it, see E.P.
Thompson, *The Making of the English Working Class*
(revised edition, Harmondsworth, Penguin Books,
1968).

23. Partly at first through the influence of

Carlyle, who introduced him to Mazzini. For
Dickens's relationships with Gallenga, Mazzini and
other Italian exiles in London, see Letters, III,
472n and IV, 485n.

Chapter Eight

NARRATIVE PERSPECTIVE AND THE GROTESQUE:
MASTER HUMPHREY'S CLOCK, THE CHRISTMAS BOOKS
AND *THE UNCOMMERCIAL TRAVELLER*

By the early 1840s, if not before, Dickens had
begun to show considerable interest in certain
aspects of narrative technique, in particular in
the question of his narrators' angle of vision.
Master Humphrey's Clock, which evolved between the
summer of 1839 and the spring of 1840 as a pet
project designed to continue the phenomenal success
of the early novels with less sweat and fewer tears,
returns to the formula of *Pickwick Papers*[1] - the
club of peripatetic observers gathering insights
into human 'nature' - whilst foregrounding through
first-person narration the grotesque perspectives
from which such wisdom is here to be culled. "I am
a misshapen, deformed old man," announces Master
Humphrey at the opening of his clock-case (*MHC*, i,
7); he lives apart from the hubbub of things in a
"silent, shady place" full of echoes of the past and
present, for whose depiction George Cattermole was
engaged.[2] He is thus an essential outsider,
despised and even feared because of his monstrosity:
"Mothers caught up their infants and ran into their
houses as I passed; men eyed me spitefully, and
muttered threats and curses." (i, 6)
    But this marginal position in society gains
compensatory rewards in the form of special relationships to otherwise neglected realities whose mode of
existence Master Humphrey will attempt to explore.
To begin with, he has developed a special affinity
to the things that form his material environment:
"... I have all my life been attached to the
inanimate objects that people my chamber, and ... I
have come to look upon them rather in the light of
old and constant friends, than as mere chairs and
tables which a little money could replace at will."
(i, 9) This faculty is shared by his chief
companion, a deaf old man with a "facility of

conceiving and enlarging upon odd ideas" in which he
is aided by a large pipe apparently descended from
E.T.A. Hoffmann, for it "once belonged to a German
student" and has "grim figures ... carved upon its
bowl". (ii, 38)[3] More than this, however, the pair
share similar insights into the scenes that confront
them as they walk the streets as flâneurs (ii, 37),
heeding the moral that seems to be contained in the
bells of St. Pauls: "... I seem to hear a voice
within thee which smiles into my heart, bidding me,
as I elbow my way among the crowd, have some thought
for the meanest wretch that passes, and, being a
man, to turn away with scorn and pride from none
that bear the human shape." (vi, 109)

The idea, then, that the fragmentary *Master
Humphrey's Clock* seems to have been intended to
pursue is the ironic truthfulness of the bizarre
angle of vision of a grotesque outsider. This
notion is most effectively presented in a scene
where Master Humphrey pursues his love of clocks to
the dome of St. Paul's, from whence he is able to
obtain a synoptic vision of the whole of the city
of London worth quoting at some length:

> Draw but a little circle above the clustering
> house-tops, and you shall have within its
> space everything, with its opposite extreme
> and contradiction, close beside. Where yonder
> feeble light is shining, a man is but this
> moment dead. The taper at a few yards'
> distance is seen by eyes that have this instant
> opened on the world. There are two houses
> separated by but an inch or two of wall. In
> one, there are quiet minds at rest; in the
> other, a waking conscience that one might
> think would trouble the very air. In that
> close corner where the roofs shrink down and
> cower together, as if to hide their secrets
> from the handsome street hard by, there are
> such dark crimes, such miseries and horrors,
> as could be hardly told in whispers. In the
> handsome street, there are folks asleep who
> have dwelt there all their lives, and have no
> more knowledge of these things than if they
> had ever been, or were transacted at the
> remotest limits of the world, - who, if they
> were hinted at, would shake their heads, look
> wise, and frown, and say they were impossible,
> and out of Nature, - as if all great towns were
> not. (vi, 108)

Here, the favourite theme of the proximity of incongruities in a large city is worked up into a concentrated anticipation of Disraeli's "Two Nations" perception, and given its distinctive Dickensian emphasis - that for the Victorian middle classes the submerged life of the poor is simply monstrous, unnatural, fanciful, and 'grotesque'. Dickens's object, in the series of experiments with narrative perspective that has its shaky inception in *Master Humphrey's Clock*, would be to find a way of shaking this perception of the world through a panoramic overview that opens up the mutually exclusive divisions within society.

The idea of the grotesque, misshapen Master Humphrey sitting up at the top of St. Paul's looking down at society may recall Hugo's *Notre-Dame de Paris*; but for Dickens the essential model for this narrative angle was the demon Asmodeus in Lesage's *Diable Boiteux (The Devil on Two Sticks)*.[4] Asmodeus has his origin, for Christian tradition, in the book of Tobit, where he takes possession of Tobias's wife, Sarah, and prevents her from marrying any of seven husbands by killing them; traditionally he is the demon of marital discord, lust and anger. But in a Spanish tradition stemming from Quevedo's *Sueños* he also has the power to take off rooftops and reveal the secrets within, and in Lesage's version, which draws quite heavily upon Spanish sources, he rewards a Spanish nobleman named Don Cleophas, who releases him from imprisonment within a glass bottle, by allowing him to travel as a companion on a nightflight over Madrid. Taking off rooftops, he reveals crimes, sexual misdemeanours, secret vices and fantasies; he is a satiric device to criticise society by exposing its hypocrisies.[5]

This ironic, rationalist way of handling the supernatural became enormously popular in England after Smollett's translation,[6] and it is quite clear that Dickens, constantly thinking of questions of narrative technique, continually returns to the conception in the 1840s. The first instance is in *The Old Curiosity Shop*, where, to link the Jarley wax-work baconstreak with Sampson and Sally Brass, "the historian takes the friendly reader by the hand, and springing with him into the air, and cleaving the same at a greater rate than ever Don Cleophas Leandro Perez Zambullo and his familiar travelled through that pleasant region in company, alights with him upon the pavement of Bevis Marks". (*OCS*, xxxiii, 244) *Barnaby Rudge* likewise frees its narrator from the usual constraints upon mobility, ironically enabling him to follow Miggs "into the sanctity of her chamber" in less overt emulation of Asmodeus: "Chronicles are privileged to enter where they list, to come and go through keyholes, to ride upon the wind, to overcome, in their soarings up and down, all obstacles of distance, time, and place." (*BR*, ix, 69) *American Notes* observes the abuse of this license by the newspapers of New York, "pulling off the roofs of private houses, as the Halting Devil did in Spain ... pimping and pandering for all degrees of vicious taste" (*AN*, vi, 88) in their pursuit of sensation, but contrasts the truthful perspective on human affairs gained by Swift when he has Gulliver, returned from the land of the Houyhnhnms, look down on his fellow creatures from a height ("That travelled creation of the great satirist's brain, who fresh from living among horses, peered from a high casement down upon his own kind with trembling horror ..." - ix, 136-7).[7] And *Martin Chuzzlewit* arranges its narrative transitions from the U.S. to the U.K. in a manner that permits with some frequency possibilities of enforcing and commenting upon the proposition advanced in its preface, that "that which is commonly called a long-sight, perceives in a prospect innumerable features and bearings non-existent to a short-sighted person". (*MC*, xv)

These references to the flying demon and his synoptic powers of vision reach their apogee, perhaps, in the famous call for a "good spirit" to take the house-tops off in chapter 47 of *Dombey and Son*.[8] Yet for the moment at least our attention must be focussed on earlier works in which the motif has a central role to play - the Christmas books of 1843 and 1844. Both Scrooge and Trotty Veck, in *A Christmas Carol* and *The Chimes* respectively, are whisked off by spirits who take the lids off houses to reveal what is within ("stone and brick, and slate, and tile, became transparent to him as to them" - *CB, The Chimes*, 120). They are thus privileged to see areas of reality, past, present, and future, that they had hitherto ignored or mis-understood, and to experience a vision of the nature of 'Nature' that breaks down categories like 'monstrous', 'unnatural' and 'grotesque'.

A Christmas Carol gives strategic employment to a first person narrator who appears to lack omniscient knowledge and authority over what he narrates. "Mind: I don't mean to say that I know of my own knowledge, what there is particularly dead about a door-nail" is his comment on the statement that

Marley is as dead as a door-nail (i, 7), and a little later it appears that he does not count himself amongst those 'knowing ones' who are aware that "to edge his way along the crowded paths of life, warning all human sympathy to keep its distance, was what the knowing ones call 'nuts' to Scrooge". (i, 8) In this ironic limitedness of viewpoint the narrator places himself in a position that is very precisely analogous to Scrooge's wilful, culpable 'ignorance' of the poor: "If they would rather die ... they had better do it, and decrease the surplus population. Besides - excuse me - I don't know that." (i, 12)

The story will ask, in fact, what kind of 'knowledge' it is that is required to see the reality of the great city, and how this may be achieved. At the outset the irony teasingly complicates the relations between the real and the marvellous: "There is no doubt that Marley was dead. This must be distinctly understood, or nothing wonderful can come of the story I am going to relate." (i, 1) That 'wonderful' is a pun, referring both to the ghosts and spirits who inhabit the work and to the moral transformation it will describe and, moreover, aim to prompt in its readers. The machinery of goblins and fairies, in fact, is made as whimsical as possible to leave the way clear for other, more devastating nightmares whose existence is strangely close to hand. The climax of *A Christmas Carol* may be said in fact to occur when the Spirit of Christmas Present produces from under its skirts grotesque allegorical representations of the children that roam the city streets at night:

> They were a boy and girl. Yellow, meagre, ragged, scowling, wolfish; but prostrate, too, in their humility. When graceful youth should have filled their features out, and touched them with its freshest tints, a stale and shrivelled hand, like that of age, had pinched, and twisted them, and pulled them into shreds. Where angels might have sat enthroned, devils lurked, and glared out menacing. No change, no degradation, no perversion of humanity, in any grade, through all the mysteries of wonderful creation, has monsters half so horrible and dread. (iii, 56)

Here, in the familiar rhetoric of the Dickensian grotesque, are the paradoxically fantastic

realities of the urban, industrialised society of
Victorian England, documenting metamorphoses that
overhaul Ovid and Dante. The book attempts to
infiltrate them into the everyday, ordinary language
monstrosities that surround and determine their
existence. Led by the spirit into the low-roofed
abode of the Cratchits, Scrooge sees Master Peter
Cratchit appearing to eat his "monstrous shirt
collar" (iii, 44), a Christmas hand-me-down from
his father - the obvious, initial grotesque product
of capitalistic avarice. 'Monstrosity' reappears
in Tiny Tim's perception of Scrooge ("Scrooge was
the Ogre of the family" - iii, 48), and at another
Christmas party where Fred Scrooge's sister-in-law
is much engaged in the erotic innuendos of blindman's-buff, and declares that her captor's bourgeois
advances to possess her are "vile, monstrous!" (iii,
54) And in an anticipation of the art of Tolstoy's
Death of Ivan Ilyich Scrooge foresees the everyday
monstrosity of reactions to his death amongst his
fellow merchant:

> 'No,' said a great fat man with a monstrous
> chin, 'I don't know much about it either way.
> I only know he's dead.'
> 'When did he die?' inquired another.
> 'Last night, I believe.'
> 'Why, what was the matter with him?' asked a
> third, taking a vast quantity of snuff out of
> a very large snuff-box.
> 'I thought he'd never die.'
> 'God knows,' said the first, with a yawn.
> 'What has he done with his money?' asked a red-
> faced gentleman with a pendulous excrescence on
> the end of his nose, that shook like the gills
> of a turkey-cock. (iv, 59)

The horror intensifies when he sees these
genteel speculators transposed into rag-and-bone
pickers who buy up his corpse for the value of his
clothes, "with a detestation and disgust, which
could hardly have been greater, though they had
been obscene demons, marketing the corpse itself".
(iv, 64) A vision of the 'grotesque' reorients
Scrooge's understanding and action in a manner held
out as exemplary in the art of the tale - we all
need to surmount our ignorance by adopting a more
comprehensive habit of seeing.
  The Chimes has a similar pattern, more obviously
polemical in its politics but rather less successful
in its imaginative realisation.[9] Trotty Veck, unlike

Scrooge a victim in nearly every respect of the inhumanities of the prevailing social system, is punished with a bleak vision of his personal future for his failure of response to a newspaper story about a mother who kills herself and her child. "Unnatural and cruel!" Toby cries out (ii, 117), acquiescing in that mistaken notion of 'nature' which the Cheeryble brothers, with uncharacteristic percipience, had diagnosed in Nicholas's puzzlement over Smike's lack of feeling for his father ("Men talk of nature as an abstract thing, and lose sight of what is natural when they do so" - *NN*, xlvi,595). It is a habit of thought that Trotty unconsciously borrows from the class that oppresses him, very evident in the conversation of Sir Joseph Porter and his kind, in such apparent trivia as Lady Porter's complaint about the cost of charity subscriptions: "That Charity, my love. They only allow two votes for a subscription of five pounds. Really monstrous!" (*The Chimes*, ii, 105) The statistical Mr.Filer stands for a static, 'Young England' view of nature, revering the good old times, condemning the monstrosities of the present - but *The Chimes* wishes to promote the alternative, Carlylean view that the present is the consequence of the past, its monstrosity a natural outcome of what has bred it. Mr. Trotty Veck climbs up into the steeple of the church, like Master Humphrey into the clock of St. Paul's, and there discovers these temporal coherencies in a synoptic vision of what is to come.

Yet the most interesting aspect of this episode, perhaps, is its detailed attempt to explain the kind of imaginative mental process that enables one to see things afresh, going beyond conventionalised perception:

> Black are the brooding clouds and troubled the deep waters, when the sea of Thought, first hearing from a calm, gives up its Dead. Monsters uncouth and wild, arise in premature, imperfect resurrection; the several parts and shapes of different things are joined and mixed by chance; and when, and how, and by what wonderful degrees, each separates from each, and every sense and object of the mind resumes its usual form and lives again, no man - though every man is every day the casket of this type of the Great Mystery - can tell. (iii, 120)

159

This is a kind of counter to the transcendental lady's hilarious philosophizing in *Martin Chuzzlewit* - the grotesque is by no means an 'arrest' of profound musings but the very condition of original thought and imaginative understanding, which arises out of 'monstrous' combinations of fragmentary perception. The positive valuation here of marginal, quasi-hallucinatory states of mind stands in a series - Mrs. Nickleby, her admirer, Barnaby Rudge, Affery, etc. - that stretches right up until *Edwin Drood*, where the insights to be had from opium smoking are scrutinised. Here, as in *A Christmas Carol*, the supernatural visions that Trotty Veck experiences enable him paradoxically to discover reality and redefine 'Nature':

> "O, have mercy on me in this hour, if, in my love for her, so young and good, I slandered Nature in the breasts of mothers rendered desperate!" (iv, 150)

The other Christmas Books are much less interesting productions. Whilst all of them, almost inevitably, contain grotesque moments and touches, only one of them, *The Cricket on the Hearth*, develops a sufficiently coherent satiric purpose to be worth commenting upon. Even here, the grotesque is of a different kind: gone are the spirits and hobgoblins affording panoramic visions of a large-scale world, to be replaced by humdrum *lares* and *penates*, a cricket and a kettle, and a humble, miniature narrator, the cricket himself, reporting on passions and events of correspondingly scaled-down dimensions (including the world of toys).

What remains, however, is a familiar theme of the Dickensian grotesque: the intended marriage of a morose old toy-maker, a relative of Gride and Quilp, to a young bride of the School of Madeline Bray. The toys that he makes are sadistic monstrosities guaranteed to frighten children out of their wits:

> Tackleton the Toy-merchant, pretty generally known as Gruff and Tackleton - for that was the firm, though Gruff had been bought out long ago; only leaving his name, and as some said his nature, according to its Dictionary meaning, in the business - Tackleton the Toy-Merchant was a man whose vocation had been

quite misunderstood by his Parents and Guardians. If they had made him a Money Lender, or a sharp Attorney, or a Sheriff's Officer, or a Broker, he might have sown his discontented oats in his youth, and after having had the full run of himself in ill-natured transactions, might have turned out amiable at last, for the sake of a little freshness and novelty. But, cramped and chafing in the peaceable pursuit of toy-making, he was a domestic Ogre, who had been living on children all his life, and was their implacable enemy. He despised all toys; wouldn't have bought one for the world; delighted, in his malice, to insinuate grim expressions into the faces of brown-paper farmers who drove pigs to market, bellmen who advertised lost lawyers' consciences, lovable old ladies who darned stockings or carved pies; and other like samples of his stock in trade. In appalling masks; hideous, hairy, red-eyed Jacks in Boxes; Vampire Kites; demonical Tumblers who wouldn't lie down, and were perpetually flying forward, to stare infants out of countenance; his soul perfectly revelled. They were his only relief and safety-valve. He was great in such inventions. Anything suggestive of a Pony-nightmare was delicious to him. He had even lost money (and he took to that toy very kindly) by getting up Goblin slides for magic-lanterns, whereon the powers of darkness were depicted as a sort of supernatural shell-fish, with human faces. In intensifying the portraiture of Giants, he had sunk quite a little capital; and, though no painter himself, he could indicate, for the instructions of his artists, with a piece of chalk, a certain furtive leer for the countenances of those monsters, which was safe to destroy the peace of mind of any young gentleman between the ages of six and eleven, for the whole Christmas or Midsummer Vacation. (*The Cricket on the Hearth*, i, 174)[10]

By the end of the story, this nursery Scrooge has been transformed, by unspecified means that seem here not to involve fairy agency, into a faithful expression of the philosophy of Christmas. But for the time being interest focusses on how toy-making is part of the commercial system of Victorian England, its styles dictated by the pressures of the market, its magic circumscribed and delimited by the psychological make-up of toy-making entrepreneurs, themselves anything but attuned or sympathetic to children's fantasies. Moreover, Tackleton's lack of talent as a maker of toys - his artistic ability is confined to the designing of monstrous leers - introduces the theme of bad professionalism and bad art, so prominent in *Martin Chuzzlewit*. This is worked out in the contrast that is developed between Tackleton and his intermediary, Caleb Plummer, a real artist who is skilful, not only at making toys, but at constructing a whole imaginary life-line around his blind daughter Bertha who is persuaded that she lives in comfortable and lively surroundings furnished by the kind-hearted Tackleton.

In Plummer's workshop the grotesque has a central place:

> As it would have been hard to count the dozens upon dozens of grotesque figures that were ever ready to commit all sorts of absurdities on the turning of a handle, so it would have been no easy task to mention any human folly, vice, or weakness that had not its type, immediate or remote, in Caleb Plummer's room. And not in an exaggerated form, for very little handles will move men and women to as strange performances as any toy was ever made to make. (ii, 184)

It is a passage where we can be sure of Dickens's consciousness of himself and his aims as a grotesque satirist. Plummer is a representative of the novelist as artist, creating marionette - like figures who show forth the operations of society and its values upon them, reducing and simplifying their motives and desires so that they behave like clock-work. This doll and puppet world is perhaps the only strongly imagined feature of *The Cricket on the Hearth* - exploring as it does the contamination of the 'hearth' through the marketing of Tackleton's debased Christmas grotesqueries - and in it we find Dickens once more attempting a firm rebuff to those critics of *Martin Chuzzlewit* who had accused him of creating "grotesque impossibilities".

It may be that the turning away from Lesage's synoptic vision after *The Chimes* is symptomatic of a general change in the direction of Dickens's work. Henceforth the notion of transcendent height rarely connotes any transcendent insight. Increasing reference is made to the stars as spectators of

human actions; but, like Estella, they appear
indifferent to what they see: "some, so remote
from this little earth that the learned tell us it
is doubtful whether their rays have even yet
discovered it" (*TOTC*, I, vi, 48).[11] The good spirit
called for in *Dombey and Son* never quite appears
(unless it is in the guise of such thoroughly
secular modern institutions like the police-force,
providing detective-heroes like Bucket in *Bleak
House*); indeed *A Tale of Two Cities*, in the powerful
meditations on human secrecy at the opening of
chapter three, seems to have abandoned the search
for someone to raise the roofs of the city ("A
solemn consideration, when I enter a great city by
night, that every one of those darkly clustered
houses encloses its own secret; that every room in
every one of them encloses its own secret; that
every beating heart in the hundreds of thousands of
breasts there, is, in some of its imaginings, a
secret to the heart nearest it!" - 1, iii, 10).
From *David Copperfield* onwards, first person
narration becomes more frequent, and with it,
perhaps, a greater degree of tentativeness, partial-
ness and uncertainty in the construction of an
authoritative narrative metalanguage.[12]
    Thus, to turn to Master Humphrey's equivalent
in later Dickens, the narrative persona of *The
Uncommercial Traveller*, is to encounter a figure
uneasily, and perhaps guiltily conscious of his
marginality, and unable to transcend it in ideal-
istic embrace of those who resemble him. Autobiographical factors ("actually the sketches grew
out of the Author's increasing infirmities. He was
greatly troubled with insomnia, and he hoped to
cure it by long walks at night. His wanderings took
him all over London at a time when the great city
was a different subject for observation than during
the day"[13]) may help to explain the sombre, brooding
tone of many of the sketches, and their narrator's
relationship to two favourite reference-points of
Dickens's childhood reading - Ahasuerus and Haroun
er Reshid.[14] The conceit of the traveller who works
and sells without profit ("Figuratively speaking, I
travel for the great house of Human Interest
Brothers, and I have rather a large connection in
the fancy goods way" - *UT*, i, 1-2) generates a
series of constant paradoxes that highlight the
contradictions of the activity in which he is
engaged. "My day's no-business," he calls it at an
early stage (*UT*, iii, 18), reviving the description
in a new series of 1868 ("I remain in the same idle

employment" - xxxi, 309); it is work that essentially
involves isolation and marginality: "No one looks
at us while we plait and weave these words" (xi,
111). Neither the angle of vision nor the status
of the observer is in any way privileged now; what
we have instead is a description of "wretched me,
peeping in at the door out of the mud of the
streets and of my life". (iv, 39)[15]
   And what, essentially, does the narrator of
The Uncommercial Traveller see, on his peregrina-
tions about the city? The answer, taking the most
powerful and influential class of images, might be
"corpses". It is a book dominated by visits to the
victims of shipwreck (i, 7) or death at birth (xii,
118-9) or cholera in the East End (xxxii, 319).
Two sketches from different series take us to the
Paris morgue to see the grotesque monstrosities that
the city creates and puts on display - "a large dark
man whose disfigurement by water was in a frightful
manner comic" is one example.(viii, 65)[16] But the
line drawn between the corpses of the dead and of
the living is often a thin one - for instance in
the vicinity of the Thames, where the narrator
meets "a creature remotely in the likeness of a
young man, with a puffed sallow face, and a figure
all dirty and shiny and slimy, who may have been
the youngest son of his filthy old father, Thames,
or the drowned man about whom there was a placard
on the granite post like a large thimble, that
stood between us". (iii, 19) Even in its high
moments of gaiety - a Christmas party in the Temple
where potential lovers play Blind Man's Buff - the
city comments ironically on the proximity of death:
an old bachelor down below has fallen in a fit and
severely damaged his head, and is in his death
throes, stumbling about to find the door:

   Somebody cried, Hark! The man below must be
   playing Blindman's Buff by himself tonight!
   They listened, and they heard sounds of someone falling about and stumbling against
   furniture, and they all laughed at the conceit,
   and went on with their play, more light-hearted
   and merry than ever. Thus, those two so
   different games of life and death were played
   out together, blindfolded, in the two sets of
   chambers. (xiv, 143)

   But no less importantly, the concentration on
corpses in *The Uncommercial Traveller* emphasises
problems of observation and interpretation. The

corpse, particularly for someone like Dickens, with
such an intense sense of bodily gestural language,
represents an extreme case of interpretative
impenetrability. Moreover, to look at a corpse is
to exercise in an extreme form the position of
dominance inherent in all relationships between an
observer and a person or creature observed, as the
'uncommercial' realises in a moment of insight into
the expressions of the faces of the visitors to the
morgue: "all these expressions concurred in possessing the one underlying expression of *looking at
something that could not return a look*." (xix, 192 -
Dickens's italics)[17] It is like viewing a waxwork
in a show without a catalogue, the narrator decides,
and the image helps explain some of the guilt and
melancholy of *The Uncommercial Traveller* - its
uneasy consciousness, contained in the figure of
the corpse, of the helplessness of the victims it
observes. To be out as a nocturnal flâneur is to
enter merely into an "amateur experience of homelessness" (xii, 127) - the narrator's 'uncommercial-
ness' is not only the sign of some positive removal
from the sphere of commerce and exploitation, but
of that middle-class security and independence that
permits an amateurism that at all times threatens to
transform the creatures it observes back into mere
entertainments, grotesque objects for the gratification of middle-class taste.

Such a realisation undermines the efficacy of
any synoptic vision of a social totality. Not that
The Uncommercial Traveller completely abandons this
device, but where it uses it, it does so only
ironically and critically. Seeing the 'yellow,
meagre, ragged, scowling, wolfish' street children
that the Spirit of Christmas Present had shown to
Scrooge, the 'uncommercial' embarks on a synoptic
journey in time that offers sharp comment on middle-
class exhibitions of dinosaurs, comparing them to
the monstrosity of children scrambling after half-
pence in the mud:

> ... I looked about at the disorderly traces in
> the mud, and I thought of the drops of rain
> and the footprints of an extinct creature,
> hoary ages upon ages old, that geologists have
> identified on the face of a cliff; and this
> speculation came over me: If this mud could
> petrify at this moment, and could lie concealed
> here for ten thousand years, I wonder whether
> the race of men then to be our successors on
> the earth could, from these or any marks, by

the utmost force of the human intellect,
unassisted by tradition, deduce such an
astounding inference as the existence of a
polished state of society that bore with the
public savagery of neglected children in the
streets of its capital city, and was proud of
its power by sea and land, and never used its
power to seize and save them! (xxxv, 347)

But after these thoughts the narrator's eye
goes upwards towards St. Paul's cathedral: "I felt
as though the cross were too high up, and perched
upon the intervening golden ball too far away." (347)
Its angle of vision is now too distant to perceive
the truths of the street. Whereas in *Master
Humphrey's Clock* the bell of St. Paul's had been
thought of as a symbol of the heart of London, here
church bells merely reinforce the profound divisions
in society:

Once - it was after leaving the Abbey and
turning my face north - I came to the great
steps of St. Martin's church as the clock was
striking three. Suddenly, a thing that in a
moment more I should have trodden upon without
seeing, rose up at my feet with a cry of loneliness and houselessness, struck out of it by the
bell, the like of which I had never heard. We
then stood face to face looking at one another,
frightened by one another. The creature was
like a beetle-browed hair-lipped youth of
twenty, and it had a loose bundle of rags on,
which it held together with one of its hands.
It shivered from head to foot, and its teeth
chattered, and as it stared at me - persecutor,
devil, ghost, whatever it thought me - it made
with its whining mouth as if it was snapping at
me, like a worried dog. Intending to give this
ugly object money, I put out my hand to stay it
- for it recoiled as it whined and snapped -
and laid my hand upon its shoulder. Instantly,
it twisted out of its garment, like the young
man in the New Testament, and left me standing
alone with its rags in my hands. (xiii, 133)

In this astonishing and appalling passage the
idea of the grotesque as 'inverse sublimity' is
quite left behind. The narrator becomes aware of
the absolute impossibility of his position as
observer of the victims of the society he represents.
If the youth appears like the ghost of Hamlet's

father (startled by a bell) to him, he in turn is
an untouchable "persecutor, devil, ghost" with whom
all contact must be refused, even at the cost of
what rags the youth possesses. The only truly
neglected Dickensian masterpiece, *The Uncommercial
Traveller* takes us far beyond the problems of
narrating the grotesque that are explored in the
minor writings of the 1840s, reformulating them in
terms that only *Great Expectations* and *Our Mutual
Friend* are able to develop.

NOTES

        1. See Steven Marcus, *Dickens: from
Pickwick to Dombey* (London, Chatto and Windus,
1965), p.131: "Master Humphrey's club is a bizarre
distortion of the Pickwickians," etc.
        2. Master Humphrey's hideaway is thus
clearly related to those out-of-the-way nooks and
crannies of London that are a favoured locus of the
grotesque in Dickens. It is the narrator of
Sketches by Boz who first informs us "that we
entertain a strong partiality for the queer little
old streets which yet remain in some parts of
London" (see Duane Devries, *Dickens's Apprentice
Years* (Hassocks, Harvester Press, 1976), p.169).
This partiality, if it can be attributed to
Dickens as well, appears to emerge again in
Pickwick Papers, where Sam Weller makes his first
appearance in a hotel in one of the "secluded
nooks" of the obscurer quarters of the town:
"Great, rambling, queer old places they are, with
galleries, and passages, and staircases, wide
enough and antiquated enough to furnish materials
for a hundred ghost stories ..." (*PP*, x, 118), and
where, in particular, the Inns of Court seem to be
an essential reference point ("Curious little
nooks in a great place, like London, these old
inns are" - xx, 277). It is hardly surprising,
then, that Cattermole - Dickens's specialist
illustrator for grotesque architecture - should
have been used in *Master Humphrey's Clock*. Cf.
also Chapter 6, fn. 12, p. 137.
        3. Phiz's illustration of the pipe (see
MHC, ii, 37) quite clearly emphasises its
grotesqueness, in support of the text.
        4. First published in 1707, Lesage's book
was based upon a Spanish book, *El Diablo Cojuelo*
(1641) by Luiz Velez de Guevara. It was almost
immediately translated into English (for Jacob
Tonson, in 1708) and appeared in several editions

during the 18th century (e.g. 1730, 1759, 1770, 1777 and 1780). Two later editions in Dickens's lifetime were those of Joseph Thomas and William Strange, both appearing in 1841.

5. Cf. Roger Lauffer, *Lesage ou le métier de romancier* (Paris, éditions Gallimard, 1971), who analyses the novel in the intellectual context of the Quarrel of the Ancients and the Moderns and sees Lesage aligning himself with the 'Moderns' by mocking superstition and tradition.

6. That Smollett is in fact responsible for the translation that has been attributed to him has never been conclusively proved; all that is known for certain is that he corrected the 1759 translation. Yet writers like Smollett and, later, Scott helped to disseminate Lesage in England, so that later authors could use Asmodeus as a familiar satiric reference point. In 1832, for instance, during the passing of the Reform Bill, Bulwer Lytton wrote his *Asmodeus at Large*, and a journal called *Asmodeus in London* ran for 37 numbers (see Jonathan Arac, *Commissioned Spirits* (New Brunswick, N.J., Rutgers University Press, 1979), pp.22, 112.

7. Dickens's admiration for Swift, his predecessor as a grotesque satirist, is evident throughout his work - cf. e.g. Letters, III, 266 (to Lady Holland, 11/7/42) praising Albany Fonblanque as "another Swift".

8. *DS*, xlvii, 648. Another interesting later reference to *Le Diable Boiteux* is in a *Household Words* article of 1853, "In and Out of Jail", which, in reflecting upon penal reform, remarks upon the need for a synoptic vision of the relation of criminals to society at large: "But when they have got into prison, and when we are considering how to provide for them there, we must mount with the aid of a Good Spirit to the highest tower in the jail; we must let that beneficent Asmodeus unroof the houses for us, and show us how the people live, and toil, and die; and we shall then know that we must not stretch out a hand to touch a privation or a hardship in the criminal's condition, without a just consideration for every humble figure in the great panorama." (Quoted from Harry Stone, *The Uncollected Writings of Charles Dickens* (London, Allen Lane, 1969; 2 volumes), II, 488.

9. For the political dimensions of *The Chimes* see Michael Slater's edition of *The Christmas Books* (Harmondsworth, Penguin Books, 1971), and his essay 'Dickens's Tract for The Times' in *Dickens 1970*,

ed, Michael Slater (London, Chapman and Hall, 1970).

10. A similar passage about the grotesqueness of toys, taken from the 1850 Christmas Story *The Christmas Tree*, is quoted in Angus Wilson's *The World of Charles Dickens*, pp.9-10.

11. Cf. Chapter 5, fn. 23 above.

12. Arac's *Commissioned Spirits* is especially stimulating on the loss of confidence in an authoritative single-perspective point of view in nineteenth century writing.

13. Quotation from John C. Eckel, *The First Editions of the Writings of Charles Dickens* (London, Chapman and Hall, 1913), p.142.

14. Amongst innumerable references to Ahasuerus the 'wandering Jew' pride of place must go to Sam Weller's: "... here am I a walkin' about like the wandering Jew - a sportin character you have perhaps heard on, Mary, my dear, as wos always doin' a match agin' time, and never vent to sleep ..." (*PP*, xxxix, 549).

15. It should perhaps be stressed here that *The Uncommercial Traveller* is being treated as a text with a degree of coherence and unity much greater than that which is usually allowed.

16. The other sketch, "Railway Dreaming", collected in *Miscellaneous Papers*, ed. B.W. Matz (London, Chapman and Hall, 1914) compares the display of the corpses to an imaginary Dance of Death illustration: "All the world knows this custom, and perhaps all the world knows that the bodies lie on inclined planes within a great glass window, as though Holbein should represent Death, in his grim Dance, keeping a shop, and displaying his goods like a Regent-Street or Boulevard linen-draper." (p.592)

17. Again Arac, *op. cit.*, p.18 and note, has a stimulating discussion of systems of unseen observation in the nineteenth century, and the guilt they entailed. See also Marc Shell, *The Economy of Literature* (Baltimore, Johns Hopkins University Press, 1978), pp.30-1.

Chapter Nine

THE CHILD'S PERCEPTION OF THE GROTESQUE:
DOMBEY AND SON AND *DAVID COPPERFIELD*

Discussion of the grotesque in *Dombey and Son* and
David Copperfield must start from the familiar
assessment of these works that sees them as markers
for substantial advances in Dickens's art, and that
links these developments with the idea of a greater
concentration and penetration in the representation
of the child. Childhood itself (so runs such a
view) had been a distinctive focus of Dickens's
writing from the beginning, but in earlier works
like *Oliver Twist* and *The Old Curiosity Shop* a
primitive, eighteenth century psychology of humours
and static essences had prevailed, preventing the
formation of effects of complexity and profundity
through the exploration of the child as an
individual experiencing the world with special
emotional and intellectual resources. "With Paul
Dombey," writes Angus Wilson, "Dickens begins that
extraordinary study of the child's view of life,
which is one of his great achievements in fiction";[1]
he echoes Kathleen Tillotson's opinion that in
Dombey and Son, where the theme of childhood is by
no means the only centre of attention, "the child's
view of the world ... is more important than in
Oliver Twist and *The Old Curiosity Shop*, though the
children there are hero and heroine, and do not grow
up".[2]
     That such a position reflects a fundamentally
realist approach to the novel, and to Dickens's
place in its history, can be demonstrated, perhaps,
by comparison with some relevant contemporary
reactions to the new developments apparent in these
works. As Gifford (following Katarsky) has shown,
"it was *Dombey and Son* (in Vvedensky's translation)
that truly established Dickens for the Russian
reader".[3] Belinsky, the critical eminence of both
radicalism and realism in Russia, who (like Ruskin)

had seen in *The Old Curiosity Shop* evidence of a
decline in Dickens's talent, was its enthusiastic
champion; according to Gifford, it "revealed Dickens
to him in a new, almost a blinding, light".[4] Hence-
forward the representation of childhood as a major
phase of human development was to be a significant
preoccupation of Russian realist writing. The
testimony of Turgenev, whose story 'Bezhin Lea' of
1851 is one of the first, and most remarkable
tributes to Dickens's influence in Russian
literature, is instructive; asked why he didn't
portray children more often, he replied, "They are
so hard to portray. They never come out quite
natural. Even little Dombey is no exception to
this."[5] For this realist, Dickens was the master
(albeit a flawed one) in a mimetic school of intense
difficulty.
     But Turgenev's emphasis upon 'naturalness' as
a desirable aim of representations of children in
literature emphasises the difficulty of equating
such an approach with an adequate recognition of
the grotesque in the novels in question. One view,
in fact, consorting with an emphasis on the triumphs
of realism in *Dombey and Son*, is that the grotesque
now begins its decline in the latter half of
Dickens's career. One source for such a view could
be Charles Kent's review of *Dombey and Son* in April
1848, with its complimentary reference to the
"occasional grotesqueness" of the novel[6] - implying,
perhaps, that on this occasion the author had struck
a right balance in which the grotesque was not too
prominent. (It is interesting that Dickens respond-
ed warmly to this praise, writing to Kent to thank
him, and averring "that I have never addressed a
similar communication to anybody, except on one
occasion!"; the exception was his letter to Hood
during the publication of *The Old Curiosity Shop*,
thanking him for a review that had emphasised the
grotesque features of that novel.)[7] Michael Steig
is one of its notable proponents; he uses the
evidence of Phiz's illustrations, arguing that
these "like the novels' texts themselves, display a
development from an essentially caricatural style
to a more complex and realistic one". Taking
Captain Cuttle, Mrs. Skewton and Major Bagstock as
the major grotesques of *Dombey and Son*, he attempts
to show that "except for the latter, even they are
less grimacing and more natural than figures in the
early novels".[8]
     Yet this evidence - assuming as it does a more
or less complete harmony of intention and execution

between novelist and illustrator - need not be compelling. Whilst Dickens certainly wanted to guard against any caricaturing of Dombey himself, he appears on another occasion, in the case of a character who must unquestionably be counted among the major grotesques of *Dombey and Son* - Mrs. Pipchin - to complain that Phiz's illustration of her is insufficiently vivid in its *changing* of the essential features of her appearance (so much so, in fact, that he gives Browne detailed instructions for the next illustration in the novel in which he takes pains to emphasise such eminently caricatural features of Toots's physiognomy as "a swollen nose and an excessively large head").[9]

Nor is the evidence of the text of *Dombey and Son* anything like unequivocal in its support of Steig's thesis. Since completing his last novel (*Martin Chuzzlewit*) Dickens had spent a year in Italy, during which his consciousness of the grotesque in art had certainly increased: the immediately preceding work, *Pictures from Italy*, contains more direct reference to the grotesque than anything else Dickens ever wrote.[10] This consciousness is certainly reflected in *Dombey and Son*, most particularly in aspects of the novel that are closely connected with Florence and Paul Dombey. For the most distinctive thing about the grotesque in *Dombey and Son* is that it appears to be the child's special privilege to share the omniscient narrator's perception of it.

To begin with a crude and banal yardstick: the word 'grotesque' occurs four times in *Dombey and Son*, and on each occasion the context involves a child's consciousness. Two references concern Paul, one Florence, and one Rob the Grinder, and the two characters who are directly referred to as 'grotesque' are Mrs.Pipchin and Mrs. Brown. In the case of Mrs. Pipchin, it is clear that the familiar "attraction of repulsion" operates in Paul's relationship to her:

> He was not fond of her; he was not afraid of her; but in those old, old moods of his, she seemed to have a grotesque attraction for him. (*DS*, viii, 103)

Rob the Grinder finds himself a good deal less at ease with Mrs. Brown, who seems to have a mesmeric hold over him:

> ... finding it uncomfortable to encounter the

yellow face with its grotesque action, and the
ferret eyes with their keen old wintry gaze,
so close to his own, he looked down uneasily
and sat shuffling in his chair, as if he were
trying to bring himself to a sullen declarat-
ion that he would answer no more questions.
(liii, 735)

The case of Florence's perception of Mrs. Brown is
more complex - it is invoked by the narrator, in an
ironic fashion, to express the 'grotesque' truth
about that good lady:

If Florence could have stood within the room
and looked upon the original of the shadow
thrown upon the wall and room, as it covered
this over the fire, a glance might have
sufficed to recall the figure of good Mrs.
Brown; notwithstanding that her childish
recollection of that terrible old woman was as
grotesque and exaggerated a presentment of the
truth, perhaps, as the shadow on the wall.
(xxiv, 484)

But the most interesting instance doesn't
concern any human grotesque in the novel. At Dr.
Blimber's, deprived of the company of Mrs. Pipchin
(he "had no such curiosity in any living member of
the Doctor's household, as he had had in Mrs.
Pipchin" - xii, 166), Paul takes to inventing his
own grotesques out of the objects that surround him:

He was intimate with all the paper-hanging in
the house; saw things that no one else saw in
the patterns; found out miniature tigers and
lions running up the bedroom walls, and squint-
ing faces leering in the squares and diamonds
of the floor-cloth. (106)

This activity of the mind is referred to first
as the "arabesque work of his musing fancy" (166):
it was Goethe who, in his essay on the Papal loggias
decorated by Raphael, had urged the substitution of
the term 'arabesque' for 'grotesque', and Poe,
responding pre-eminently to the influence of
Germany, who had gathered the two together for the
title of his *Tales of the Grotesque and Arabesque.* [11]
But later the same imaginative play activity is
referred to again, with a shift of terminology:

He had to think - would any other child (old-fashioned, like himself) stray there at any time, to whom the same grotesque distortions of pattern and furniture would manifest themselves; and would anybody tell that boy of little Dombey, who had been there once? (xiv, 194)

The important thing here is the new psychological approach to the grotesque. No doubt the passage would yield returns to an autobiographical approach, reminiscent as it is of the confession to Lytton of an "infirmity to fancy or perceive relations in things which are not apparent generally", with its relevant metaphor of illness.[12] More importantly, though, it refuses to separate off the grotesque from the workings of Paul's mind and imagination; it can't be dismissed as the province of inferior or insignificant characters or aspects of the novel. It's right in there, as part of what makes the novel distinctive and new, and as an aspect of central themes in the novel, to which we must now turn.

The title of *Dombey and Son* makes it plain that this is a novel about a relationship - in this respect, at least, it anticipates *Our Mutual Friend*. The first sentence provides some clues about the nature of that relationship:

Dombey sat in the corner of the darkened room in the great arm-chair by the bedside, and Son lay tucked up warm in a little basket bedstead, carefully disposed on a low settee immediately in front of the fire and close to it, as if his constitution were analogous to that of a muffin, and it were essential to toast him brown while he was very new. (i, 1)

A contrast is developed - between a person in a 'great' armchair and a person in a 'little' basket bedstead on a 'low' settee. The one who is named first - whose name opens both the sentence and the novel - obviously dominates the relationship, and others besides, perhaps: the sound of his name in fact echoes the word *dominance* and also suggests, with its *by* ending hinting at some Northern industrial town,[13] the idea of commercial or mercantile power. At this stage, in fact, 'Son' has no other name but 'son' - and in fact he will be given the same name as his father. The relationship appears first as a power relationship between ontologically superior and inferior forces - a relationship that will be frequently expressed in the novel as that between a person and a thing. It is already presented in this way, in fact, in the first sentence itself, which compares 'son' to something to eat, the 'muffin' which soon modulates, via Dickens's assonating and associating imagination,[14] to the 'muffled' sounds - here of Dr. Parker Peps's voice (4), later of schoolchildren (xii, 153) - demanded in Dombey's *sombre*, proper, Victorian world.

The notation of these commodity-style middle-class relationships offers considerable scope in *Dombey and Son* for the play of a grotesque imagination. Children themselves are property: at Dr. Blimber's academy, which is portrayed as a kind of botanical forcing-house producing the monstrous cacti of which Mr. Pipchin is fond, "the owners of the plants were always ready to lend a helping hand at the bellows, and to stir the fire". (xii, 166 - the fire image of the first sentence is still active here) Other human creatures in a dependent relationship seem to be articles produced by processes reminiscent of manufacture - Miss Tox, for example, "wearing such a faded air that she seemed not to have been made in what linen-drapers call 'fast colours' originally, and to have, by little and little, washed out". (i, 6) Dombey himself - "one of those close-shaved close-cut moneyed gentlemen who are glossy and crisp like new bank-notes" (ii, 17) - ironically sets the tones for habits of reification of the self and others that are to have tragic consequences.

For the major structural function of the grotesque in *Dombey and Son* is to reveal the Dombey lifestyle, setting itself up as normal, respectable, natural, inevitable, as essentially monstrous and irrational. Over and over again, what Dombey abhors as distasteful, vulgar, romantic, 'grotesque' returns to haunt and torment him in the consequences of his conduct. And in the new art of this novel the grotesque is not only a way of seeing the industrial processes of the manufacturing society of Victorian England in fresh and disturbing lights: it is also a way of understanding its psychological disasters.

Thus, for instance, we may trace the ironic patterns of Dombey's obsession with the possible substitution of one of Polly Toodles's children for his son. It's a paranoia that's essentially based in a conservative notion that what motivates people is money - but as Toodles had shown in confronting

return of ✓ repressed - 175
"   "   " *grotesque*

Dombey's version of the word 'afford' with his own[15]
there's no likelihood of his wanting to gain such
disembodied material advantage for the children he
loves. But Dombey persists with his irrational
precautions - the suppression of Toodles's name,
the injunction forbidding her to take Paul to her
home - as if magical forces threaten and surround
him.[16] In some sense or another, he may be right:
as in Sterne, or the prose of German Romanticism,[17]
the narrator is a kind of ghostly presence, torment-
ing him with the recurrent use of the word
'substitute', and ironic parallels with fairy-
stories. Upset at her mother's death, Florence is
"naturally substituted" (iii, 21) by Polly for one
of her own children, the adverb indicating the
precision of the irony, Dombey himself looking to
something other than nature as a possible means of
sparing Paul from the dangers of childhood illness:
"if he could have bought him off, or provided a
substitute, as in the case of an unlucky drawing for
the militia, he would have been glad to do so on
liberal terms." (viii, 90) At the level of plot,
there is something close to a real substitution
when Florence, instead of Paul, is abducted by Mrs.
Brown, stripped of her clothes, and almost of her
hair; but Dombey is not concerned about that,
because she is a mere girl and Paul is safe and
"unchanged". At any rate, superficially; Paul will
later undergo his own, grotesque kind of 'substitution': "he had a strange, old-fashioned, thought-
ful way, at other times, of sitting brooding in his
miniature armchair when he looked and talked like
one of those terrible little beings in the Fairy
Tales, who, at a hundred and fifty or two hundred
years of age, fantastically represent the children
for whom they have been substituted." (viii, 91)
At Miss Pipchin's he will metamorphose yet further
into fairyland: "The good old lady might have been
- not to record it disrespectfully - a witch, and
Paul and the cat her two familiars, as they all sat
by the fire together." (viii, 104) Thus Dombey,
paranoid in his concern to prevent the substitution
of his child by another creature, in fact achieves
the very thing he fears through his policies for
the child's education.

But in any event, Dombey himself is portrayed
as a monstrosity.[18] This is true, not only of his
later struggles with Edith, where he shows himself
"as hard a master as the Devil in dark fables",
appearing literally to be "possessed by a moody,
stubborn, sullen demon" (xl, 560, 562), but of his

earlier solitary pride, in which Polly Toodles glimpses him as "a strange apparition that was not to be accosted or understood". (iii, 23) His office is presented as a fantastic submarine world, in which "a mouldy little strong room in the obscure perspective, where a shady lamp was always burning, might have represented the cavern of some ocean-monster, looking on with a red eye at these mysteries of the deep". (xiii, 169)

One irony here, of course, is that young Paul is very fond of sea-monsters, but that these are frowned upon by those whom Dombey has chosen to educate his son. He has a special expert to accompany him on the beach, and give him instruction in sea-monsters; from his kind of knowledge, Paul learns far more than from the classical scholars at Dr. Blumber's school:

> '... He knows all about the deep sea, and the fish that are in it, and the great monsters that come and lie on rocks in the sun, and dive into the water again when they're startled, blowing and splashing so, that they can be heard for miles. There are some creatures,' said Paul, warming with his subject, 'I don't know how many yards long, and I forget their names, but Florence knows, that pretend to be in distress; and when a man goes near them, out of compassion, they open their great jaws and attack him.' (vii,152)[19]

Mrs. Blimber, of course, thinks of Glubb as an unclassical monster, but Paul's reply - "he's no more a monster than you are" (152) - penetrates to the heart of the matter. In the handy-dandy world of *Dombey and Son* it is Dombey himself who is the Gorgon Medusa, turning other people - his daughter Florence in particular - into stone with his monstrous basilisk eye:

> 'What is the matter?' he said sternly. 'Why do you come here? What has frightened you?' If anything had frightened her, it was the face he turned on her. The glowing love within the breast of his young daughter froze before it, and she stood and looked at him as if stricken into stone. (xviii, 256)

Thus it is essentially the children of *Dombey and Son* who perceive the 'grotesque truth' of this society - their perspective containing also a kind of compassion that prevents these "monsters" from becoming ogres and villains. It is Florence, who, right at the start, had taken in her father with the sharp, 'true' eye of the caricaturist: "The child glanced keenly at the blue coat and stiff white cravat, which with a pair of creaking boots and a very loud ticking watch, embodied her idea of a father" (i, 3);[20] from a satiric point of view that is manifestly Carlylean, clothes make the man. And Paul, probing into the nature of Dombey's power, asking essential questions - "'Papa! what's money?'" (viii, 92) - that explode the mystificatory abstraction of Dombey's dominating discourse, manages to uncover the essential, irrational contradictions of the system:

> Mr. Dombey having recovered from his surprise, not to say his alarm ... expounded to him how that money, though a very potent spirit, never to be disparaged on any account whatever, could not keep people alive whose time was come to die. (viii, 93)

Money is a 'potent spirit' - Dombey is forced to concede those unromantic, unscientific 'essences' that in fact, as we have seen, possess him. Paul's question, and Dombey's reply, push forward to the famous Lesage passage in the novel, that prays "for a good spirit who would take the house-tops off, with a more potent and benignant land than the lame demon in the tale, and show a Christian people what dark shapes issue from amidst their homes, to swell the retinue of the Destroying Angel, as he moves forth among them!" (xlvii, 643) We have seen plenty of those 'dark shapes' generated by the fetishistic worship of the 'potent spirit' money - Carker, for instance, who looks at Dombey "with the evil slyness of some monkish carving, half human and half brute; or like a leering face on an old water-spout". (xlii, 597) It is the tragedy of Paul, with his own 'old-fashioned shyness'[21] to be condemned to observe, comment upon and suffer this grotesqueness with the piercing sharpness of the child's eye and mind but with a helpless inability to affect it.

One last irony permits a glimpse at the personal, autobiographical emotions stirred during the writing of *Dombey and Son*, and their relation to these themes. Cryptically and strangely, Dombey's office resembles the London home of the young Dickens, broken up as it was by the father's bank-

ruptcy. Walter Gay describes the odd contents of
the room where he works; these include "an old bird-
cage (I wonder how *that* ever came there!) and a coal-
scuttle" (iv, 36), which also crop up in a more
obviously autobiographical Christmas story where a
child is suddenly taken out of school (like David
Copperfield) because of a death at home:

> I was taken home, and there was Debt at home
> as well as Death, and we had a sale there. My
> own little bed was so superciliously looked
> upon by a Power unknown to me, hazily called
> "The Trade", that a brass coal-scuttle, a
> roasting-jack, and a birdcage, were obliged to
> be put into it to make a lot of it, and then
> it went for a song. ("The Haunted House", *CS*,
> 251)

Debt takes a good deal longer to arrive at the
House of Dombey. By the time it arrives, the son
and heir is not just left an orphan, exposed,
vulnerable and humiliated: he's long since dead.
But the same 'potent spirit' is responsible - Money,
or the lack of it. What takes the rooftop off in
Dombey and Son is no "good spirit"; once more
grotesque demons haunt the house:

> herds of shabby vampires, Jew and Christian,
> over-run the house, sounding the plate-glass
> mirrors with their knuckles, striking dis-
> cordant octaves on the Grand Piano, drawing
> wet forefingers over the pictures, breathing
> on the blades of the best dinner-knives ...
> There is not a secret place in the whole
> house. (*DS*, lix, 832-3)

Superficially at least, *David Copperfield*
might seem a novel with a rather narrower focus
than *Dombey and Son*, and a more exclusively
individual, psychological emphasis. Its invoking
of social and historical dimensions, for all its
qualitative distinction - the brilliant description
of London at *DC*, xlvii, 679-80, for instance,
strikingly anticipating *Our Mutual Friend* in its
comprehension of the extent to which cities are
built on the production of waste - may appear
unusually curtailed, or economical. Yet the preoccupation with perception that links the novel with
Dombey and Son does carry important overtones of

issues in nineteenth century radical politics -
issues that involve art, imaginative vitality, and
the social meaning of the growth of the human
individual. *David Copperfield* is a *Bildungsroman*
about the development of an artist,[22] in which to
be imaginatively perceptive as an adult is to retain
traces of faculties seen in Florence and Paul Dombey,
that "power of observation in numbers of young
children ... quite wonderful for its closeness and
accuracy". (ii, 13) The mature David comes to
believe

> ... that most grown men who are remarkable in
> this respect, may with greater propriety be
> said not to have lost the faculty, than to
> have acquired it; the rather as I generally
> observe such men to retain a certain freshness
> and gentleness, and capacity of being pleased,
> which are also an inheritance they have
> preserved from their childhood...(13)

and that these qualities represent values absent
from contemporary society, in urgent need of
recovery.
     The early chapters of *David Copperfield*
explore the nature of childhood perception as
Dickens conceives it. It is distinguished first of
all by its freedom from conventional logic, its
unconsciousness of habitual classificiations of
experience into abstract categories like real and
fantastic, strange and familiar, terrifying and
ludicrous - divisions that inhibit recognition of
the grotesque in 'cultivated' sensibilities. Each
act of perception is an exploration of the
particular, immediately apprehended nature of its
object: "I could observe, in little pieces, as it
were; but as to making a net of a number of these
pieces, and catching anybody in it, that was, as
yet, beyond me." (ii, 21) Hence the luminous
intensity of 'unnecessary' details (Orwell's
'gargoyles'[23]) like Peggotty's "workbox with a
sliding lid, with a view of St. Paul's cathedral
(with a pink dome) painted on the top" (ii, 16); it
is the precision of the perception that allows the
development of critical perspectives capable of
recognising and laughing at the idealised picture.
     The honorific term, both for the state in
which the child is able to produce such perceptions
and for the quality of the perceptions themselves,
is 'freshness'. Steerforth's nickname for David
contains not only a mocking awareness of a naiveté

to exploit but an appreciation of an enviable
spontaneity: "I am never contented, except with
your freshness, my gentle Daisy." (xxii, 324)
Memories that are particularly alive, in which the
potency of childhood perception is particularly
strong, are felt to be 'fresh' - in terms that
evade cliché: "The delight with which Traddles
propounded this plan to me, and the sense he had of
its uncommon artfulness, are among the freshest
things in my remembrances." (xxxiv, 495)

The hallmark of 'fresh' perception is, first
of all, its unpremeditated, uncalculated immediacy
- as when David crosses the threshold of Ham
Peggotty's boat/house, and takes in its contents
all at once: "All this I saw in the first glance
after I crossed the threshold - childlike, according
to my theory." (iii, 30) Moreover,the 'fresh'
perception of the child establishes new connections
between things and thereby often attains penetrating
insights or discriminations. Mr. Murdstone, for
instance, is unmasked on the occasion of David's
first encounter with him because "a squareness about
the lower part of his face, and the dotted indication of the strong black beard he shaved close every
day, reminded me of the wax-work that had travelled
into our neighbourhood some half-a-year before".
(ii, 22)[24] The incongruous association, dependent
upon disinterested, experimental styles of perception (David is exploring the relations between
things that have only recently been registered in
his consciousness) conveys the 'grotesque truth'
about Murdstone, bracketing him with hollowness and
insincerity. The same faculty is apparent in adult-
hood, in its trace version, when David meets Mr.
Spenlow, and observes his gold watch-chain - "so
massive, that a fancy came across me, that he ought
to have a sinewy golden arm, to draw it out with,
like those which are put up over the goldbeaters'
shops." (xxiii, 380) He too is a grotesque
exhibit - "obliged ... to move his whole body, from
the bottom of his spine, like Punch" (350) -
fraudulently displaying, as a sign of wealth, the
gold watch-chain; swiftly and unexpectedly, 'fancy'
unveils him, linking him with a street sign that
(here at least) conveys essential imposture.[25]

And constantly in these early chapters, a
contrast between the child's way of inquiring about
the world - a spontaneous and 'philosophical' undertaking, because focussed essentially upon a search
for truth - is contrasted with cynical, manipulative,
mystificatory deployments of thought and language

for the purpose of acquiring or maintaining power. Following Rousseau,[26] David takes verbal signs, in their 'natural' state, to be pure and truthful indicators of the realities they represent. Names evoke specific times and places: "I never hear the name Yarmouth, but I am reminded of a certain Sunday morning on the beach, the bells ringing for church, little Emily leaning on my shoulder, Ham lazily dropping stones into the water." (iii, 40) When he sees a sailor with 'Skylark' on his chest, he imagines his name to be 'Mr. Skylark' (ii, 24); and when Ham announces his house, he can't see it at first, because a boat isn't for him a truthful referent for the word 'house'. (iii, 29)

The contrast is shown in Murdstone's habits of language. He invents a 'Mr. Brooks of Sheffield' to convey to his friends (and conceal from Copperfield) that David is sharp-witted; once again, David at first assumes the truthfulness of his language, and wonders who this Mr. Brooks might be. His analogies display intimidatory shufflings of categories involving humans and animals, or humans and things; about to punish David for disobedience, he situates him with other chattel: "If I have an obstinate house or dog to deal with, what do you think I do?" (iv, 46) Habitually, in fact, he reifies David - for the amusement of his friends, for instance, he calls him "bewitching Mrs. Copperfield's encumbrance" (ii, 23), a phrase which David, with finer sensitivity, edits for the sake of his mother in his account of the incident, leaving only the reference to her physical charm.

Elsewhere in the novel, similar, symptomatic habits of language are to be observed. At Creakle's school, for instance, there is a child named "Exchange or Barter": "I heard that one boy, who was a coal-merchant's son, came as a set-off against the coal-bill, and was called, on that account 'Exchange or barter' - a name selected from the arithmetic book as expressing this arrangement." (vi, 87) No wonder, then, that Steerforth regards David as a possession ("I feel as if you were my property" - xx, 290); a materialistic conception of human beings as commodities to trade and exchange governs personal and class relationships in *David Copperfield* no less than in *Dombey and Son*, and is reflected in linguistic practice.

By contrast again, the child's perception tends to animate the world - to imagine intelligence in animals, and vital energy in things. David attributes volition to Barkis's horse, imagining

182

that he keeps people waiting deliberately: "I fancied, indeed, that he sometimes chuckled audibly over this reflection, but the carrier said he was only troubled with a cough." (iii, 28) Like Paul Dombey, when no live creatures are available, for 'fancy' to operate upon, he turns his attention to the mundanest of surrounding objects, even - or especially - when 'imprisoned' in his room:

> I thought of the oddest things. Of the shape of the room, of the cracks in the ceiling, of the paper on the wall, of the flaws in the window-glass making ripples and dimples on the prospect, of the washing-stand being ricketty on its three legs, and having a discontented something about it, which reminded me of Mrs. Gummidge under the influence of the old one. (iv, 44)

And unlike Paul - more, in fact, like John Baptist Cavaletto, keeping up his spirits in captivity through the exercise of the imagination ("I can cut my bread so-like a melon. Or so-like an omelette. Or so-like a fried fish. Or so-like lyons sausage" - *LD*, I, i, 7) - this faculty enables him in some measure to withstand and survive intense suffering. The child's mode of perception, working upon things to metamorphose them, has a political significance; it sees the world as essentially fluid and therefore alterable, capable of being trans- formed into something other than itself. David's habit of "reading as if for life" (iv, 56) during the time of his persecution is a discipline of attention to how things *might* be; the books that his father left "kept alive my fancy, and my hope of something beyond that place and time". (55) They are to do so, as well, during David's trials in London when, in his roaming about the streets, David claims to have "fitted my old books to my altered life, and made stories for myself, out of the streets, and out of men and women". (xi, 168) Vile things become precious to him in this stage of growth, "making his imaginative world out of such strange experiences and sordid things". (169)

The journey to Dover that follows - indebted to, but decidedly developing upon earlier versions of the modern *Pilgrim's Progress*, like that in *The Old Curiosity Shop* - bears very marked resemblances to patterns of myth.[27] David first loses his clothes, returning, it seems, to the state in which he was born. He is in fact to die and be reborn,

and the journey is, as it were, the harrowing of
hell that comes between death and resurrection. But
the monsters he meets are inevitably grotesques -
mixtures of satire and horror, like the clothes-
dealer with hands "which were like the claws of a
great bird" (xiii, 184) and a grin that is
(synaesthetically) "a fierce, monotonous whine". He
swears by separate organs of the body - 'oh, my
lungs and liver ... oh, my eyes and limbs' -
comically ringing mechanical changes upon the
repertoire of them, and screws goroos out of himself. Even when he arrives, the first person he
sees, at an upstairs window, is "a florid pleasant-
looking gentleman, with a grey head, who shut up one
eye in a grotesque manner, nodded his head at me
several times, shook it at me as often, laughed, and
went away." (190)

Mr. Dick, in fact, has an important function in
the pattern of David's development from child to
artist. A sketch of this is provided by the passage
that relates the fate of Blunderstone after David's
departure:

> It was occupied, but only by a poor lunatic
> gentleman, and the people who took care of him.
> He was always sitting at my little window,
> looking out into the churchyard; and I wondered
> whether his rambling thoughts ever went upon
> any of the fancies that used to occupy mine,
> on the rosy mornings when I peeped out of that
> same little window in my night-clothes, and
> saw the sheep quietly feeding in the light of
> the rising sun. (xxii, 320)

Children and lunatics (as in other Romantic writing)[28]
appear connected by their capacity of 'fancy', their
common station the window, as they look out upon the
world beyond them, offering scope for the imagination (it is not only associated with David, Dick,
and this other madman, but also with Aunt Betty -
who first appears at it). Mr. Dick's creativity is
expressed, not in the 'memorial' he is writing (an
authoritative text that has more in common with
Micawber's 'Deed' than with anything else in the
novel), but in his Cavaletto-like capacity for
bricolage:

> He was an universal favourite and his
> ingenuity in little things was transcendent.
> He could cut oranges into such devices as none
> of us had an idea of. He could make a boat

out of anything, from a skewer upwards. He could turn crampbones into chessmen; fashion Roman chariots from old court cards; make spoked wheels out of cotton reels, and bird-cages of old wire. But he was greatest of all, perhaps, in the articles of string and straw; with which were all persuaded he could do anything that could be done by hands. (xvii, 251)

But Dick not only possesses these capabilities, he also stands as a model for their exercise. When David first meets him, he has already been reborn, and renamed; later he is to go through an additional stage of development, when Aunt Betsy is ruined, and it becomes necessary to earn money: "He was like one under the propitious influence of a charm, from the moment of his being usefully employed." (xxxvi, 529) Dick discovers the meaning of work - a very important theme in the novel, and an essential complement to the theme of imaginative perception, for without this latter becoming harnessed to determination and purpose, the "inheritance of childhood" is wasted.

Steerforth is the great study of this problem in the novel. His is a case of failed imagination; he is bored with life, and searches constantly for new sensations, because he can't find anything to do (he just "steers forth", in accord with his name). His problem is essentially connected with the status of the gentleman and amateur, who must be above work - he is imprisoned, in fact, by the class relationships that prevail in the novel, just as much as other characters. He is portrayed throughout in an essentially sympathetic way, for (as in *Master Humphrey's Clock*[29]) empathy is an essential aspect of the right way of perceiving things, as (once more) Mr. Dick exemplifies:

... as I have recorded in the narrative of my school days, his veneration for the Doctor was unbounded; and there is a subtlety of percep-tion in real attachment, even when it is borne towards man by one of the lower animals, which leaves the highest intellect behind. To this mind of the heart, if I may call it so, in Mr. Dick, some bright ray of the truth shot straight. (xlii, 623)

If Dick is the central 'innocent' grotesque of *David Copperfield*, Uriah Heep is unquestionably its central 'demonic' or 'terrible' grotesque. He too appears first at a window - but in his case this links him with the pantomimic Quilp, especially because of the proximity of medieval carvings: "he certainly did look uncommonly like the carved face on the beam outside my window." (xxi, 235) What shows in that first glimpse is a "cadaverous face" (xv, 218) - enough to link Heep to the skeleton in the Dance of Death; he plays a kind of hideous music upon himself, in fact, "beating a little tune on his chin as he walked on, with the two forefingers of his skeleton right hand" (xvii, 254), stalking his prey and seeming to charm it with mesmeric power. He appears, in fact, to be possessed by a diabolic spirit, and the writhings of his body seem to express the movements of the 'supernatural' element within him: "I looked at him, sitting all away as if his mean soul griped his body." (xxv, 381)

Once more, then, this theme emerges in this novel. Demons have not gone out of the world - the medieval nightmare continues on in an ironic modern vein, worse, more horrifying and frightening, for instead of falling victim to external powers of evil, people demonise themselves, and prey upon their own bodies. There is "a certain gloomy, arrogant, devil's humour in the Murdstones" (iv, 49); and, according to the trick business habits of Spenlow, "The heart and hand of the good angel Spenlow would have been always open, but for the restraining demon Jorkins". (xxii, 351) Even Micawber's 'Deed' carries these diabolical associations, confused in David's mind "with those demoniacal parchments which are held to have, once upon a time, obtained to a great extent in Germany". (xi, 167) Romantic Germany lives on in unromantic Victorian England.

Yet as David develops, he has to learn to distinguish between types of romance. He isn't to be a conventional hero by any stretch of the imagination, and the kind of Biedermeier conception of romance with which Dickens had been familiar in the 1830s comes in for some sharp criticism. The false fairy world of Dora Sperlow, idealised by David into an impossible, ethereal dream - "she was more than human to me. She was a Fairy, a Sylph, I don't know what she was" (xxvi, 390) - is placed as something altogether worse, in class terms, than the pink dome of St. Paul's on Peggotty's workbox. The reality is that Dora suffers the fate of early Victorian middle-class

girls: stuffed up in cotton wool, she can take no
serious part in life, inhabiting a false world of
pagodas, harps, and mechanical toys in which she
too appears almost like a grotesque piece of clock-
work: "Dora seemed by one consent to be regarded
like a pretty toy or plaything." (xli, 603-4)
Once this artificial fairy-story collapses - "all
the romance of our engagement put away upon a shelf,
to rust" (xliv, 634), and replaced by mundane
reality - practical problems develop with which she
is ill-equipped to cope.

No, once again the 'romance of real life' is
played against such thin 'castles in the air', as
the only true subject of the artistic imagination,
and its recovery, the only way for the child's
habits of vision to survive in adult life. One
last, special instance may be adduced. The dwarf
Miss Mowcher, at her first appearance, belongs with
Dickens's most brilliant grotesques. She inhabits
peculiarly mixed categories; with the status of a
child, she has an adult knowingness that at times
even threatens to shade off into the supernatural
(she's described as an "imp" of supernatural
knowingness at xxii, 328 linking her to Heep); an
essential outsider (like Dick the lunatic and in
another sense, David at school, isolated from his
fellows through the bitterness of his sufferings)
she nonetheless has access to secrets that are
denied to others. She operates like the fool in a
Shakespearean play, commenting on misdemeanours and
frauds, speaking about sex with a Regency frankness
that has no parallel in Dickens outside of *Nicholas
Nickleby*. But her significance is inherently *social*;
without understanding her in this way - treating her
for instance as some gargoyle in the margin of a
realist text - she is misunderstood.

Harry Stone, in fact, has some useful remarks
concerning the focus of his own concerns in *David
Copperfield*, which may be of relevance here:

> The magical atmosphere in *Copperfield* is more
> domesticated, more naturally and unobtrusively
> fused to the central realism of the story,
> than is the reverberant ambiance of the ground-
> breaking *Dombey and Son*.[30]

The same might reasonably be claimed of the
grotesque in *David Copperfield*. It's at any rate
likely to give impetus to a more rewarding approach
to Dickens in mid-career than that which would see
the grotesque in the process of dying out.

NOTES

1. Wilson, *op. cit.*, p.205.
2. See *Novels of the Eighteen-Forties* (Oxford, Clarendon Press, 1954), p.51. Wilson and Tillotson are also agreed that *Dombey and Son* and *David Copperfield* are linked as autobiographical; thus Wilson: "Working on *Dombey and Son* undoubtedly woke Dickens up to that recall of his own childhood that culminated in the next novel, *David Copperfield*" (p.206), and thus Tillotson, commenting on Paul's stay with Mrs. Pipchin: "probably the first of his reminiscent confidences, the seed from which grew the 'autobiography' and the childhood chapters of *David Copperfield*" (Letters, IV, xii).
3. Quoted from "Dickens in Russia: The Initial Phase" in Stephen Wall, ed., *Charles Dickens: A Critical Anthology* (Harmondsworth, Penguin Books, 1970), p.512.
4. *ibid.*, p.510. Belinsky died before he could complete his reading of *Dombey and Son*.
5. See Patrick Waddington, *Turgenev and England* (London, Macmillan, 1980), p.76.
6. Philip Collins, ed., *Dickens: The Critical Heritage*, p.228. Kent was also the editor, in 1884, of an anthology entitled *The Humour and Pathos of Charles Dickens: With Illustrations of his Mastery of the Terrible and the Picturesque*.
7. See Letters, V, 284 (18/4/48).
8. This at any rate is his view in "Dickens, Hablot Browne, and the Tradition of English Caricature", *Criticism* XI, 3, 219-235 (quotations in the text are from pages 225 and 232). In *Dickens and Phiz* (Bloomington, Ind., Indiana University Press, 1978) it seems to have evolved into something less schematic.
9. Letters, IV, 671 (to Forster, November-December 1846) and 677 (to H.K. Browne, 6/12/46). Of Dickens's dissatisfaction with the portrayal of Mrs. Pipchin, Tillotson comments "The real trouble no doubt was that CD had a clear picture in his memory of Mrs. Roylance."
10. Cf. Chapter 7 above.
11. See Kayser, *op. cit.* (English edition), pp.21, 49, 76-81.
12. Cf. p.22 above.
13. Characteristic of Dickensian names for businessmen: cf. Nickleby, Casby, Fledgeby, etc.
14. Cf. e.g. the description of the House of Clennam (*LD*, I, iii, 31), where the "gigantic

crutches" that support the house clearly become a "gymnasium for the neighbouring cats" through a similar alliterative process.

15. 'You have a son, I believe?' said Mr. Dombey.
'Four on 'em, Sir. Four hims and a her. All alive!'
'Why, it's as much as you can afford to keep them!' said Mr. Dombey.
'I couldn't hardly afford but one thing in the world less, Sir.'
'What is that?'
'To lose 'em, Sir.' (*DS*, ii, 17)

16. Cf. Harry Stone, *Dickens and the Invisible World*, Chapter 6.

17. In particular the work of Jean Paul. In *Des Feldpredigers Schmelzle Reise nach Flätz*, for example, the paranoid central character, on his way to Flätz to prove that he isn't a coward, is haunted by the presence of a fellow-traveller by the name of Jean Paul - who knows, of course, that he is a coward (see the edition by J.W. Smeed, Oxford, Oxford University Press, 1952, p.52). This story was translated by Carlyle, and Forster's reference to Jean Paul in his biography of Dickens (adopting a definition of humour attributed to the German writer) presumably reflects the prevalence of Carlyle's ideas and aesthetic principles in the Dickens circle.

18. This is a strategic irony, and doesn't mean that Dombey is caricatured. The conception of Gradgrind in *Hard Times* is not dissimilar - both figures become sympathetic as the novel progresses and their illusions are stripped away. (It is striking how frequently the pattern of *Great Expectations* is anticipated in these later novels.)

19. In a letter of a slightly later date (during the writing of *David Copperfield*) Dickens mentions a pair of infants with a very comparable affinity for sea monsters: "We were dreadfully shocked, at Broadstairs, by seeing the Baldwinian Twins, whom I have taken the liberty of calling The Measeliese Twins - as opposed to the Siamese. Oh the apparent age of those young Codgers! They were on the sands, in the blue stage of rickets, with their small noses very red, and pinched up sharp at the ends. They slobbered as they dangled over the nurse's shoulder, and, feebly crooning, looked out to sea, as if they were expecting the Marine Goblins who had changed them at their birth, to come and fetch them away to bowers of slime and seaweed.

It was a dreadful spectacle - with a vague smell of cheese about it - and one I never can forget." (to Beard, 18/7/49).

20. Compare later in *Our Mutual Friend*, "Miss Podsnap's early views of life ... principally derived from the reflections of it in her father's boots." (*OMF*, I, xi, 131).

21. As Dickens's frequent recourse to the 'antique' illustrator George Cattermole implies, 'old-fashioned' and 'grotesque' are near-synonyms in his work. They appear to be mediated, in fact by the word 'antic', used in its Elizabethan sense to describe the 'old-fashioned' Jenny Wren in *Our Mutual Friend*. For a valuable study of the inter-changeability of 'antic' and 'grotesque' in Renaissance England, see Reinhard Lengeler, *Tragische Wirklichkeit als Groteske Verfremdung bei Shakespeare* (Cologne, Böhlau Verlag, 1964), esp. pp.6-23,.42-55.

22. The best work on the *Bildungsroman* in England is Jerome Buckley's *Season of Youth: the 'Bildungsroman' from Dickens to Golding* (Cambridge, Mass., Harvard University Press, 1975). Yet there is scope for further comparative work (involving English and German Literature) in this area.

23. See the essay on Dickens in *The Collected Essays, Journalism and Letters of George Orwell*, eds. Sonia Orwell and Ian Angus (London, Secker and Warburg, 1968: 4 vols.), I, 413-460, esp. 450 and 454.

24. Cf. Chapter 11 below.

25. "... a fancy came across me, that he ought to have a sinewy golden arm, to draw it out with, like those which are put up over the gold-beaters' shops." (*DC*, xxiii, 350). Cf. *A Tale of Two Cities*, where a number of streetsigns near Dr. Manette's house are detailed: "In a building at the back ... church-organs claimed to be made, and silver to be chased, and likewise gold to be beaten by some mysterious giant who had a golden arm starting out of the wall of the front hall - as if he had beaten himself precious, and menaced a similar conversion of all visitors." (II, vi, 87). There is a suggestion of fraudulence about nearly all these streetsign references in Dickens, presumably owing something to the Warrens' sign that stood in the Strand to suggest a posher address than Hungerford Stairs.

26. Rousseau made a very influential distinction between language in its pristine state, as a purely oral/aural institution, incapable of

deception, because available to immediate
validation, and 'fallen', written language, which
could be untruthful because of techniques of
dissemination and storage. See the *Essai sur
l'Origine des Langues* in the critical edition of
Charles Porset (Bordeaux, Guy Ducros, 1970).

27. Harry Stone has some good pages on myth
in *David Copperfield* in *Dickens and the Invisible
World* (esp. pp.211ff.)

28. Wordsworth's *The Idiot Boy* is a paradigm
- see *The Poetical Works*, ed. E. de Selincourt,
Oxford, Oxford University Press, 1944; 4 volumes),
II, 67-80.

29. Cf. Chapter 8 above.

30. *op. cit.*, p.211.

Chapter Ten

IRONIC INFERNOS : *BLEAK HOUSE, HARD TIMES* AND
RUSKIN'S CONCEPTION OF THE GROTESQUE

It is perhaps surprising that discussions of
Dickens's work in relation to the aesthetic and
political writings of John Ruskin are quite hard to
come by.[1] The situation is in marked contrast to
that which obtains in the case of the admittedly
much more important connection between Dickens and
Carlyle, where a substantial body of work, in
quantity and quality, is available. Yet Carlyle
was a 'mutual friend' of Dickens and Ruskin, and
the three of them were linked by many of their
contemporaries as critics of political economy and
laissez-faire capitalism. To some, like Edwin
Whipple, they formed an unholy trinity of reaction-
aries whose influence must be combatted: "the
fact that men like Carlyle, Ruskin and Dickens can
write economic nonsense without losing intellectual
caste shows that the science of political economy,
before its beneficent truths come to be generally
admitted, must go through a long struggle with
benevolent sophisms and benevolent passions ...."[2]
Stephen Wall reminds us that in the complacent and
affluent 1850s and 60s such views began to constitute
an ideological consensus that may have promoted a
solidarity between its three most prominent critics:
"Carlyle and Ruskin remained sympathetic, but
Dickens was often under attack in his later years
from other intellectual critics of his day, and he
was especially liable to criticism from those
connected with an administrative Establishment to
which Dickens had become increasingly hostile."[3]
    Nevertheless, the record of the relationship
between Dickens and Ruskin is a chequered one. It
begins with the testimony of *Praeterita* II (1886)
concerning the impact of reading Dickens as a young
man:

no word has been said of the dawn and sunrise
of Dickens on us; from the first syllable of
him in the *Sketches*, altogether precious and
admirable to my father and me; and the new
number of *Pickwick* and following *Nickleby*
looked to, through whatever laborious or
tragic realities might be upon us, as unmixed
bliss, for the next day.[4]

The praise, though generous, is mixed; it implies,
and will go on to say, that at this stage Dickens
was for him primarily an entertainer (Ruskin, with
Arnold, being one of the sources of that still
familiar limiting recognition of Dickens's achieve-
ment shared by F.R. Leavis at the time of *The Great
Tradition*, and classically expressed in that book[5])
and not a great artist, because of his tendency
towards caricature, "so that he never became an
educational element of my life, but only one of its
chief comforts and restoratives".
    Yet it would be reasonable, perhaps, to
speculate that Ruskin's lifelong dialectical preoccupation with the grotesque - later to be associated with the mind at play, resting from "laborious
or tragic realities" - was not uninfluenced by this
exposure to the "joyful and triumphant hilarity" of
Dickens's first writings. In a very youthful work,
The Poetry of Architecture (1837-8), he begins to
explore the grotesque, characteristically discrimin-
ating between alternative forms that are held to be
'true' and 'false' respectively:

> Though the grotesque of Elizabethan
> architecture is adapted for wood country,
> the grotesque of the clipped garden, which
> frequently accompanies it, is not. The
> custom of clipping trees into fantastic forms
> is always to be reprehended: first, because
> it can never produce the true grotesque, for
> the material is not passive, and, therefore,
> a perpetual sense of restraint is induced,
> while the great principle of the grotesque
> is action.[6]

Any connection with Dickens here must at first
sight seem remote, and yet by 1841 it is clear that
the terms 'true' and 'false' grotesque - the latter
clearly associated with the idea of the 'picturesque'
- are integral to Ruskin's critical assessment of
the novelist. In that year he writes to W.H.
Harrison (a would-be contributor to the *Pic Nic*

Papers in 1838, his paper mentioned in Dickens's
diary for 31 December 1840[7]), discussing *The Old
Curiosity Shop* in a rather censorious vein, lamenting in particular "a want of his former clear truth,
a diseased extravagance, a violence of delineation,
which seem to indicate a sense of failing power in
the writer's own mind".[8] Already, it seems, a
pattern of decline and fall has set in with
Dickens's creativity, in Ruskin's eyes - and this
is to be a *leitmotif* of later work on the Gothic
and the Grotesque.

     During the 1840s Ruskin's career develops in a
fashion that offers fascinating glimpses of
connection and parallel with Dickens's own. Both
of them, with their Protestant backgrounds
(Ruskin's was Evangelical), reacted against the
Oxford Movement, Ruskin's satiric portrait of Pusey
in June 1843 (a "sickly and rather ill put together
English clerical gentleman who never looked one in
the face or appeared aware of the state of the
weather"[9]) every bit as sharp as Dickens's
invective in a letter to Fonblanque earlier that
year ("Good God, to talk in these times of most
untimely ignorance among the people, about what
Priests shall wear, and whither they shall turn
when they say their prayers."[10]). And both spent
crucial years in Italy in the mid 1840s (Dickens
in Genoa in 1844-5, and Ruskin, alone for the first
time, and without his parents, in 1845), during
which they developed remarkably similar critiques
of the idea of the picturesque. Ruskin's letter
to his parents from Parma in July 1845, explaining
why it is so difficult for him to write poetry in
Italy ("I don't see how it is possible for a person
who gets up at four, goes to bed at 10, eats ices
when he is hot, beef when he is hungry, gets rid of
all claims of charity by giving money which he
hasn't earned - and those of compassion by treating
all distress more as picturesque than as real - I
don't see how it is at all possible for such a
person to write good poetry."[11]) bears close
comparison to Dickens's recognition that in Italy
"the conventional idea of the picturesque is
associated with such misery and degradation that a
new picturesque will have to be established as the
world goes onward".[12]

     At other points, however, it could be said,
with some understatement, that their views on art
were divergent. Dickens's close friend Clarkson
Stanfield ("Stannie") figured in *Modern Painters I*
(1843) as a worthy follower of Turner - only to be

194

dropped in the second edition of 1846, after
Ruskin's stay in Italy, and to be criticised in
1848 for the painting of Amalfi he exhibited at
the Royal Academy.[13] Conversely, Dickens's famous
1850 attack, in *Household Words*, upon Millais'
"Christ in the House of His Parents" - chiming in,
as it did, with a whole series of hatchet jobs
against the Pre-Raphaelites, appearing in *The Times*,
The Atheneum and elsewhere during 1850-1 - forms
part of the background to Ruskin's equally famous
defense of the Brotherhood in letters to *The Times*
in May 1851.[14] As Angus Wilson suggests,[15] what
was at least partly at issue was an attitude
towards the past: this surfaces quite clearly in
Ruskin's letter to Norton at the time of Dickens's
death: "Dickens was a pure modernist - a leader of
the steam-whistle party *par excellence* - and he had
no understanding of any power of antiquity except a
sort of jackdaw sentiment for cathedral towers."[16]

Yet of particular relevance and fascination
here is the extent to which this debate also
centres around notions of the grotesque. The year
1850 can be seen, in fact, as a marker for certain
shifts in Dickens's attitude towards the grotesque,
in which a response to mid-Victorian *pudeur* and
high-mindedness is discernible. These could be
seen as beginning with the *Examiner* article of 30
December 1848 on John Leech (a Victorian caricaturist also greatly admired by Ruskin) with its attack
upon "personal ugliness" in the work of Rowlandson
and Gillray, and praise of Leech as "the very first
English caricaturist ... who has considered beauty
as being perfectly compatible with his art";[17] as
continuing with Dickens's anodyne 'rehabilitation'
of Miss Mowcher between November 1849 and March
1850;[18] and as culminating in the attack upon
Millais'

> hideous, wry-necked blubbering red-haired boy
> in a nightgown who appears to have received a
> poke in the hand from the stick of another boy
> with whom he has been playing in an adjacent
> gutter, and to be holding it up for the
> contemplation of a kneeling woman, so horrible
> in her ugliness that (supposing it were
> possible for any human creature to exist for
> a moment with that dislocated throat) she
> would stand out from the rest of the company
> as a monster in the vilest cabaret in France,
> or the lowest gin-shop in England.[19]

The timetable of Ruskin's altogether more weighty and intellectually complex major wrestlings with the idea of the grotesque, issuing forth as they do in the publication of *The Stones of Venice* and *Modern Painters III*, is only slightly in arrears. Work on the former began in the winter of 1849-50, with a period of residence in Venice; its first volume appeared in the spring of 1851 and its second and third, following another Venetian winter in 1851-2, in the spring and autumn (respectively) of 1853, just as the serialization of *Bleak House* came to a conclusion. It is the third volume that contains the chapter on the 'Grotesque Renaissance', to which subject Ruskin also returned in chapter eight of *Modern Painters III* published in January 1856, and in appendix one of *Modern Painters IV* (April, 1856). Meanwhile, *Hard Times* had appeared, in 1854; it is this novel above all, among Dickens's later works, that claimed Ruskin's attention, and provoked the major celebration of his work appearing in *Unto this Last* (1860).

So Ruskin, in the process of thinking and writing about the grotesque, unquestionably had Dickens on his mind: he mentions him, in fact, both in 'Grotesque Renaissance' and in *Modern Painters III*, treating him in both places as the inheritor of a medieval tradition of the grotesque, devolved as this now is through profound alterations in the means of production: "The classical and Renaissance manufactures of modern times having silenced the independent language of the operative, his humour and satire pass away in the word-wit which has of late become the especial study of the group of authors headed by Charles Dickens; all this power was formerly thrown into noble art, and became permanently expressed in the sculptures of the cathedral."[20] And it is tempting to think of Dickens tacitly acknowledging the ambiguously complimentary recognition - depicting him as the head of a school, a brotherhood (like the Pre-Raphaelitic) dedicated in 'hard times' to the perpetuation of a tradition[21] - in his famous assertion, to Forster, "that the very holding of popular literature through a kind of popular dark age, may depend on such fanciful treatment".[22]

Nevertheless, other indications of the inter-penetration of Ruskin's and Dickens's thoughts on the grotesque in the 1850s may seem, in their familiarity, more substantial. In considering the decline of the gothic and grotesque in *The Stones of Venice* and *Modern Painters III* Ruskin has constantly in

mind an ideal, 'noble' grotesque expressing *truth* -
its pre-eminent model is Dante - from which later
derivations have lapsed.[23] ('Truth' had been
Ruskin's touchstone from his earliest writings, as
Hewison attests: "the great theme of the first
volume of *Modern Painters* is not beauty, but
truth."[24]) And in praising *Hard Times* the same
emphasis is apparent; Dickens's writing, though
imperfect (a category that plays an important role
in *The Stones of Venice*[25]) because of its dependence
upon grotesque exaggeration, is inherently *true*:

> The essential value and truth of Dickens's
> writings have been unwisely lost sight of by
> many thoughtful persons, merely because he
> presents his truth with some colour of
> caricature. Unwisely, because Dickens's
> caricature, though often gross, is never
> mistaken. Allowing for his manner of telling
> them, the things he tells us are always true.[26]

Interestingly, similar emphases begin to appear
in Dickens's work at the end of 1849, when he
writes to Forster concerning Number VIII of *David
Copperfield*, which includes the account of David's
night on the tiles with Steerforth in Chapter 24:
"His first dissipation, I hope, will be found
worthy of attention as a piece of grotesque truth."[27]
In outline at least, the development of Dickens's
conception of the grotesque in his later work
parallels Ruskin's in its essentially binary
structure. In the novels that succeed *Dombey and
Son*, there is frequently a confrontation between
two alternative grotesques, one positive, one
negative, one inherently 'true' or 'innocent', the
other debased, or as in *Hard Times* (the novel in
which this pattern can be most clearly discerned),
'disgraceful'. They tend to stand for two phases
of the imagination - on the one hand the imagination
'in a state of nature', as it were, perceiving the
grotesque from the perceptions of the child, or the
artist who has retained sufficient childhood powers
of vision, and on the other hand, the imagination
as it must express itself, in and through monstrous
distortion, out of radically diseased social
conditions and relations.

In this contrast, then, something of Ruskin's
'noble' and 'ignoble' grotesque, albeit in
dissociation from any nostalgic myth of historical
decline and fall,[28] can be sought. Furthermore,
there are other terms from *The Stones of Venice*

that may be serviceable in the consideration of the
Dickensian grotesque - the 'ludicrous' and 'fearful',
for instance, as contrasting elements within
grotesque art, and the related notions of 'sportive'
and 'terrible' grotesque:

> First, then, it seems to me that the grotesque
> is, in almost all cases, composed of two
> elements, one ludicrous, the other fearful;
> that, as one or the other of these elements
> prevails the grotesque falls into two branches,
> sportive grotesque, and terrible grotesque;
> but that we cannot legitimately consider it
> under these two aspects, because there are
> hardly any examples which do not in some
> degree combine both elements; there are few
> grotesques so utterly playful as to be over-
> cast with no shade of fearfulness, and few so
> fearful as absolutely to exclude all idea of
> jest.[29]

One might perhaps think of Dickens's development,
in fact, as a passage from the 'sportive grotesque'
of *Pickwick Papers* to the 'terrible grotesque' of
later novels like *Bleak House* and *Hard Times* -
bearing in mind, of course, Ruskin's own caveat
that the two are never properly separable.

Ruskin's own preference seems to be for the
'terrible grotesque' - a category that may in fact
partly overlap with the idea of the 'noble
grotesque'. The most interesting and pertinent
consideration of these terms occurs during a
discussion of representations of hell and its
diabolical inmates. Ruskin regards the comic or
satiric mode as essential to these: it is an
expression of the Christian confidence in the overthrow of Lucifer by Christ that the devil should be
made fun of. The gargoyles of medieval cathedrals,
then, express that satiric spirit of playfulness of
which Dickens is the modern inheritor; in them,
"the fiends are oftener ludicrous than terrible".
Ruskin regards this as a "degradation of conception",
and yet is equally critical of Milton, who "makes
his fiends too noble, and misses the foulness,
inconstancy, and fury of wickedness".[30]

The right balance between the 'ludicrous' and
'fearful', according to Ruskin, is to be found in
Bunyan, and above all Dante, "the central man of
all the world": "in him the grotesque reaches at
once the most distinct and the most noble development to which it was ever brought in the human

mind."[31] It is clear that the representations, in the *Inferno*, of the degradations that the sinners in hell must endure, stand at the pinnacle of grotesque art:

> ... I think the twenty-first and twenty-second books of the *Inferno* the most perfect portraitures of fiendish nature which we possess; and, at the same time, in their mingling of the extreme of horror (for it seems to me that the silent swiftness of the first demon, 'con l'ali aperte e sovra i pie leggiero', cannot be surpassed in dreadfulness) with ludicrous actions and images, they present the most perfect instances with which I am acquainted of the terrible grotesque.[32]

The interest of this assessment of Dante's *Inferno* for the study of Dickens may lie in the extent to which, in the later novels, the deployment of a "terrible grotesque" may be bound up with the development of portrayals of modern industrial cities as hellish infernos. The connection is by no means unique to Dickens among nineteenth and even twentieth century writers. Indeed the city/inferno topos which writers as various as Shelley, Balzac, Gissing and Brecht find so attractive[33] has almost the character of a cliché in the modern novel, and the mere fact of its frequency in Dickens's work cannot suggest the presence of that *terribilità* admired by Ruskin in Dante. Yet a study of its essentially ironic workings in two representative mature novels, *Bleak House* and *Hard Times*, may suggest some further points of contact between the Dickensian and Ruskinian notions of the grotesque. It is upon these works, at any rate, that attention is now focussed.

The Dantean dimensions of *Bleak House* reveal themselves soon enough in the first 'glimpse' of Jarndyce and Jarndyce afforded in chapter one. The novel is fond of a Ruskinian 'suddenness', and it begins with a series of bacon-streaks which move from one incongruous scene to another.[34] These individual locations are described as 'circles' - the Dedlock world will become, habitually, a 'brilliant and distinguished circle' (e.g. *BH*, xii, 153, 159) - with the notion that Chancery stands as their centre. As embodied in the case of Jarndyce and Jarndyce, it becomes clear at once that Chancery is rather like hell, and its mode of effect rather like a temptation to sin: "... and even those who have contemplated its history from the outermost circle of such evil, have been insensibly tempted into a loose way of letting bad things alone to take their own bad course ..." (I, 5)

The connection will be strategically reinforced as the novel progresses. There is the testimony of reliable witnesses like Boythorn, declaring that "There never was such an infernal cauldron as that Chancery, on the face of the earth!" and identifying as its son the Accountant General and its father the Devil. (ix, 118) The 'Mace and Seal' of Chancery, are (according to Miss Flite) "cold and glittering devils" that "draw people on, my dear. Draw peace out of them. Sense out of them. Good looks out of them. Good qualities out of them." (xxxv, 498); the imagery comes from the lowest depths of hell, as represented by Dante and painted by Signorelli in Orvieto.[35] For Richard Carstone, classically educated at a public school, the experience of waiting for its lawyers to complete their circles ("We have put our shoulders to the wheel, Mr. Carstone, and the wheel is going round") is like the infernal torments of Greek mythology: "Yes, with Ixion on it." (xxxix, 550)

Yet the circles of this Inferno manifestly extend far beyond Chancery. An atmosphere envelops the city which seems like the 'dunnest smoke of Hell' - to Esther, at least, experiencing London for the first time, and therefore registering its truths with fresh, 'innocent' perceptiveness: "I asked him whether there was a great fire anywhere? For the streets were so full of dense brown smoke that scarcely anything was to be seen." (iii, 28) In the area of Tom-all-Alone's are "streets and courts so infamous that Mr. Snagsby sickens in body and mind, and feels as if he were going, every moment deeper down, into the infernal gulf". (xxii, 310) When the same party (Snagsby and the policemen) return, it is as if from a harrowing of hell: "here, the crowd, like a concourse of imprisoned demons, turns back, yelling, and is seen no more." (xxii, 314)

Here, perhaps, in this mythical journey, is the first glimpse of a 'terrible grotesque'. For the moment, however, it is necessary to document the extent to which these parallels serve satiric purposes. Dickens's famous assertion, that "in Bleak House I have purposely dwelt upon the romantic

side of familiar things" (xiv), may mislead if it
suggests that what occurs is a glamorising and
aggrandising of mundanities; in deploying the idea
of hell, the novel emphasises, in mock-heroic
fashion, the absence of anything grandly Miltonic
in its demons and sinners. The circles of these
infernos are small - the fashionable world, for
instance, is a "tremendous orb, nearly five miles
around" (xlviii, 650), resembling "the circle the
necromancer draws around him" (xii, 161) rather
than anything on an epic scale. Milton is in fact
quoted with ironic effect, to suggest the scaled-
down architectonics of Chesney Wold: "Not to know
that there is something wrong at the Dedlocks' is
to argue yourself unknown." (lviii, 786)³⁶ And
when Esther recovers from her illness at Boythorn's
cottage, riding her pony Stubbs, "the circle of
tantalising little gnats" (xxxvi, 506) that attack
his ear appears to mock the bigger ones up the road,
reducing them, like the devils of Pandemonium, to an
appropriate size.

    Fashionable intelligence is ironically limited
too - "like the fiend", it "is omniscient of the
past and present, but not the future". (ii, 9)
The phrase may serve to introduce the numerous and
various comic devils who stalk their prey in *Bleak
House*. Sir Leicester Dedlock "receives the gout as
a troublesome demon, but still a demon of the
patrician order" (xvi, 218); Lady Dedlock's cognate
hell is 'Boredom'.³⁷ Bucket is distinguished by a
fat forefinger which he appears to consult like a
"familiar demon". (liii, 712) And the Smallweeds,
rummaging among the ruins of Krook's shop, "present
a fiendish appearance not relieved by the general
aspect of the room". (xxxix, 558)

    Yet the most brilliant satiric devils in the
novel are the lawyers of Chancery. They appear
first as a kind of ironic priesthood of the rites,
dressed in black and looking like "that sedate and
clerical bird, the Rook" (*ED*, ii, 5); Mr.
Tulkinghorn, for instance, "may be seen walking
before breakfast like a larger species of rook",
(xii, 162) and Jarndyce is described looking
suspiciously at Mr. Vholes, "eyeing his black
figure, as if he were a bird of ill-omen". (xlv,
615) They are portrayed as necromancers describing
magic circles around the professional 'mysteries'
they wish to protect from rational investigation
and reform - Volumnia Dedlock is convinced, for
instance, that Mr. Tulkinghorn "must be a free-
mason. Is sure he is at the head of a lodge, and

wears short aprons, and is made a perfect idol of,
with candlesticks and trowels." (xl, 568) This in
fact, in one of Dickens's familiar historical ironies,[38] is the Druidical priesthood that *A Child's
History of England*, mocking Victorian complacency,
had declared dead ("But it is pleasant to think
that there are no Druids now who go on in that way,
and pretend to carry Enchanters' Wands and
Serpents' Eggs - and of course there is nothing of
the kind anywhere" - *CHE*, 132-3).

But the chief point of such a remarkable
triumph of Dickens's grotesque imagination as the
portrayal of Mr. Vholes is to highlight the banality
of Victorian legal evil. "A sallow man, with
pinched lips that looked as if they were cold, a
red eruption here and there upon his face" (xxxvii,
533): the 'red eruption' offers an absurd hint of
the infernal, volcanic metaphors that surround a
character like Smallweed, which the sallowness of
face - denoting indigestion - serves to render yet
more farcical. Vholes's indigestion appears to
have 'terrible' origins: it is connected with
Gothic motifs like bloodsucking and cannibalism.
His bags stuffed with Chancery documents look like
"the larger sort of serpents in their first gorged
state" (xxxix, 549); Esther perceives "something of
the vampire in him" (lx, 820); and at the end of
the novel, in which he has druidically pursued
Richard Carstone "as if he were looking at his prey
and charming it" (xxxvii, 535), Vholes bids farewell "with one last gasp as if he had swallowed the
last morsel of his client". (lxv, 867) Yet this
mythic, quasi-supernatural register is also juxta-
posed with the utter mundanity of Vholes's clerkly
soul: "My digestive functions, as you may have
heard me mention, are not in a good state, and rest
might improve them." (xxxix, 553)

Here indeed the 'ludicrous' and the 'terrible'
are combined. Vholes's pimples, for instance, are
simultaneously a joke kind of jewelry - he is
described exercising his aesthetic faculties by
feeling "the pimples on his face as if they were
ornaments" (lx, 820) - and the stuff of nightmare
and hallucination, described in the colours of
expressionist painting: "he secretly picked at one
of the red pimples on his yellow face with his black
glove." (xlv, 615) At his druidical work,
describing his magic circles around Richard Carstone
("Mr. Vholes, after glancing at the official cat
who is patiently watching a mouse's hole, fixes his
charmed gaze again on his young client, and

proceeds in his buttoned up half-audible voice, as
if there were an unclean spirit in him that will
neither come out nor speak out" -- xxxix, 551), he
is a wizard with a cat as familiar (like Krook) -
only the cat from whom he takes his cue has to be
'official' - and a man possessed by a demon which
can only express itself in pimples.

If Vholes epitomises the sportive, mock-heroic
grotesque of *Bleak House*, we must then look elsewhere for something grander - to the incongruous
figure of Phil Squod, perhaps. "A little grotesque
man with a large head" (xxi, 303), Squod is clearly
related in appearance and name (with suitable
military transformations) to the Squeers/Quilp
school of grotesques. Yet he is quite devoid of
sadistic impulse: "he has never hurt anybody but
himself," George Rouncewell assures Mr. Smallweed.
(xxvi, 370) What is distinctive about him, in
fact, is that his grotesque appearance is the
product of the industrial environment of Victorian
England:

> I was passable enough when I went with the
> tinker, though nothing to boast of then; but
> what with blowing the fire with my mouth when
> I was young, and spileing my complexion, and
> singeing my hair off, and swallering the smoke;
> and what with being naturally unfort'nate in
> the way of running against hot metal, and
> marking myself by sich means; and what with
> having turn-ups with the tinker as I got
> older, almost whenever he was too far gone in
> drink - which was almost always - my beauty
> was queer, very queer, even at that time. As
> to since; what with a dozen years in a dark
> forge, where the men was given to larking; and
> what with being scorched in an accident at a
> gas-works; and what with being blowed out of a
> winder, case-filling in the firework business;
> I am ugly enough to be made a show on! (xxvi,
> 367)

Here too is an ironic inferno, but with a
difference from those seen thus far. In the
rhetoric of *Bleak House*, Phil Squod's experiences
belong with those "realities and not phantoms"
(xii, 162) that threaten to break in upon the
necromantic circles spun out from Chancery. It is
a novel which imagines social change in infernal
terms - as a great conflagration or explosion which
will 'blast open'[39] the historical stagnation that

it chronicles.

Again, the experience of writing *A Child's History of England* may have encouraged Dickens to think in these terms. Here a beneficial fire is contemplated - even if a successful repeat is difficult to predict:

> The Great Fire .... was a great blessing to
> the city afterwards, for it arose from its
> ruins much improved - built more regularly,
> more widely, more cleanly and carefully, and
> therefore much more healthily. It might be
> more healthy than it is, but there are some
> people in it still - even now, at this time,
> nearly two hundred years later - so selfish,
> so pig-headed, and so ignorant, that I doubt
> if even another Great Fire would warm them up
> to do their duty. (*CHE*, 503)

And in *Bleak House* there are various signs of this recurrence of this event. 'Spontaneous combustion' is the most obvious of these, foreshadowed as it is by Krook's breath at his very first appearance, "issuing in visible smoke from his mouth, as if he were on fire within" (v, 50); but the process is not confined to him - Chadband, for instance, appears to run on train oil, and to be smoking. There is so much human wood in the novel - Judy Smallweed is half a walking-stick, her mother "a clattering broomstick that ought to be burnt" (xxi, 298), and there is even *Lignum Vitae* - that a conflagration seems imminent: when Krook is discovered burnt, he is described as "a small charred and broken log of wood sprinkled with white ashes, or is it coal". (xxxii, 455) As in *Barnaby Rudge* the household fires appear ready to revolt - even the druidical oaks of Chesney Wold: "The blazing fires of faggot and coal - Dedlock timber and antediluvian forest - that blaze upon the broad wide hearths, and wink in the twilight on the frowning woods, sullen to see how trees are sacrificed, do not exclude the enemy." (xxviii, 389) The grotesque Guy Fawkes's who inhabit the novel (Smallweed chief amongst them) also carry a historical variant of the political theme - Smallweed is "a person without the use of his lower-extremities, carried upstairs similarly to a Guy" (lv, 757), and Judy, "the lean female with a face like a pinched mask" who accompanies him on his visit to Rouncewell, "might be expected immediately to recite the popular verses, commemorative of the time when they did contrive to blow Old England up alive". (xxvi, 368) But it is Boythorn, in his denunciation of Chancery, who calls in the loudest and clearest voice for the necessary explosion:

> Nothing but a mine below it on a busy day in term time, with all its records, rules, and precedents collected in it, and every functionary belonging to it also, high and low, upward and downward, from its son the Accountant-General to its father the Devil, and the whole blown to atoms with ten thousand hundred weight of gunpowder, would reform it in the least. (ix, 118)

And what will force this explosion is the familiar paradoxical 'fantastic reality' in which the 'terrible grotesque' of *Bleak House* resides. "It surely is a strange fact," muses Allan Woodcourt, trying to find a refuge for Jo, "that in the heart of a civilised world this creature in human form should be more difficult to dispose of than an unowned dog", and the narrator reflects: "But it is none the less a fact because of its strangeness, and the difficulty remains." (xlvii, 636) Likewise, the burial of Nemo in a graveyard that will breed disease is "a shameful testimony to future ages, how civilization and barbarism walked this boastful island together". (xi, 151) A 'terrible grotesque' thrives, in a society that imagines itself to represent the avant-garde of progress.

Hard Times announces itself as an ironic epic at the end of chapter 2:

> Say, good M'Choakumchild. When from thy boiling store, thou shalt fill each jar brim full by-and-by, dost thou think that thou wilt always kill outright the robber Fancy working within - or sometimes only maim him and distort him? (*HT*, I, ii, 8)

The delicious style of invocation ("sing, heavenly muse") and the command of blank verse offer an evident parody of Milton: M'Choakumchild fits Beelzebub nicely. As a muse, though, he clearly makes a poor showing, unable, for all his store of fact, to foretell the outcome of the epic action;

and the Arabian Nights reference stands for a proper imaginative outlet that M'Choakumchild, seeking to extirpate, may in fact only distort, and turn into something monstrous. The novel shows us two forms of the grotesque - its true, 'innocent' form as embodied in the circus, and its distorted form, ironically reflected over and again in the monstrosities of the industrial north that include, as a central exhibit, the 'hell' of Coketown (seen in full glare, for instance, when Tom comes to persuade Louisa to marry Bounderby for his sake, and she accompanies him to the door, "whence the fires of Coketown could be seen, making the distance lurid" - I, xiv, 94). This mirror image is an expression of a central Dickensian perception about the grotesque - that, facing in Victorian England a central threat to its existence, it has simply metamorphosed and resurrected itself in the new world from which it is supposedly expelled.

There are immediate suggestions of these ironic patterns in the novel. Mr. Gradgrind, the representative of fact, has a strangely grotesque physiognomy: his forehead, like a square wall beneath which his eyes find "commodious cellarage" (I, i, 2), is a derivative of Sampson Brass's "protruding forehead, and retreating eyes". (OCS, xi, 84) Appearances also tell in the case of Bounderby: his great "puffed head and forehead, swelled veins in his temple" (iv, 14) hark back to Dr. Creakle in David Copperfield with his "thick veins in his forehead, a little nose, and a large chin". (DC, vi, 81) Mrs. Sparsit, who has the bushy eyebrows of a Miss Murdstone, and is described by Mr. Harthouse as a "griffin" (II, ii, 227 - like Mrs. Pipchin) has an even more remarkably grotesque relative, Lady Scadgers ("an immensely fat old woman, with an inordinate appetite for butcher's meat, and a mysterious leg which had now refused to get out of bed for fourteen years" - I, vii, 42 - that leg, it appears, one of those Dickensian limbs with its own volition). Add to the 'school of fact' grotesques Bitzer, continually associated with insects (e.g. at I, ii, 5), skeletal in appearance, "fit colourless servitor at Death's door (II, ix, 196) and making strange mechanical noises at night in lieu of snores ("I have heard him on such occasions produce sounds of a nature similar to what may be sometimes heard in Dutch clocks" - II, viii, 182), and the opposition - even Mr. Sleary himself, with his "one fixed eye, and one loose eye", and "a voice (if it can be called so) like the efforts of a broken old pair of bellows" (I, vi, 35) - begins to look remarkably tame. In this ironic perspective, anything the circus can do, Coketown can do better, it seems.

The infernal world that these creatures foster and promote through their philosophies, then, is inevitably fantastical. As often before (cf. *Nicholas Nickleby* and *Dombey and Son*) high speed travel provides a good angle for seeing grotesque truth - Coketown is glimpsed in its essence from the express train: "The lights in the great factories which looked, when they were illuminated, like Fairy palaces - or the travellers by express-train said so - were all extinguished." (I, x, 64) Its chimneys produce "monstrous serpents of smoke" (I, xi, 69) - hellish enough, indeed, and ironically like the fantastic forms that had emerged from the twisted chimneys of *The Maypole* - that symbol of conservative, old England - in *Barnaby Rudge*. The pistons of its steam-engines are first compared to an elephant, and then assimilated to it, so that the town takes on a fantastically exotic appearance, with strong Eastern suggestions, especially in the summer, when its atmosphere was "like the breath of the simoom". (II, i, 111) Yet essentially "all seasons are alike" to it - the essential point of Coketown being that its time is more like that of eternity, in hell, than that of growth and change. 2

Like *Bleak House*, the novel is full of demonic figures preying upon souls in torment. Gradgrind may be the mildest, associated ironically with the eastern theme of the novel through the statistical blue books that line his study ("although Mr. Gradgrind did not take after Blue Beard, his room was quite a blue chamber in its abundance of blue books" - I, xv, 96). Mrs. Sparsit is naturally related more to classical demons as she insinuates the difference of age between Bounderby and Louisa, "and, as she bent her again contracted eyebrows over her steaming cup, rather looked as if her classical countenance were invoking the infernal gods" (I, vii, 44); later, interrogating Tom Gradgrind about the whereabouts of Harthouse, she is unmasked, "mentally devoting the whelp to the Furies for being so uncommunicative". (II, xi, 208) Stephen Blackpool is tormented by his wife - or rather the "demon in her shape" that has possession of him. (I, xii, 81)

But the most extended ironic working-out of the idea of diabolical possession centres upon the relationship of Harthouse and Tom. Harthouse

arrives in Coketown "weary of everything and putting
no more faith in anything than Lucifer". (II, i,
119) The talismanic power of alcohol and cigars
quickly enables him to assume dominance over Tom;
he is soon found "looking pleasantly at the whelp,
as if he knew himself to be a kind of agreeable
demon who had only to hover over him, and he must
give up his whole soul if required". (II, iii,
133) Harthouse's skill (and Tom's obtuseness) is
such that it is soon possible for him to transfer
these metaphors to Tom, making him the devil ("if
you will open your bedevilments to me when they
come thick upon you, I may show you better ways out
of them than you can find yourself" - II, vii, 177).
The driving out of Harthouse from Coketown, then,
represents a kind of secular exorcism: as soon as
Sissy exerts *her* power, the rhetoric of 'natural'
influence and persuasion replaces the rhetoric of
possession.

The psychological subtlety with which such
themes are explored in Dickens's mature work is
well illustrated in the case of Louisa. With her,
the language of demonic possession is present at an
internal level, manifest first in her 'tiredness'
(I, iii, 13), her preoccupation with eschatology,
with mutability and apocalypse. In her case, 'self-
possession' does the work of possession: as she
explains to her father, she has been engaged in a
confused struggle with a demon whose side is
unclear:

> With a hunger and thirst upon me, father,
> which have never been for a moment appeased;
> with an ardent impulse towards some region
> where rules, and figures, and definitions were
> not quite absolute; I have grown up, battling
> every inch of the way ... in this strife I
> have almost repulsed and crushed my better
> angel into a demon. (II, xii, 217)

There is a poignancy in her recognition of the
'regions of pain' that surround her, and something
of the 'terrible grotesque' in the particular
maiming and distortion of fancy that goes on in her.
What appears quite evident, then, is that the
reign of fact is far from having established itself
in Coketown, or killed off the robber Fancy. The
hypocrisy of utilitarianism is revealed, in fact,
at an even more direct level - it has its own
cherished fictions. The central 'philosophical'
characters in the novel are engaged in manufacturing

their own epic structurings of events in a rhetoric whose flimsiness generates some delicious parodic 'sportive grotesqueness'.

The most obvious instances of such fictions are the evasive lies of the Coketown capitalists:

> Whenever a Coketowner felt he was ill-used - that is to say, whenever he was not left entirely alone, and it was proposed to hold him accountable for the consequences of any of his acts - he was sure to come with the awful menace, that he would 'sooner pitch his property into the Atlantic'. (II, i, 110-111)

Part of the irony is in the word 'popular' - this kind of imaginative work is miles away, in fact, from the art of the circus; the perpetrators of these fictions trample upon anything truly 'popular'. But we see how, where it suits their interests, their imaginative powers are active enough: witness of course Bounderby's fairy story of his deprived upbringing, of his ogrish mother - he describes her, unwittingly, as "an old woman who seems to have been flying into town on a broomstick" (II, viii, 185) - and drunken grandmother.

But the most extended and brilliant example concerns Mrs. Sparsit's epic *Inferno* for Louisa and Harthouse. She is the obverse of those characters who, from Martin Chuzzlewit to William Dorrit to Pip, build themselves castles in the air - her fantasy is a staircase into hell. It is appropriate that in a novel where a systematic attack is mounted upon the imagination, the major fantasies of its protagonists should be vindictive and cruel:

> Now, Mrs. Sparsit was not a poetical woman; but she took an idea in the nature of an allegorical fancy, into her head. Much watching of Louisa, and much consequent observation of her impenetrable demeanour, which keenly whetted and sharpened Mrs. Sparsit's edge, must have given her as it were a lift, in the way of inspiration. She erected in her mind a mighty staircase, with a dark pit of shame and ruin at the bottom; and down these stairs, from day to day and hour to hour, she saw Louisa coming. (II, x, 201-2)

Mrs. Sparsit is presented here, ironically, as an alternative novelist, with her own epic structure of beginning, middle and end, and her own private

access to the muse M'Choakumchild. Yet her
inspirational 'lift' is in fact a descent, and her
'edge' is not a sharpness of wit or observation;
she wants to get her knife in, in a fairly literal
way, playing chronos in the fiction for which she
borrows organic rhetoric: "she waits for the last
fall, or for the ripeness and fulness of the harvest
of her hopes." (II, x, 205) In the manner of
Greek gods and goddesses, and according to the
canons of classical art, she participates in her
own creation, descending from those heights from
which (like 'Allegory' on Tulkinghorn's ceiling)
she observes what goes on: "she would shoot with
consummate velocity from the roof to the hall, yet
would be in full possession of her breath and
dignity on the moment of her arrival there." (II,
ix, 192) She writes her own romance of Louisa's
melodramatic fall - Dickens's command of *Erlebte
Rede* grown masterly in this novel:

> Lo, Louisa coming out of the house! Hastily
> cloaked and muffled, and stealing away. She
> elopes! She falls from the lowermost stair,
> and is swallowed up in the gulf. (II, xi, 213)

But the rhetoric is manifestly shaky: Mrs.
Sparsit's sleuthing is rewarded, not with the
dramatic descent of Louisa into hell, but with a
soaking, as she loses sight of her prey in the rain,
and harvests only "a stagnant verdure on her general
exterior, such as accumulates on an old park fence
in a mouldy lane". (214) Louisa *does* fall - at her
father's feet; and at the same time there is
Stephen's agonised torment in Old Hell Shaft. Such
real terrors - the paths around Coketown are indeed
'mouldy lanes', and later Sissy and Rachael walk in
the country, "sometimes getting over a fragment of
fence so rotten that it dropped at a touch of the
foot" (III, vi, 265) - pointedly contrast with the
impoverished fictions of a classical *grande dame*,
which appropriately issue forth in the splendid
grotesque comparison of her to a rotting fence.
Risking repetition, this discussion of *Hard
Times* may conclude by re-emphasising how such
'ignoble' Coketown grotesques - the imagery of
ghosts and phantoms often accompanies them, as when
M'Choakumchild, ironically imitating the illiterate
Krook, is described as "a dry Ogre chalking ghastly
white figures" (I, iii, 9) on the blackboard - are
mirrors or shadows of the 'true' or 'natural'
grotesque. In this form it is an essential part of

popular art, appealing to the taste for the marvellous and surprising, for forms that change and metamorphose into one another with surprise transitions that combine pleasure and horror. It is embodied of course in this novel in the circus: Sissy Jupe's father is a grotesque artist, a clown who, as a confrère of Grimaldi, is losing his touch, in symbolic expression of the difficulty, in a mechanised society, of maintaining such an art (significantly connected with Italy, the home of the *commedia dell'arte*, of Punch and Harlequin). The plan of Dickens's novel - pointedly distancing itself from Mrs. Sparsit's - will show a 'natural' reassertion of this world: Sissy becomes the major power in the latter half of the novel, vanquishing Harthouse, redeeming Louisa and her father. And the whelp Tom, unredeemable within the confines of the novel, ends up appropriately enough in a circus disguise that is described sarcastically as "disgraceful grotesqueness". (III, vii, 284) The careful art of the novel has shown how "a young gentleman, whose imagination had been strangled in his cradle, should still be inconvenienced by its ghost in the form of grovelling sensualities". (II, iii, 132) Only those forces that Coketown had sought to extirpate now appear capable of saving him.

It will be immediately apparent from this discussion of *Bleak House* and *Hard Times* that no very precise or direct relation between the two works and Ruskin's theory of the grotesque has been suggested. Despite some interesting connections and parallels between the two writers, such an approach would no doubt misfire, and founder on vague notions of influence or on the difficulties of comparing abstract ideas with concrete artistic representations. Nonetheless, it may be possible to claim a similarity in the *terms* the two writers employ for the grotesque. Sharing a language and a culture at a particular moment of history, they seem compelled to think in religious terms, to connect the grotesque with sin and hell,[40] in at least one of its phases, and to work with an essentially dualistic mode of perception of binary oppositions. In both cases, however, the terms of these oppositions are felt as shifting and unstable, combining and re-combining in ways that - despite the equally obvious *particular* differences between Dickens and

Ruskin - constitute the essential energy of both men's work.

However this may be, Ruskin's attitude towards Dickens continues to display a significant degree of admiration and respect after *Hard Times*, at least until the years of his mental instability. The terms in which he praises the novel in *Unto this Last*, for instance - "let us not lose the use of Dickens's wit and insight, because he chooses to speak in a circle of stage fire"[41] - suggest an attentive response to the figurative patterns of his imagination, which, as we have seen, focus about the circles and fires of hell as well as of the theatre. Unable to attend the Farewell Banquet to celebrate Dickens's departure for the United States in 1867, Ruskin - like Carlyle and Browning - sent a commendatory letter. Their relationship deserves further probing.

NOTES

1. Or so it would seem: Kirk H. Beetz's *John Ruskin: A Bibliography, 1900-1974* (Metuchen, N.J., The Scarecrow Press, 1976), for instance, contains no reference to any study in that period; Peter Conrad's *The Victorian Treasure-House* (London, Collins, 1973) is perhaps the exception that proves the rule. Prior to 1900, Dickens seems to have been quite frequently linked with Ruskin - by George Bernard Shaw, for instance, who praises *Hard Times* by saying "This is Karl Marx, Carlyle, Ruskin, Morris" (quoted in William Oddie, *Dickens and Carlyle*, p.143).

2. See the *Atlantic Monthly* (March, 1877) essay on *Hard Times*. Quoted from Collins, *Dickens: The Critical Heritage*, pp.315-316.

3. *op. cit.*, pp.33-34.

4. Quoted from Collins, *op. cit.*, p.445.

5. "That Dickens was a great genius and is permanently among the classics is certain. But the genius was that of a great entertainer, and he had for the most part no profounder responsibility as a creative artist than this description suggests." *The Great Tradition* (London, Chatto and Windus, 1948), p.19.

6. Quoted from *The Works of John Ruskin* (Library Edition) eds. E.T. Cook and Alexander Wedderburn (London, George Allen, 1903; 39 vols.), I, 155.

7. See Letters, II, 44, 462.

8. Quoted from Collins, *op. cit.*, p.100

(letter of 6/6/41).

9. Quoted from Derrick Leon, *Ruskin: The Great Victorian* (London, Routledge and Kegan Paul, 1949), p.44 (from *Praeterita* - *Works* (Library Edition), XXXV, 202).

10. Letters, III, 462.

11. Quoted from Robert Hewison, *John Ruskin: the Argument of the Eye* (London, Thames and Hudson, 1976), p.47. The whole chapter, "Ruskin and the Picturesque", is useful and relevant here.

12. Cf. above, Chapter 7.

13. See *Works* (Library Edition), IV, 337-9.

14. Leon, *op. cit.*, pp.137-8, has a good account of this episode.

15. *op. cit.*, p.192.

16. Collins, *op. cit.*, p.443 (letter of 19/6/70).

17. "Leech's 'The Rising Generation'." See also Ronald Paulson, "The Tradition of Comic Illustration from Hogarth to Cruikshank", *George Cruikshank: A Revaluation*, ed. Robert L. Patten (Princeton, N.J., Princeton University Press, 1974), p.58.

18. In consequence of a letter he received on 18 December 1849 from Mrs. Jane Seymour Hill, a chiropodist on whom Dickens had modelled the character. She wrote: "... widowed in all but my good name you shew up personal deformities with insinuations that by the purest of my sex may be construed to the worst of purposes." (Letters, V, 674n).

19. *Household Words*, 15/6/50. Quoted from Leon, *op. cit.*, p.138.

20. *Works* (Library Edition), XI, 173.

21. This is Ruskin's habitual style of referring to Dickens - see in particular Appendix 3 to *Modern Painters* III (*Works* (Library Edition), V, 428).

22. Cf.Chapter 1 above, p.7 and fn. 23.

23. Arthur Clayborough, in *The Grotesque in English Literature* (Oxford, Clarendon Press, 1965), pp.36-42, has a useful summary of Ruskin's position.

24. Hewson, *op. cit.*, p.42. Cf. the pre-occupation with the 'true' grotesque as early as 1837-8 in *The Poetry of Architecture*.

25. See *Works* (Library Edition), X, 214.

26. Quoted from Collins, *op. cit.*, p.314 (the source is *Unto this Last*, first published in the *Cornhill Magazine*, 1860).

27. Letters, V, 654 (to Forster, 20/11/49).

28. Here John Lucas (one of the few critics to

make much of the relation between Dickens and
Ruskin) offers some useful discriminations - see
The Melancholy Man (London, Methuen, 1970), esp.
pp.274-282.
     29. *The Stones of Venice, Works* (Library
Edition), XI, 151.
     30. *Works* (Library Edition), XI, 174.
     31. *ibid.*, 187. See also Clayborough, *op.
cit.*, p.37.
     32. *ibid.* For Dante and the Grotesque, see
also Spitzer, *op. cit.*
     33. Shelley's *Peter Bell the Third*:

> Hell is a city much like London -
> A populous and a smoky city;
> There are all sorts of people undone,
> And there is little or no fun done;
> Small justice shown, and still less
>   pity. (quoted from the Norton Critical

Edition of *Shelley's Prose and Poetry*, eds. Donald
H. Reiman and Sharon B. Powers (New York, W.W.
Norton and Co., 1977), p.330)
has had a substantial progeny, including Brecht's
Nachdenkend über die Hölle of 1943:

> Nachdenkend, wie ich höre, über die
> Hölle,
> Fand mein Bruder Shelley, sie sei ein
> Ort
> Gleichend ungefähr der Stadt London. Ich,
> Der ich nicht in London lebe, sondern
> in Los Angeles,
> Finde, nachdenkend über die Hölle, sie
> muss
> Noch mehr Los Angeles gleichen.
> (*Gedichte*, ed. E. Hauptmann and B.

Slupianek (Frankfurt-am-Main, Suhrkamp Verlag,1960;
10 volumes), VI, 52. Some aspects of Dickens's
relation to the topos are dealt with in F.S.
Schwarzbach, *Dickens and the City* (London, Athlone
Press, 1979), especially pp.1-30, 'The Genesis of a
Myth'. Cf.also M. Hollington's review of
Schwarzbach, *Durham University Journal* LXXIV no. 1
(December 1981), 149-50.
     34. Cf. Peter Conrad, *The Victorian Treasure-
House*, p.154: "Ruskin finds in Turner something
rather like the streaky bacon of Dickens's double
plots, a twisting together of the vulgar with the
noble, of Keats and Dante ..."
     35. See Dante's *Inferno*, Canto XXXIV, 10 ff,
in (e.g.) the edition of Grandgent and Singleton

(Cambridge, Mass., Harvard University Press, 1972),
p.302; Signorelli's frescoes are an illustration of
this scene.

36.   However, there are textual problems here;
Dickens's manuscript shows that he wrote 'augur' and
not 'argue' (see the Norton Critical Edition of
Bleak House, eds. Ford and Monod (New York, W.W.
Norton and Co., 1977), p.690n.   Thus the allusion
to *Paradise Lost* IV, 830-31, where Satan chides
those angels who did not recognise him ("Not to
know me argues yourselves unknown/The lowest of
your throng") is less clear.   But the phrase
structure, whether it be 'augurs' or 'argues',
seems incontestably allusive.

37.   The star/satellite imagery which
surrounds Lady Dedlock ('fashionable intelligence'
takes her as the centre of its system) is clearly
ironically related to the actual 'hells' in the
novel.

38.   Cf. Chapter 5 above.

39.   Cf. Walter Benjamin, 'Der Begriff der
Geschichte', *Gesammelte Schriften* eds. Tiedemann
and Schweppenhaüser (Frankfurt am Main, Suhrkamp
Verlag, 1974; 5 vols.), I(2), 703.

40.   According to Arieh Sachs, *The English
Grotesque* (Jerusalem, Israel Universities Press,
1969), "All English grotesques are the product of a
peculiarly Western (or should one say Northern?)
conception of evil."   (xix).

41.   Quoted from Collins, *op. cit.*, p.314.

Chapter Eleven

THE GROTESQUE AND TRAGICOMEDY: *GREAT EXPECTATIONS*

"Such a very fine, new and grotesque idea has opened upon me, that I begin to doubt whether I had better not cancel the little paper, and reserve the notion for a new book." These are the words that announce, in a letter to Forster, the origins of *Great Expectations*, a major novel generated, like Joyce's *Ulysses*, from a much smaller component of another work (*The Uncommercial Traveller*).[1] At least one writer has challenged their significance: Frederick Page, writing in the introduction to the Oxford Illustrated Dickens, argues that they are hasty and ill-chosen, and that "the critic who should adopt them would write himself down an ass".[2] Yet Dickens appears to have stuck to them over a period of weeks, if not months, in 1860, returning to them after the completion of the first number of the new novel, and jogging Forster's memory: "Of course I have got in the pivot on which the story will turn too - and which indeed, as you remember, was the grotesque, tragicomic conception that first encouraged me."[3]

The words 'grotesque' and 'tragicomic' seem to refer, above all, to the relationship between Magwitch and Pip, which is characterised from the start by mixed emotions. Magwitch terrifies Pip in the first scene with his threats to have his "heart and liver out" (*GE*, i, 3); but he is also a comic ogre, his sadistic bullying, to an adult reader, transparently fictitious. When it comes to the recognition scene, where Magwitch unmasks himself as Pip's benefactor, the roles are partly reversed, but the feelings similarly complicated. Perplexed and apprehensive, Magwitch speaks "with a smile that was like a frown, and a frown that was like a smile" (xxxix, 303); and Pip reacts to his repeated apologies for 'lowness' with nervous giggling:

216

"Some sense of the grimly-ludicrous moved me to a
fretful laugh ...".(xi, 314) Both scenes contain
those "grotesque features" that at Dotheboys Hall
"in a less interested observer than Nicholas, might
have provoked a smile" (*NN*, viii, 88-9), and that
for Dickens, visiting the poor in the East End of
London, caused embarrassment: "I was wretched,
looking on; and yet the boiler-maker and the poor
man with the legs filled me with a sense of drollery
not to be kept down by any pressure."[4]

Yet at the same time, if we take the scene
(which Harry Stone refers to as a 'magical
inversion'[5]) to be that 'pivot' on which the novel
turns, more than merely local effects are involved.
With Magwitch's appearance, essentially, Pip's
"great expectations had all dissolved, like our own
marsh mists before the sun". (*GE*, lvii, 445); the
fantasy narrative he has constructed for himself,
as Miss Havisham's heir, destined to marry Estella,
is revealed as the equivalent of the many 'castles
in the air' of previous novels (*Martin Chuzzlewit,
Little Dorrit*, etc.). A complex of ironies unfolds:
the contrast between the 'low' Magwitch and the
'high' Miss Havisham collapses, both of them having
attempted the creation of a 'gentleman' or 'gentle-
woman', with equally disastrous consequences, as a
revenge for the wrongs they have suffered, and both
of them regarding the products as their possessions
("All on you owns stocks and land: which on you
owns a brought-up London gentleman?" - xxxix, 306).
At the same time, paradoxically, the loss of his
expectations is to offer to Pip for the first time
an opportunity for real change and personal development through the acceptance of and assumption of
responsibility for his despised benefactor.

Paradoxicality, in fact, is one of the most
important and distinctive features of the novel.[6]
It has its genesis in the special combination of
grotesque and tragicomic effects that the first
person narrative is so skilfully calculated to
articulate. Pip's is at once the most self-conscious
first-person narrative in Dickens's work (more so
than David Copperfield's, and certainly than
Esther's in *Bleak House*), and yet at the same time
the consciousness it records is the most self-
deluding. "All other swindlers upon earth are
nothing to the self-swindlers" (xxviii, 213): this
is perhaps the crucial formulation of a paradox
whose significance is more than merely psychological.
It serves also to illumine the subtle, profound and
profoundly depressing contradictions of a society

where oppression has become learned behaviour and internalised as self-suppression. 'Voluntarily' dedicating himself to money, class and status, the hero does his own self-exploiting, losing himself in a labyrinth of mistaken needs and desires, from which he can only be liberated by the destruction of his most cherished hopes.

Great Expectations, like *David Copperfield*, is thus a *Bildungsroman*,[7] asking the central question: how does the young human individual change and develop, in an unpropitious physical and social environment? This stress on constraining material conditions is of considerable significance, even if (characteristically, for this stage of Dickens's career) its expression is at least partly symbolic. The formative conditions of life in which Pip grows up, the surroundings out of which his mistaken perceptions are developed, are the Romney marshes, a "flat dark wilderness" (I, i) which is worked into a many-sided allegory and determinant of consciousness.

The first significance-bearing aspect of the marsh landscape - its dull monotony - had been used in earlier works. In *David Copperfield*, Steerforth expresses his bitter sense of the futility of life with an appeal to the countryside of Yarmouth: "Look to the right, and you'll see a flat country, with a good deal of marsh in it; look to the left, and you'll see the same." (*DC*, xxiii, 342) In *Bleak House*, Phil Squod has only been outside the city once - to see what he describes as '*the* marshes' - and his view of them is taciturnly unromantic: "They was flat. And miste." (*BH*, xxvi, 365) In *Great Expectations*, the convicts are almost as terse, but more emphatic: "A most beastly place. Mudbank, mist, swamp, and work: work, swamp, mist, and mudbank." (*GE*, xxviii, 217) Pip is glad to leave such a flat and tedious world behind, its 'lowness' interpreted in terms of a class hierarchy: "No more low wet grounds, no more dykes and sluices ... farewell monotonous acquaintances of my childhood." (xix, 139)

A second, paradoxically distinctive feature of the marsh countryside is its indistinctness. It is almost a *tabula rasa* upon which the mind may project its own significances: "The marshes were just a long black horizontal line then, as I stopped to look after him; and the river was just another horizontal line, not nearly so broad, nor yet so black; and the sky was just a row of long angry red lines and dense black lines intermixed." (i, 4)

218

Pip certainly does so, first gloomily, like
Steerforth ("I remember that at a later period of
my 'time', I used to stand about the churchyard on
Sunday evenings, when night was falling, comparing
my own perspective with the windy marsh view, and
making out some likeness between them by thinking
how flat and low both were, and how on both there
came an unknown way and a dark mist and then the
sea" - xiv, 100) but later increasingly optimistic-
ally, as he weaves Miss Havisham and Estella into
the *Gestalt:* "When we had passed the village and
the church and the churchyard, and were out on the
marshes, and began to see the sails of the ships as
they sailed on, I began to combine Miss Havisham
and Estella with the prospect, in my usual way."
(xvii, 120) What he in fact succeeds in doing is
to compose for himself a conventionally 'picturesque'
(the word is associated with the inmates of Satis
House at xv, 103) landscape out of the hitherto
intractable materials that surround him: "... I
loitered into the country on Miss Havisham's side of
town ... thinking about my patroness, and painting
pictures of her plans for me." (xxix, 219)
     Yet as in other novels, the 'grotesque' is to
be preferred as a truer mode of representation as
the third emphasis that is placed upon the marsh
landscape in this novel, highlighting the mists and
the visual tricks that they play, suggests. Going
out to meet Magwitch in the early morning, Pip
encounters all manner of ghosts and hallucinations
in the mist:

     ... the marsh-mist was so thick, that the wooden
     finger on the post directing people to our
     village - a direction which they never accepted,
     for they never came there - was invisible to me
     until I was quite close under it. Then, as I
     looked at it, while it dripped, it seemed to my
     oppressed conscience like a phantom devoting me
     to the Hulks.
     The mist was heavier yet whenI got out upon the
     marshes, so that instead of my running at every-
     thing, everything seemed to run at me. (iii, 14)

     The passage suggests, not only the illusoriness
of 'prospects' and 'expectations' - in the marsh-
world, nothing reveals itself for what it is until
one comes upon it - but the weird and fantastical
shapes that are constructed by an intense imagination. The mists accompany Pip indoors - especially
to Satis House, where "the reluctant smoke which

hung in the room seemed colder than the clearer air - like our own marsh mist" (xi, 78); there, they provide further fuel to the active shaping of fantasies: "Is it to be wondered at if my thoughts were dazed as my eyes were, when I came out into the natural light from the misty yellow rooms?" (xii, 89)

And in this interior, the most powerful grotesque images of *Great Expectations* are presented. The lighting is in fact an important aspect of the effects created; everything takes place "in a pretty large room, well lighted with wax candles. No glimpse of daylight was to be seen in it". (viii, 52) The central figure is dressed in white, "faded and yellow", herself associated with the wax of the candles:

> Once, I had been taken to see some ghastly waxwork at the Fair, representing I know not what impossible personage lying in state. Once, I had been taken to one of our old marsh churches to see a skeleton in the ashes of a rich dress, that had been dug out of a vault under the church pavement. Now, waxwork and skeleton seemed to have dark eyes that moved and looked at me. I should have cried out, if I could. (viii, 53)

In this brilliant image, Miss Havisham appears as an intensified version of another grotesque - Mr. Murdstone, whose "squareness about the lower part of his face, and the dotted indication of the strong black beard he shaved close every day, reminded me of the waxwork that had travelled into our neighbourhood some half-a-year before". (*DC*, ii, 22)[8] Others like her also make an appearance before Pip in the surreal colours of Satis House - in particular the Arcimboldesque Sarah Pocket, "a little dry brown corrugated old woman, with a small face that might have been made of walnut shells" (xi, 80), metamorphosing when she sees Pip in his London gentleman's outfit ("her walnut-shell countenance likewise turned from brown to green and yellow" - xix, 148).

But of course the important, essential tragicomic feature of *Great Expectations* is that Pip, perceiving Miss Havisham's grotesqueness, nevertheless accepts it and her as a suitable benefactress. In *David Copperfield*, the connection David makes between Murdstone and the waxwork exhibition is the sign of quick, live (and artistically valid)

perception - it places Murdstone as a monstrosity.
But in *Great Expectations* Miss Havisham's ghastliness is simply a particularly vivid version of a
much more organised and systematic pattern of
relationships. Society as a whole, it could be
said, is represented as an *exhibition* of freaks.
   At any rate Miss Havisham's self-incarceration
- which represents Mrs. Clennam's, *Great Expectations* being a novel that (like *Little Dorrit*)
explores the ironic parallels of the world "convict
and free" (xxviii, 214) - is certainly to be linked,
in the first instance, with those convicts who
travel to the dockyard in Pip's company, together
with their keeper, who has "an air as if the
convicts were an interesting Exhibition not formally
open at the moment, and he the Curator". (xxviii,
214) The waxwork image spreads beyond the
'curiosity shop' of Satis House- to the Lord Chief
Justice in the London lawcourts, where "an exceedingly dirty and partially drunk minister of
justice" accosts Pip, "mentioning that awful
personage like waxwork, and presently offering him
at the reduced price of eighteenpence" (xx, 155);
to the "dreadful casts on a shelf, of faces
peculiarly swollen, and twitchy about the nose"
(154), that adorn Mr. Jagger's office and stand as
monuments to his 'professionalism' ("Famous clients
of ours that got us a world of credit" - xxiv, 189);
and to Wemmick's Walworth chamber of horrors:
"They're curiosities. And they're property." (190)
   But its intensest moment of tragicomedy may
come as Pip reads to Magwitch:

> ... he, not comprehending a single word, would
> stand before the fire surveying me with the
> air of an Exhibitor, and I would see him,
> between the fingers of the hand with which I
> shaded my face, appealing in dumb show to the
> furniture to take notice of my proficiency.
> The imaginary student pursued by the misshapen
> creature he had impiously made, was not more
> wretched than I, pursued by the creature who
> had made me, and recoiling from him with a
> stronger repulsion, the more he admired me and
> the fonder he was of me. (ix, 320)

Here Magwitch exhibits his reified 'curiosity' as
a property eligible to incite the admiration of
other objects: "which on you owns a brought-up
London gentleman?" is here, as it were, addressed
to the chairs. It is the evident consequence of

the treatment of convicts ("the great numbers on
their backs, as if they were street doors" - 214) -
Magwitch shows his man as he had been shown. Pip is
both Frankenstein and monster, made into a grotesque
by his master, and experiencing him likewise.

     In this novel Dickens thus makes acute and
sustained probings of that "fantastic paradox" that
had fascinated him at the outset of his career.[9] He
goes beyond the complex relations of the 'real' and
'fantastical' to consider the fundamental contradictions of Victorian society. Progress, material
wealth, comfort, power- the novel shows how these
bring, not contentment but newer and greater
unhappiness: "I drew away from the window, and sat
down in my one chair by the bedside, feeling it very
sorrowful and strange that this first night of my
bright fortunes should be the loneliest I had ever
known." (xviii, 137) Paradox engulfs Pip's
relationship to Joe, as soon as the consciousness of
money, class and status set a barrier between them,
causing Pip to feel ashamed at being seen by Bentley
Drummle in the company of Joe: "So, throughout
life, our worst weaknesses and meannesses are
usually committed for the sake of the people whom we
most despise." (xxvii, 206) And Pip's love for
Estella is shot through with a paradoxical
consciousness of its dubiety:

          Once for all; I knew to my sorrow, often and
          often, if not always, that I loved her against
          reason, against promise, against peace,
          against hope, against happiness, against all
          discouragement that could be. Once for all;
          I loved her none the less because I knew it,
          and it had no more influence in restraining me
          than if I had devoutly believed her to be
          human perfection. (xxix, 219)

     This, then, is Pip's "poor labyrinth". (219)
As soon as he leaves Joe and Biddy, he finds himself
"lost in the mazes of my future fortunes" (xviii,
133) as he follows a false star - Estella.
     Elsewhere in Dickens's work stars are felt as
remote and indifferent to human suffering.[10] Even
in this novel Pip recognises what is implied in her
name before he meets her:

          A man would die to-night of lying out on the
          marshes, I thought. And then I looked at the
          stars, and considered how awful it would be
          for a man to turn his face up to them as he

froze to death, and see no help or pity in all
the glittering multitude. (vii, 46)

He is to experience this 'awfulness' (at a psychological level) soon enough at Satis House, baying
to the stars, perhaps, "... in the dark in a
mysterious passage of an unknown house, bawling
Estella to a scornful young lady neither visible
nor responsive, and feeling it a dreadful liberty
so to roar out her name". (viii, 54) Set up on a
pinnacle by Pip (she makes his rustic stars appear
'low' by comparison at xviii, 136) she inevitably
causes unhappiness. "Oh she is thousands of miles
away from me," declares Pip in Werther-like fashion
at xxx, 234; until the revised ending of the novel,
the only stars he appears likely to achieve are
those offered by Orlick as a *quietus*: "I'll let
you go to the moon. I'll let you go to the stars."
(liii, 402)

The chief point of this mournful tragicomedy,
of course, is that Pip learns to accept the class
divisions of the Victorian social hierarchy through
his contact with Estella. "Why he is a common
labouring-boy!" (viii, 55) is the taunt that
wounds him; instead of rebelling against it - as
earlier heroes from Oliver Twist to David Copperfield do - Pip accepts the categories and power
relationships involved. As an apt pupil, he very
quickly learns to employ them himself, even in the
supposedly 'free' and rebellious lies he tells
about Satis House, in which his fantasies are shown
to centre upon his enslavement: "And we all had
cake and wine on gold plates. And I got up behind
the coach to eat mine, because she told me to."
(ix, 63) Later, he multiplies fetishes and debases
himself in front of others - eating with Herbert
Pocket, for instance, at a fashionable restaurant:
"We went and had lunch at a celebrated house which
I then quite venerated, but now believe to have
been the most abject superstition in Europe."
(xxii, 175)

Learning to look up, Pip also learns to look
down; at this stage at least, his is unquestionably
an 'authoritarian personality'.[11] But his assertions
of power and dominance remain largely at the level
of fantasy - chafings that other impulses have to
suppress. Like Dombey he wants money to be all-
powerful, and finds it isn't - in cases like
keeping Joe away from him, for instance: "If I
could have kept him away by paying money, I
certainly would have paid money." (xxviii, 206)

Like Dorrit he learns that the 'shame' of the past -
"I had been brought up a blacksmith in a country
place" (xxii, 168) - isn't easily erased; when an
oarsman praises Pip for the strength of his arm,
economic sanctions have again to be held in check:
"This practical authority confused me very much, by
saying I had the arm of a blacksmith. If he could
have known how nearly the compliment lost him his
pupil, I doubt he would have paid it." (xxiii, 184)

But in *Great Expectations* the tragicomic
effects are, if anything, sharper. Autobiography is
close at hand, and *blacksmithery* an obvious encoding
of the *blacking* factory, the transmutation from
uncreative to creative labour expressing that
revaluation of childhood suffering upon which
Dickens in this novel (as other critics have noted)[12]
appears to be engaged. The most immediate impression, however, is that Pip - covering up, not the
bitterest experiences of his life, but the most
joyous - is more pitiful than Dorrit. Especially
since (now like Merdle rather than Dorrit) he
creates for himself a servant in *boots* to haunt and
torment:

> I had even started a boy in boots - top boots -
> in bondage and slavery to whom I might be said
> to pass my days. For after I had made this
> monster (out of the refuse of my washerwoman's
> family) and had clothed him with a blue coat,
> canary waistcoat, white cravat, creamy
> breeches, and the boots already mentioned, I
> had to find him a little to do and a great
> deal to eat; and with both of these horrible
> requirements he haunted my existence. (xxvii,
> 207)

Here Pip appears in the position of the fowl
that Mr.Pumblechook serves up to celebrate his "well-
deserved" fortune, congratulated in phrases that
reverberate deliciously: "Ah, poultry, poultry.
You little thought ... when you was a young fledg-
ling, what was in store for you." (xix, 146) The
grotesque art of the novel generates such connections between people and animals, or people and
things. As a child Pip is both - "I often served
as a connubial missile." (ii, 7); and as the
Gargery's and Pumblechooks sit down to supper, they
torture him by comparing him to the pig they eat,
elongating the sadism with their slow narrative
elaboration of the slaughter: "You would have been
disposed of for so many shillings according to the

market price of the article, and Dunstable the butcher would have come up to you as you lay in your straw, and he would have whipped you under his left arm, and with his right he would have tucked up his frock to get a penknife from out of his waistcoat-pocket, and he would have shed your blood and had your life." (iii, 24) (By comparison, the cannibalism of Magwitch appears mild, and excusable: "You young dog ... what fat cheeks you ha' got ... Darn me if I couldn't eat 'em" - i, 2).

From this reification, Pip learns to reify himself and others. The heartlessness that Kafka noted as a feature of Dickens's style[13] is to be noted in Pip's language - the servant is from "the refuse of my washerwoman's family", and later he is replaced by "an inflammatory old female, assisted by an animated rag-boy whom she called her niece". (xl, 309) Magwitch is imagined as a clock - "something clicked in his throat as if he had works in him like a clock, and was going to strike"(iii, 16), and Wemmick's mouth is a slit into which he throws biscuits "as if he were posting them". (xxiv, 188) People seem to work on mechanistic rather than organicist principles - the convicts met in the stagecoach seem "to have more breathing business to do than another man" (xxviii, 216), and one of Mr. Pocket's pupils seems to have an electric head ("Startop ... was reading and holding his head, as if he thought himself in danger of exploding it with too strong a charge of knowledge." - xxiii, 179).[14] Animate and inanimate matter is frequently left undistinguished - Jaggers laughs with his boots, and Wemmick produces a key from his coat-collar that is "like an iron pigtail". (xxiv, 188)

So that when Joe arrives in London and vigorously clasps Pip by the hands, "working them straight up and down, as if I had been the last-patented Pump" (xxvii, 207), the ironies are sharp. Pip perceives the accost as an affront that reifies him - yet he'd wanted to keep Joe away, by paying money. The vigour of the blacksmith's arm is again an uncomfortable reminder of the past, as are the implications of 'work', for which Pip as a gentleman has now conceived a distaste. It is for him now - personified in Joe - a form of "dull endurance" (xiv, 100), assimilated to the routines of a convict-like existence ("mudbank, mist, swamp and work; work, swamp, mist and mudbank" - xxviii, 217).

For the conceptions of work dominant in *Great Expectations* form an essential part of the analysis

of the reification of the self and others. Miss
Havisham's 'employment' of Pip sets the tone: she
needs someone to watch at play, engaged in meaning-
less and destructive activity (neighbour-beggaring)
with Estella, in order to fill the voids of her
'leisure'. She gets angry when this occupation
appears not to inspire him (xi, 77-78), and proposes
other unproductive labour - walking her around in
a circle. 'Gentlemen' mustn't do anything useful,
though brewing (presumably because its end product
is stupefaction) appears to be all right, as Herbert
Pocket explains: "While you cannot possibly be
genteel and bake, you may be as genteel as never was
and brew." (xxii, 169) And so Pip quickly learns
"loitering along the High-Street" (xv, 109) -
ironically, like Orlick - in anticipation of his
preferment; whilst his female counterparts are
brought up in the manner of Mrs. Pocket, who "in
the nature of things must marry a title, and who
was to be guarded from the acquisition of plebeian
domestic knowledge". (xxiii, 179)

     Bourgeois distortions of work take a different
form. Mr. Jaggers is the opposite of the gentleman
amateur, collapsing distinctions between the world
and his work. Where Wemmick separates the personal
from the professional, he scrambles them, so that
even in his dining-room "in a corner was a little
table of papers with a shaded lamp; so that he
seemed to bring the office with him in that respect
too, and to wheel it out". (xxvi, 200) People for
him are objects upon which to conduct professional
operations and manipulations - at dinner he 'works'
upon Bentley Drummle, attempting "to screw discourse
out of him". (200) Children, he acknowledges to
Pip late in the day, "he had reason to look upon as
so much spawn, to develop into the fish that were
to come into his net - to be defended, foresworn,
made orphans, bedevilled somehow". (li, 391)

     The fraudulence of such practices requires
protection, of course, through the erection of
'professional mysteries', and Jaggers is a major
exemplar of what Miss Mowcher calls "the rule of
Secrets in all trades". (DC, xxii, 332) Yet he
has colleagues - the Bow-Street Men from London,
for instance, who come to capture Mrs. Joe's
assailant, with their "mysterious manner of taking
their drink, that was almost as good as taking the
culprit" (xvi, 115), and the funeral mutes who put
on a show (the "curiosity shop" theme emerging once
more) at her funeral, "two dismally absurd persons,
each ostentatiously exhibiting a crutch done up in

a black bandage - as if that instrument could possibly communicate any comfort to anybody". (xxxv, 264) Yet the gentlemanly pursuit of leisure also has its grisly ostentations - "There was a gay fiction among us that we were constantly enjoying ourselves, and a skeleton truth that we never did" (xxxiv, 260) - and Pip too appears like a "ghastly waxwork", alienated from work and from himself.

Yet, after Magwitch's return, Pip is allowed the chance to recover the values he had lost. These of course reside in Joe - a 'true' gentleman, representing the 'real' world. He stands in the traditions of Little Nell, and the book is again a memorialising of the unremembered lives of supposedly insignificant people: "It is not possible to know how far the influence of any amiable honest-hearted duty-doing man flies out into the world." (xiv,101) There is an absence in him of any ostentation - anything to be exhibited as a 'curiosity': "Looking towards the open window, I saw light wreaths from Joe's pipe floating there, and I fancied it was like a blessing from Joe - not obtruded on me or paraded before me, but pervading the air we shared together." (xviii, 138) The mundane, humdrum pipe-smoke appears as a kind of solid counter-image to the feverish vapours conjured up in the marsh-mists.

And Joe's contentment is the sign of a capacity to recognise and create, in ordinary things, the marvellous and fantastic. For him the words 'common' and 'uncommon' carry meanings that are different from those put upon them by Pip or Pumblechook, and have no connection with class or taste: "oncommon plump" (xix, 140) means "remark- ably sudden". It is a perception of the world that can be regained by deprivation; Magwitch is to resemble Joe in the novel's later stages, apprecia- ting 'common' things because they are new to him again: "'If you knowed, dear boy,' he said to me, 'what it is to sit here alonger my dear boy, and have my smoke, arter having been day by day betwixt four walls, you'd envy me.'" (liv, 414) Like *The Old Curiosity Shop*, the novel undertakes an ironic adjectival inversion of its title - it demonstrates the virtues of 'small expectations'.

And these Pip, also by a process of rediscovery, is beginning to learn in the novel's later stages. He begins to 'see' Magwitch for what he is - not to compose him in a picturesque and self-centred prospect landscape: "in the hunted, wounded shackled creature who held my hand in his, I only saw a man who had meant to be my benefactor, and who had felt affectionately, gratefully, and generously, towards me with great constancy through a series of years." (liv, 423) Looking out of the window (that quintessential Dickensian activity, with its romantic antecedents[15]) at dawn on the day of Magwitch's escape, Pip sees a transposed world, where marshes are no longer flat and dull; the mists; in himself and out of himself, appear to be lifting:

> The winking lights upon the bridges were already pale, the coming sun was like a marsh of fire on the horizon ... As I looked along the clustered roofs, with church towers and spires shooting into the unusually clear air, the sun rose up, and a veil seemed to be drawn from the river, and millions of sparkles burst out upon the waters. From me too a veil seemed to be drawn, and I felt strong and well. (liii, 411)

The promised land glimpsed here, does not of course materialise. In the novel's first version, there is no apotheosis at the end of the novel either; an emphasis, rather, upon Pip's return to Biddy and Joe, and upon Estella's visit. Revising it, Dickens added a Miltonic close in which Pip and Estella are united at the last, and the mists are all dissipated:[16]

> I took her hand in mine, and we went out of the ruined place; and, as the morning mists had risen long ago when I first left the forge, so, the evening mists were rising now, and in all the broad expanse of tranquil light they showed to me, I saw no shadow of another parting from her. (lix, 460)

He wrote to Forster describing it - I have put in as pretty a little piece of writing as I could"[17] - and it may be felt that the prettiness is false, a relapse into the conventionally picturesque. But the novel it concludes has been of another kind, in which the grotesque and tragicomic are prominent.

NOTES

1. Quoted from Forster, *The Life of Charles Dickens, ed. cit.*, II, 284.
2. See p.vi.
3. Forster, II, 285.

4. Cf. Letters, III, 482 (to Jerrold 3/5/43), describing an awful Hospital dinner attended by "sleek, slobbering ... overfed cattle": "But if I could have partaken it with anybody who would have felt it as you would have done, it would have had quite another aspect - or would at least, like a "classical" mark (oh damn that word!) have one funny side to relieve its dismal features." In both passages, Dickens shows his awareness of the intertwining of comic and serious effects.

5. In his excellent discussion of the relationship of Pip and Magwitch (*op. cit.*, pp. 309-312, 327-337).

6. The prevalence of paradox in *Great Expectations* is also yet another manifestation of Dickens's urge to unify and integrate his novels at this stage of his career.

7. Cf. Chapter 9, fn. 22 above.

8. Cf. Chapter 9, fn. 24 above.

9. For this concept, see M. Hollington, "The Fantastic Paradox: An Aspect of the Theory of Romantic Realism", *Comparison no. 7* (Spring, 1978), 33-44.

10. Cf. (especially) Chapter 5 above. The 1863 series of *The Uncommercial Traveller* (6/6/63) contains a piece entitled "Birthday Celebrations" which describes a childhood visit to an Orrery. The atmosphere is anything but festive: "All this time the gentleman with the wand was going on in the dark (tapping away at the heavenly bodies between whiles, like a wearisome woodpecker), about a sphere revolving on its own axis eight hundred and ninety-seven thousand millions of times - or miles - in two hundred and sixty-three thousand five hundred and twenty-four millions of something elses, until I thought if this was a birthday it were better never to have been born." (*UT*, 200) Possibly this autobiographical experience has a connection with the Dickensian representation of stars.

11. A Frankfurt School concept, particularly associated with Adorno. See Paul Connerton, ed. *Critical Sociology* (Harmondsworth, Penguin Books, 1976), p.25.

12. Especially Stone, *op. cit.*

13. In his diary, 8/10/1917: "There is a heartlessness behind his sentimentally overflowing style. These rude characterizations which are artificially stamped on everyone and without which Dickens would not be able to get on with his story even for a moment." (quoted from Wall, *op. cit.*,

p.258).

14. Cf. Chapter 5, fns, 20, 31 above.

15. The visual paradigm might be Caspar David Friedrich's painting *Frau am Fenster* (see Jens Christian, *Caspar David Friedrich: Leben und Werk* (Cologne, Verlag M. DuMont Schauberg, 1974), pp.128, 244).

16. Cf. *Paradise Lost*, XII, 628ff.:

                    .... on the ground
    Gliding meteorous, as Ev'ning Mist
    Ris'n from a River ore the marish glides
    And gathers ground fast at the Labourers
      heel
    Homeward returning.

17. Forster, II, 289.

Chapter Twelve

OPIUM AND THE GROTESQUE: *OUR MUTUAL F*
EDWIN DROOD

During the writing of *The Bride of Lammermoor* in
1819 Sir Walter Scott was suffering from a painful
illness for which he took opium as a medicine. The
work was dictated from his sickbed, and the manuscript compiled by two amanuenses stationed at his
bedside. Scott's illness continued even after the
work's publication, and with it, the effects of the
medicine; when the book was first put into his
hands, according to the publisher, "he assured me,
that ... he did not recollect one single incident,
character, or conversation it contained!" Asked
what he thought of the work, he replied that he had
been reading it through with considerable unease,
"lest I should be startled by meeting something
altogether glaring and fantastic," and found it "as
a whole, ... monstrous, gross and grotesque".[1]
    The interest of this anecdote for the present
study lies in its manner of relating the grotesque
(of which Scott was one of the most significant
Romantic theorists in English[2]) as an effect of
taking opium with one of the main preoccupations of
Dickens's later writings - with the double, or split
consciousness, of criminal psychology.[3] As a writer
conscious of following in the footsteps of Scott,
and assuming his mantle as the most popular English
novelist, Dickens may have been aware of it in
writing *Edwin Drood*, in such sentences as that
concerning Miss Twinkleton and her *Doppelgänger*:
"As, in some cases of drunkenness, and in others of
animal magnetism, there are two states of consciousness which never clash, but each of which pursues
its separate course as though it were continuous
instead of broken (thus, if I hide my watch when I
am drunk, I must be drunk again before I can
remember where), so Miss Twinkleton has two distinct
and separate phases of being." (*ED*, iii, 20) More-

231

r his friend Wilkie Collins, addicted to opium by
.e late 1860s, underwent similar experiences
.uring the composition of *The Moonstone* for *All the
Year Round*, and - fully conscious of their ancestry
in Scott's career - may well have related these to
Dickens. Alethea Hayter writes that "when he had
finished, and then read through the last part of the
book, he was not only 'pleased and astonished' at
the *finale* of the story, but did not recognise it as
his own".[4]

Yet the theme of opium-smoking in *Edwin Drood*,
and the grotesque visions it produces, has significances that go beyond biography. To get these in
focus, it is necessary to take full account of the
Dublin Review's perception, in 1871, that Dickens's
last, unfinished novel was "in some respects a
singular repetition of its immediate predecessor".[5]
It may not be frequently noted that in *Our Mutual
Friend* continual reference is made to narcotics and
opiates, and that these - especially at a metaphor-
ical level- form a persistent theme whose dimensions
are primarily sociological rather than psychological.
Our Mutual Friend explores the proposition,
expressed in figurative terms that(stemming from
very similar cultural experiences) inevitably recall
Marx's, that money is the opium of the Victorian
middle classes, and that the consequences of addiction to it are grotesque visions that far outstrip
those procured by any individual addict.

The theme is announced, in its clearest form,
in the chapter in which the Lammles are married.
Lammles's 'occupation' is to go "in a condescending
amateurish way" to meetings of Directors in the City,
and to "traffic in Shares": "O mighty shares! To
set those blaring images so high, and to cause us
smaller vermin, as under the influence of henbane or
opium, to cry out night and day. 'Relieve us of our
money, scatter it for us, buy us and sell us, ruin
us, only we beseech ye take rank among the powers of
the earth, and fatten on us!'" (*OMF*, I, x, 114)
Veneering is the master of a drug-house, Chicksey,
Veneering and Stubbles ("Chicksey and Stubbles ...
had both become absorbed in Veneering, once their
traveller or commission agent" - I, iv, 33); and
Bella, imagining riches during her day out on the
river with her father, sees him "going to China in
that handsome three-masted ship, to bring home
opium, with which he would for ever cut out Chicksey,
Veneering, and Stubbles ...". (II, viii, 318) So the
suggestion that Veneering is a 'pusher' is strong -
especially since the resident *eiron* of the Veneering

household, the appropriately named "Analytical
Chemist", comments darkly to himself on the food
and drink offered at every Veneering dinner.
"'Chablis, sir?' - 'You wouldn't if you knew what
it's made of!'" (I, ii, 9) is one typical comment,
or, in inverse anticipation of Jenny Wren's "Come
up and be dead!" (I, v, 282): "Come down and be
poisoned ...". (I, ii, 10)

But there are other poisons in the novel.
Whether it's opium or not, the drug that Riderhood
administers to Rokesmith in the Limehouse area of
the docks of London (where Veneering's cargo would
be easy to come by) is clearly the indispensable
staple of the "honest trade" he plies, and links him
to his more respectable counterparts. That drug
produces visions in which the idea of fire is
dominant ("the whirling round of the room, and the
flashing of flames" is what Rokesmith remembers, and
then, a little later, "a great noise and a sparkling
and a crackling as of fires" - II, xiii, 370), as it
is, too, in the paranoid alcoholic fantasies of
'Mr. Dolls' ("Has had the horrors, too, and fancied
that four copper-coloured men in red wanted to throw
him into a fiery furnace" - III, ii, 434). That
Judas Iscariot, conscience-stricken "that he had
betrayed his sharp parent for sixty threepennyworths
of rum" (IV, viii, 714), is merely the most
obviously degraded of those who, in the novel, sell
themselves and others.

Yet the narcotics theme of *Our Mutual Friend*
also has a more humorous side. There is for
instance the redoubtable grotesque pensioner with
two wooden legs, who, at Bella's wedding, is transformed and resurrected by his urge to wish 'ji' to
the bride. The poison favoured by this quintessential Dickensian gargoyle is tobacco, insulating
him against what passes around him: "most events
acted on him simply as tobacco-stoppers, pressing
down and condensing the quids within him." (IV, iv,
665) The visionary Bella raises him above this
mundane anaesthetic level, enabling him to walk and
to stand in wonder: "And long on the bright steps
stood Gruff and Glum, looking after the pretty
bride, with a narcotic consciousness of having
dreamed a dream." (666)

But the most extended and extraordinary comic
example of this theme in the novel is Mr. Venus.
It is strange to find the astute Edmund Wilson
describing him and Wegg as "mechanical and sterile";[6]
they might also be seen as amongst the most
brilliant exhibits of Dickens's grotesque art.

Venus is an addict of a more mundane Chinese substance than Jasper's - tea; with its aid, he is able "to lower himself to oblivion-point" (III, vii, 500):

> It lowers me. When I'm equally lowered all over, lethargy sets in. By sticking to it till one or two in the morning, I get oblivion. (I, vii, 84)

Wegg, hoping to incite him to a "friendly move" against Boffin, but also - in accordance with the notion of 'friendship' predominating in *Our Mutual Friend* - eager to gain the upper hand over his friend, observes the habit, and applauds it:

> Silas took his seat in silence on the wooden box before the fire, and Venus dropping into his low chair, produced from among his skeleton hands, his tea-tray and teacups, and put the kettle on. Silas inwardly approved of these preparations, trusting they might end in Mr. Venus's diluting his intellect. (III, vii, 495)

The absurd hope that "floating your powerful mind in tea" (II, vii, 303) incites in Wegg, with his pitiful aims and low cunning, is that Venus will be rendered a stupefied prey to his designs - a fit mirror, again, of the operations of the Veneerings and Podsnaps.

In this comic mode, then, the theme of addiction consorts easily enough with the mock-heroic. Venus at his rites, poring over the sacred liquid to cool it down, stands as the joke modern priest of the goddess of love, "his head and face peering out of the darkness, over the smoke of it [tea], as if he were modernising the old original rise in his family". (I, vii, 82) This is what has happened, it seems, in modern society, to love; the frenzied, intoxicated drive to erotic satisfaction of the worshippers of Aphrodite has become the dull-witted obsession with money of characters like Fledgeby "who sees nothing written on the face of the earth and sky but the three letters L.S.D. - not Luxury, Sensuality, Dissoluteness, which they often stand for, but the three dry letters". (II, v, 272) Venery it seems, has become 'Veneering'.

Thus in his grotesque way Mr. Venus offers ironic commentary not only on the narcotic addictions of *Our Mutual Friend* but also on the related

theme of failed relationships. Its title, of
course, announces this emphasis. 'Friendship' had
been a preoccupation of Dickens's writing since the
earliest work in *Sketches by Boz* - 'Thoughts about
People' is one strong example, its themes later
developed in *Nicholas Nickleby* ("It is extraordinary
how long a man may look among the crowd without
discovering the face of a friend, but it is no less
true. Mr. Nickleby looked, and looked, till his eye
became sore as his heart, but no friend appeared..."
- *NN*, i, 1).[7] The phrase 'our mutual friend' gets
regular mocking in Dickens's writing and letters
because of its stiff and clichéd pomposity - for
instance in Flora Finching's conversation with Amy
Dorrit about Arthur Clennam ("it's better that we
should begin by being confidential about our mutual
friend - too cold a word for me at least I don't
mean that, very proper expression mutual friend" -
LD, i, xxiv, 284).[8] It stands as the appropriate
ironic title of a novel that analyses the death of
the tradition of humanist values like friendship and
love as these confront the all-pervasive reductive
materialism of modern capitalist societies.[9]
 That property and commodity relationships
replace personal relationships in *Our Mutual Friend*
in all manner of ways and in all kinds of contexts
- Silas Wegg's decision to "speculate" in Boffin
("I'll invest a bow in you" - I, v, 47), Lady
Tippins's offer of shares in the Veneerings to those
who'll vote for him ("Do come and dine with my
Veneerings, my own Veneerings, my world!" - II, iii,
250), Mr. Boffin's counterfeit exploitation of
Rokesmith (A secretary is worth so much in the
market, and I ought to give it and no more" - III,
v, 462) - has been frequently and adequately commented upon.[10] What may be less widely appreciated,
though, is the extent and subtlety of the grotesque
comedy, worked out of this perception in the banter
between the two modern Grimaldis (anticipating in
their way, Beckett's Vladimir and Estragon), Venus
and Wegg. "And how have I been going on, this long
time, Mr. Venus?" is Wegg's conversational gambit -
an ironically self-centred reversal of conventional
greetings justified, it transpires, by the fact that
Venus owns Wegg's leg. The reply - "very bad" -
also flouts polite convention, assuming that Wegg's
question concerns not health but marketability.
Venus proceeds to assure him that he has 'great
expectations': his leg may have a twist in the bone,
"but you might turn out valuable yet, as a ...
Monstrosity, if you'll excuse me". (I, vii, 82)

But Wegg has his own aspirations and wants to buy himself back, fearing the kind of embarrassment about class and status that Pip experiences when he learns that Magwitch is his benefactor if it is discovered that his leg forms part of a miscellaneous skeleton (and Venus has been disappointed in love because his fiancée did not wish to be associated with his trade). So he becomes a purchaser - Venus's professionalism extending to complimenting his client ("I am glad to restore it to the source from whence it - flowed" - II, vii, 297) - though grumbling about the legality of Venus's original purchase: "You can't buy human flesh and blood in this country, sir; not alive you can't."

The irony is a familiar one in Dickens: but of course you can. Wegg himself in fact has not the least compunction in buying and selling human flesh - not only his own, but Boffin's, "asserting a proprietorship over his soul and body that was at once more grim and more ridiculous than anything in Mr. Venus's rare collection". (IV, iii, 657) The rhetoric is familiar, too, and the language - "grim" and "ridiculous", especially in tandem, by now regular synonyms for the grotesque. The grotesque, embodied in Venus's shop, expressing itself there in a humour as wild and disturbing as anything in Dickens's work (its nearest counterpart, in fact, is Gogol's *Dead Souls*[11]), is a benchmark for the grimly ludicrous horrors of Victorian bourgeois society.

Once more, too, these are explored through an analysis of the radically impoverished opportunities of meaningful work in a society founded upon, and dedicated to waste, which is accumulated in the dustheaps about which the 'friendly moves' cluster. The point is established, in part, by contrast with Paris, "where nothing is wasted, costly and luxurious city though it be, but where wonderful human ants creep out of holes and pick up every scrap ...".(I, xii, 144) In London, on the other hand, characters from Eugene Wrayburn downwards lack purpose and activity. The solicitors' clerk Blight, "wearing in his solitary confinement no fetters that he could polish, and being provided with no drinking-cup that he could carve" (I, viii, 87) is an anticipatory study of the kind of despair in inactivity that Jasper voices in *Edwin Drood*: "No wretched monk who droned his life away in that gloomy place, before me, can have been more tired of it than I am. He could take for relief (and did take) to carving demons out of the stalls and seats and desks. What can I do? Must I take to carving them out of my heart?" (*ED*, ii, 14) And Wegg, imagining himself to offer Venus a stimulant antidote to his dependence on an anodyne narcotic - "Since I called upon you that evening when you were, as I may say, floating your powerful mind in tea, I have felt that you required to be roused with an object. In this friendly move, sir, you will have a glorious object to rouse you" (II, vii, 303) - foreshadows Durdles's absurd claim that, in employing Deputy to throw stones at him, "I took him in hand and gave him an object". (*ED*, v, 44)

For in the professional activity in Venus, in a remarkably pessimistic and ironic way, Dickens seems to explore misgivings about his own creative work in the 1860s. This kind of feeling emerges in the following exchange:

> 'You seem very low, Mr. Venus. Is business bad?'
> 'Never was so good.'
> 'Is your hand out at all?'
> 'Never was so well in, Mr. Wegg. I'm not only first in the trade, but I'm *the* trade ...'
> (I, vii, 83)

- or in Venus's Hamlet-like soliloquy that follows shortly upon it:

> And so a man climbs to the top of the tree, Mr. Wegg, only to see that there's no lookout when he's up there! I sit here of a night surrounded by the lovely trophies of my art, and what have they done for me? Ruined me.

Even Wegg's praise of Venus's art - "you with the patience to fit together on wires the whole framework of society - I allude to the human skelinton" (III, vi, 478) - seems to mock the achievements of Dickens's career. A feeling that these have been purchased at the expense of self-fulfilment seems to surface here - to be worked out more fully of course, and in a not totally dissimilar mode, in the case of Jasper. And it may also be reasonable to speculate that in Venus Dickens expresses the *mea culpa* of the grotesque artist, the sense of working with and upon inert and mechanical dolls - corpses even, like the "fishers of men" who in *Our Mutual Friend* travesty New Testament Christian Humanism - that Kafka acutely diagnosed as Dickens's 'heartlessness'.[12]

237

At any rate, some autobiographical sediment seems to be present in at least one strand of the work-themes in *Our Mutual Friend*. For Dickens, the paradigm of useless work was inevitably connected with boot-blacking, and the period of intense suffering he spent as a child pasting labels on bottles of blacking in a factory in the Strand.[13] So it is instructive that polishing work should be so prominent in this novel. Young Blight, again, in his torment of useless activity, has "no fetters that he could polish"; in Veneering's house, "all things were in a state of high varnish and polish". (I, ii, 6) In the novel, there is so much human wood - Wegg, Veneering, the "Rocking-Horse" Mrs. Podsnap, the "Secretary" Rokesmith - and apparently so much polishing to be done (Wegg exclaims to Boffin "*Your* varnish is fading" - III, vii, 501).[14]

And the theme of narcotics, of opiates to deaden pain, relates of course to this torment from the past that seems to have always been in Dickens's mind. "And you needn't, Mr. Venus, be your black bottle," sings Wegg in one of the ghastly unrhythmical ballads he improvises to lift his 'friend' from his depression (III, vi, 477); he might be one of the poets employed to write advertising jingles for Warrens of the Strand.[15] At the furthest remove it would seem, from meaningful work - depending on leisure, and rendering one incapable of labour - opium and its use seem nevertheless to be the consequence and product of the kind of pointless exploited toil that Dickens had experienced as a child. At any rate, it is significant that, visiting the opium dens of the East End with Inspector Field, he should have noted that 'Princess Puffer' dispenses her product in pipes constructed from ink-bottles, and worked this detail (together with her very Warren's-like warning to beware imitations) into the novel.[16]

Nevertheless, one of the main values of the approach to *Edwin Drood* through *Our Mutual Friend* is the extent to which it offers a corrective to the many thoroughly privatizing readings of that novel.[17] In common with other later works, it offers a much more complex account of psychological processes than do the earlier novels; but to move from the opium visions or mesmeric trances of *Edwin Drood* to an exclusive concentration on Jasper's interior life and its relation to Dickens's own is to risk misreading. Opium was a fact of Victorian social life, a commodity available as a consequence of British colonialist policy, about which a war had been fought.

Though very considerable interpretative caution is an axiomatic principle of approaches to the unfinished novel, *Edwin Drood* appears to reflect as much upon these realities as upon issues of personal psychology.

Thus, for instance, the novel is all too easily described in terms of the split personality of Jasper, divided as it is between his respectable daylight activity as a cathedral organist and his opium-smoking nightlife, in neglect or oblivion that these psychological spheres also involve two locations: Cloisterham, or Rochester, and London, especially its East End. The 'Tale of Two Cities' structure is in fact a favoured one in Dickens's work - London and Paris, London and Italy, England and America had all done duty as alternating streaks of the bacon - with the not infrequent aim of uncovering hidden similarities between ostensibly dissimilar worlds.[18] Even in this fragmentary text, there seems to be evidence of a similar pattern, as the two worlds are shown to be moving closer together - on the very last page, for instance, where the Princess Puffer infiltrates the Cloisterham world, penetrating its holy of holies, the Cathedral, and appearing to blend easily with her new surroundings. She seems there to be establishing a pointedly ironic link between the homespun 'picturesque' of Cloisterham and the grotesque phantasmagoric world of opium dens. The novel seems to hold these two in complementary relationship, allowing us to see the 'ordinariness' of the world of opium and the 'extraordinariness' of the everyday world of Cloisterham, in a manner not dissimilar to the dialectic of surrealism as this is analysed by Walter Benjamin.[19]

As Nancy Hill suggests,[20] the operative word for the presentation of Cloisterham in the novel is "picturesque". "Still picturesque suggestions of Cathedral Town," wrote Dickens in the number plan for Chapter III,[21] suggesting once more how conscious he was of such terms and such effects. It is a place for tourists to come and look at curiosities, and for residents to pretend to enthuse about. Edwin Drood himself, an amateur artist, goads Neville Landless with coolly indifferent whistling "and a stop now and then to pretend to admire picturesque effects in the moonlight before him" (viii, 71); Jasper makes sure that Sapsea harbours no suspicions about his nighttime excursions with Durdles by reminding him of what prompted them - "'You remember suggesting, when you

brought us together, that, as a lover of the
picturesque, it might be worth my while?'" (xii,
129); and Dick Datchery - appearing to feign similar
interests, and therefore perhaps also a Cloisterham
resident - announces "that he had a mind to take a
lodging in the picturesque old city for a month or
two, with a view of settling down there altogether".
(xviii, 206)

Already then, there's a hint of something sham
about Cloisterham's picturesque - glimpsed perhaps
by Crisparkle in his meditations upon the relationship between Rosa Bud and Helena Landless, which he
things of as "the picturesque alliance between those
two, externally so very different" (x, 99; at
profounder levels, it would seem, they may be more
alike). It is the essential product of the past, of
the city as a kind of palimpsest of various architectural styles from various periods of history:
"Fragments of old wall, saint's chapel, chapter-
house, convent and monastery, have got incongruously
or obstructively built into many of its houses, much
as kindred jumbled notions have become incorporated
into many of its citizens' minds." (ii, 19) As
such, it seems to submit readily enough to an
allegorical reading in which its physical complex-
ities stand for psychological knots and twists - or
at least the hostel where Deputy lives, "currently
known as the Travellers' Twopenny:- a house all
warped and distorted, like the morals of the
traveller" (v, 47), certainly does. The jumble,
incongruity and obstructiveness of this architecture,
by the way, is also a marked feature of Jasper's
opium vision on the novel's first page, in which
the central focus is the Cathedral Tower of Cloisterham Cathedral.

The point of this 'picturesque' presentation of
Cloisterham, in fact, is to show how beneath its
quiet surface respectability and normality, strange
monsters and grotesques are bred. Durdles, for
instance, "prowling among old graves, and ruins,
like a Ghoule" (xii, 132), is a joke monstrous
cannibal, like Mrs. General and Jerry Cruncher,
carrying his lunch about with him even at night-time
and recommending quicklime to Jasper in fee-fi-fo-
fum terms: "quick enough to eat your boots. With
a little handy stirring, quick enough to eat your
bones." (132) Deputy is a kind of juvenile Quilp,
doing a kind of "demon dance" to goad Datchery
(xviii, 209), and mocking Jasper's murderous assault
upon him with a mime: "With a diabolical insight
into the strongest part of his position, he is no

sooner taken by the throat, and screws his body, and twists, as already undergoing the first agonies of strangulation." (141) He seems the Cloisterham counterpart of those London street urchins - violent, savage, unprincipled, compelled to live off their wits in the struggle for survival on the streets - that had so disturbed the narrator of *The Uncommercial Traveller*. And Jasper, too, seems to belong to this family - "so quickly roused, and so violent, that he seems an older devil himself". (140)

Jasper, of course, has another, more attractive, mesmeric side, to illustrate the principle of the "attraction of repulsion" that is emphasised in the novel. Yet in general the grotesques of London (unusually, for late Dickens, and surely with ironic intent) are less diabolical and more attractive than those of Cloisterham. Grewgious is the major example, his face (very much like Wegg's) carved out of wood, "sculpted by Nature" and described in a passage uncannily like one in Gogol's *Dead Souls*:

> The little play of features that his face presented was cut deep into it, in a few hard curves that made it more like work; and he had certain notches in his forehead, which looked as though Nature had been about to touch them into sensibility or refinement, when she had impatiently thrown away the chisel, and said: 'I really cannot be worried to finish off this man; let him go as he is.' (ix, 84)

He is a self-conscious grotesque - "The fact is, I am a particularly Unnatural man" (89) - like Wemmick, a modern urban creature, living as he can in the margins of his work. His wooden mask, significantly enough, permits a comparison to the world of opium - he is "like the carved image of some queer Joss or other coming out of its reverie" (xi, 123) - and also, via the novel's ironic logic, to the wooden misericords among which the Princess Puffer stands at the close of the fragmentary novel. Grewgious's legal environment - "behind the most ancient part of Holborn, London, where certain gabled houses some centuries of ages still stand looking on the public way" (112) - also carries ironic reminders of the Cloisterham 'picturesque'. And his grotesque clerk Bazzard, "a fabulous Familiar", "possessed of some strange power over Mr. Grewgious" (114), carries forward the theme of possession and power relations also explored in the triangle of Rosa, Edwin, and Jasper.

So this strategic placing and comparing serves to point up the difficulty of life in Cloisterham. For all his diabolism, the situation of Jasper is manifestly "attended with some real suffering, and is hard to bear", as Edwin Drood concedes (ii, 15). The problem of Jasper in Cloisterham is the problem of the artist in the complacent, philistine, provincial society of England in the late 1860s - the world of Podsnappery, in fact.

"You are evidently going to write a book about us, Mr. Jasper ... to write a book about us." (xii, 128) Thus quoth the Dean, unable to resist pompous self-repetition. He represents a church patently not mediating anything that might be termed Christian values to his society (*Edwin Drood*, it seems, was in part triggered off by a visit to Canterbury Cathedral, during which Dickens was disgusted at the empty ritualism of the service).[22] Patronisingly admonishing Crisparkle for his eagerness to take Neville's side after the murder, and assert his willingness to face accusations, he prevaricates: "I *don't think* I would state it emphatically. State it? Ye-e-es! But emphatically? No-o-o." (xvi, 188) He is the ironic 'fetch' or double of that other secular pillar of the class establishment of Cloisterham Mr. Sapsea, who, like Wegg with Boffin and his mounds, "likes to pass the churchyard with a swelling air of proprietorship, and to encourage in his breast a sort of benignant landlord feeling, in that he has been bountiful towards that meritorious tenant, Mrs. Sapsea, and has publicly given her a prize". (xii, 127)

Sapsea, of course, represents an obvious and ludicrous example of the racism and jungoism of Cloisterham: "I have put my finger on the North Pole before now, and said 'Spear of Esquimaux make, for half a pint of pale sherry!'" (iv, 33) Jasper finds it expedient to keep well in with "my friend the Mayor" (xviii, 210) and others of his class in Cloisterham, "giving him the genuine George the Third home-brewed; exhorting him (as 'my brave boys') to reduce to a smashed condition all other islands but this island". (xii, 128) But of course savagery flourishes at the centre of this island of 'civilization': Deputy is "own brother to Peter the Wild Boy" (v, 44), living in a jungle world of "hideous small boys ... [who] as if attracted by some carrion-scent of Deputy in the air, start in the moonlight, as vultures might gather in the desert, and instantly fall to stoning him and one

another". (48) The pretensions to geographical
superiority are scuppered, then - as are the
historical ones, for "Christians are stoned on all
sides, as if the days of Saint Stephen were revived".
(48) More literally than the London of *Our Mutual
Friend*, Cloisterham is a world where bones are
ground to make bread. (iii, 18)

So it's enough, as it were, to make you smoke
opium. In justified alienation from the society he
is supposed to represent in glowing and flattering
terms, the artist seeks compensatory visions in the
world of narcotics. Only here the obverse begins
to obtain: just as the tame and provincial world
of Cloisterham holds monstrosities, so too the
world of opium is oddly like those unbearable
realities it purports to escape.

There's royalty at the head of it, for a
start - a Princess Puffer, a kind of ironic, inverse
Queen Victoria, ruling over the empire of night.
She too has her competitors - Jack Chinaman over the
way - experiences economic problems, finds 'work'
difficult, unsatisfying: "Ah, poor me, the business
is slack, is slack!" (i, 2) Hers too is a *class*
world, just as much as Cloisterham, and she
congratulates Jasper for his rise in it: "But you
got on in the world, and was able by and by to take
your pipe with the best of 'em, warn't ye?" (xxiii,
265) And he in response feels the same 'artistic'
contempt for the mundanity of her preoccupations:

> What visions can *she* have? ... Visions of
> many butchers' shops, and public-houses, and
> much credit? Of an increase of hideous
> customers, and this horrible bedstead set
> upright again, and this horrible court swept
> clean? What can she rise to, under any
> quantity of opium, higher than that? (1, 3)

The point - reaching back through the aesthetics of
Dickens's novels - is that in the end opium, like
the grotesque, is merely *real*. It may give
"Paradises and Hells of visions" (xix, 22),
"changes of colours and the great landscapes and
glittering processions" (xxiii, 268), but these
have their base in a foul rag-and-bone shop to which
vision constantly returns: "Look at it! Look what
a poor, mean, miserable thing it is! *That* must be
real." (269) "It's opium, deary. Neither more
nor less," is what the Princess Puffer has to say by
way of apologia; "And it's like a human creatur so
far, that you always hear what can be said against

it but seldom what can be said in its praise." (273)

And so when she appears once more, on the last page that Dickens ever wrote, the irony is Blakean. "Is this a holy thing to see?" seems the right question to ask of Princess Puffer in Cloisterham Cathedral; Datchery has to look twice, to believe his eyes:

> Mr. Datchery looks again, to convince himself. Yes, again! As ugly and withered as one of the fantastic carvings on the under brackets of the stall seats, as malignant as the Evil One, as hard as the big brass eagle holding the sacred books upon his wings (and, according to the sculptor's representation of his ferocious attributes, not at all converted by them), she hugs herself in her lean arms, and then shakes both fists at the leader of the Choir. (278)

The extremes that touch here - opium *madame*, holy sanctuary, grotesque demon, human form - are part of the same system. They shape its indictment.

NOTES

    1. I owe this information to Alethea Hayter, *Opium and the Romantic Imagination* (London, Faber and Faber, 1968), pp.292-3.

    2. Cf. Chapter 1 above, especially p.21 and fn. 91.

    3. Cf. M. Hollington, *Dickens and the Double.*

    4. Hayter, *op. cit.*, p.259.

    5. Philip Collins, *Dickens: The Critical Heritage*, p.543.

    6. In "Dickens: The Two Scrooges", *The Wound and the Bow* (London, Martin Secker and Warburg, 1941), pp.74-5.

    7. Cf. Chapter 3 above, especially fn. 27.

    8. The phrase "mutual friend" is a misusage (in which the word 'mutual' is used incorrectly in place of 'common'), and it characterises, in Dickens, the illiterate attempt to appear formal (in *Our Mutual Friend*, it is coined by Boffin in response to Mrs. Wilfer's distaste for "the low expression", Lodger - I, ix, 111). Dickens signals his own consciousness of its dubiousness when, in a letter of 1845 to Clarkson Stanfield concerning the difficult courtship of Christiana Weller pursued by T.J. Thompson (their fellow-actor in *Every Man in His Humour*), he places the phrase in

inverted commas: "on the very eve of his marriage
with a very beautiful girl - the ring purchased,
wedding dresses made, and so forth - finds the
whole contract shattered like Glass, in an instant,
under the most inexplicable circumstances that ever
distracted the head of a 'mutual friend.'" (Letters,
IV, 398; 4/10/45)

9. Friendship is a major theme of Dickens's
work, and the word 'mutual' occurs frequently in
connection with it. "We - we - have a mutual
interest, Bill, - a mutual interest" (*OT*, xv, 104),
claims Fagin in *Oliver Twist*; and in *The Old
Curiosity Shop* it is used in connection with the
remarkable friendship between Tom Scott and Quilp
("between this boy and the dwarf there existed a
strange kind of mutual liking" - v, 42).
Frequently, in the adjective/noun frames that
Dickens constructs to express friendship and
relationship, the adjective is suspect (e.g.
General Choke, introducing Martin and Mark Tapley
to Zephariah Scadder - "these air partickler
friends" (*MC*, xxi, 354); Louisa Chick, introducing
Miss Tox to Mr. Dombey - "my very particular friend
Miss Tox" (*DS*, i, 6); or , commenting chorically
like Mrs. Merdle's parrot on Dr. Blimber's greeting
to Paul Dombey, the clock in the hall: "how, is,
my, lit, tle, friend?" (*DS*, xi, 145)).

10. Especially by John Lucas, *The
Melancholy Man*, pp.315ff, and H.M. Daleski, *Dickens
and the Art of Analogy* (London, Faber and Faber,
1970), pp.270ff.

11. The relationship between Dickens and
Gogol has been insufficiently explored, yet Donald
Fanger's *Dostoevsky and Romantic Realism* offers an
invaluable starting-point.

12. Cf. Chapter 11, fn. 13 above.

13. See Forster, The Life of Charles Dickens
I, 19ff.

14. Jokes about wood and flesh in Dickens
are too numerous to be more than sampled. Matthew
Bagnet, alias "Lignum Vitae", in *Bleak House* is
perhaps the most memorable grotesque figure to
appear to be made of wood; but there is also
Hannibal Chollop in *Martin Chuzzlewit* ("His face
was almost as hard and knobby as his stick; and so
were his hands. His head was like an old black
hearth-broom." - *MC*, xxxiii, 518), and Jack Bunsby
in *Dombey and Son* ("... there appeared, coming
slowly up above the bulk-head of the cabin, another
bulk-head - human, and very large - with one
stationary eye in the mahogany face, and one

revolving one, on the principle of some light-houses." - *DS*, xxiii, 334). Wooden legs are particular specialities, worked in at every available opportunity, as when Dick Swiveller remodels a popular ballad to produce: "Her name is Cheggs now, Sophy Cheggs. Yet loved I as man never loved that hadn't wooden legs, and my heart, my heart is breaking for the love of Sophy Cheggs." (*OCS*, 1, 374)

15. One of them figures as Mr. Slum in *The Old Curiosity Shop*. See Wilfred Partington, "The Blacking Laureate: The Identity of Mr. Slum, A Pioneer in Publicity", *The Dickensian* XXXIV (June, 1938), pp.199-202.

16. See Collins, *Dickens and Crime*, pp.213, 354.

17. Edgar Johnson's, in the first edition of *Charles Dickens: His Tragedy and Triumph*, is one example, Fred Kaplan's, in *Dickens and mesmerism: the hidden springs of fiction* (Princeton, N.J., Princeton University Press, 1975), another.

18. Cf. Chapters 5, 6 and 7 above.

19. In the essay "Surrealism: The Last Snapshot of the European Intelligentsia". See Benjamin, *Reflections*, ed. Demetz (New York, Harcourt Brace Jovanovich, 1978), pp.189-90.

20. In *A Reformer's Art* (Athens, Ohio, Ohio University Press, 1981), p.120.

21. See Appendix B to the Clarendon edition of *The Mystery of Edwin Drood*, ed. Margaret Cardwell (Oxford, Clarendon Press, 1972), p.221.

22. *ibid.*, xvii-xviii.

BIBLIOGRAPHY

This is not an attempt at a comprehensive or exhaustive list of references to the subject of this book; it is simply a compilation of works, chiefly secondary, consulted and/or referred to in this text. Section A covers items on Dickens and his work; Section B, items of relevance to the grotesque and Section C, general and miscellaneous works.

Section A: Dickens

William F. Axton, *Circle of Fire: Dickens's Vision and Style and the Popular Victorian Theatre* (Lexington, Ky., University of Kentucky Press, 1966).
John Butt and Kathleen Tillotson, *Dickens at Work* (London, Methuen, 1957).
Philip Collins, *Dickens and Crime* (London, Macmillan, 1965; 2nd edition).
_____, "Dickens and London", *The Victorian City: Images and Realities*, eds. H.J. Dyos and Michael Wolff (London, Routledge and Kegan Paul, 1973; 2 vols.).
_____, "Dickens on Ghosts: An Uncollected Article", *The Dickensian* LIX (January, 1963), 5-14.
_____, ed. *Dickens: The Critical Heritage* (London, Routledge and Kegan Paul, 1971).
H.M. Daleski, *Dickens and the Art of Analogy* (London, Faber and Faber, 1970).
Duane Devries, *Dickens's Apprentice Years: The Making of a Novelist* (Hassocks, Harvester Press, 1976).
George H. Ford and Lauriat Lane, jr., *The Dickens Critics* (Ithaca, N.Y., Cornell University Press, 1961).
John Forster, *The Life of Charles Dickens*, ed. A.J.

Hoppé (London, J.M. Dent and Co., 1966; 2 vols.).
George Gissing, *Charles Dickens: A Critical Study*
(London, Blackie and Son, 1898).
Michael Goldberg, *Carlyle and Dickens* (Athens,
Georgia, University of Georgia Press, 1972).
Virgil Grillo, *Charles Dickens's 'Sketches by Boz'*
(Boulder, Colo., University of Colorado Press,
1974).
John Gross and Gabriel Pearson, eds., *Dickens and
the Twentieth Century* (London, Routledge and Kegan
Paul, 1962).
Nancy K. Hill, *A Reformer's Art: Dickens's
Picturesque and Grotesque Imagery* (Athens, Ohio,
Ohio University Press, 1981).
Michael Hollington, *Dickens and the Double* (Ann
Arbor, Michigan, University Microfilms, 1967).
_____, "Dickens and the Dance of Death", *The
Dickensian* LXXIV (May, 1978), 67-76.
_____, "Dickens's Conception of the Grotesque",
The Dickensian LXXVI (Summer, 1980), 91-99.
_____, "Dickens the Flâneur", *The Dickensian*
LXXVII (Summer, 1981), 71-87.
_____, "Dickens and Grotesque Art", *Dickens
Studies Newsletter* XIII, no. 1 (March, 1982), 5-11.
Humphrey House, *The Dickens World* (Oxford, O.U.P.,
1942).
Edgar Johnson, *Charles Dickens: His Tragedy and
Triumph* (London, Allen Lane, 1977; abridged version).
Fred Kaplan, *Dickens and mesmerism: The hidden
springs of fiction* (Princeton, N.J., Princeton
University Press, 1975).
Arnold Kettle, "Dickens and the Popular Tradition",
Zeitschrift für Anglistik und Amerikanistik III
(1961); reprinted in David Craig, ed., *Marxists on
Literature* (Harmondsworth, Penguin Books, 1975),
pp.214-244.
Michael C. Kotzin, *Dickens and the Fairy Tale*
(Bowling Green, Ohio, Bowling Green University
Popular Press, 1972).
John Lucas, *The Melancholy Man* (London, Methuen,
1970).
Steven Marcus, *Dickens: From Pickwick to Dombey*
(London, Chatto and Windus, 1965).
Richard C. Maxwell, jr., "G.M. Reynolds, Dickens
and the Mysteries of London", *Nineteenth Century
Fiction* (September,1977), 188-213.
J. Hillis Miller, *Charles Dickens: The World of
his Novels* (Cambridge, Mass., Harvard University
Press, 1958).
_____, "The Fiction of Realism; *Sketches by Boz,
Oliver Twist*, and Cruikshank's Illustrations",

Charles Dickens and George Cruikshank: Papers Read at a Clark Library Seminar on May 9, 1970 (Los Angeles, William Andrews Clark Memorial Library, University of California, 1971), pp.1-69.

Robert Newsom, *Dickens on the Romantic Side of Familiar Things: 'Bleak House' and the Novel Tradition* (New York, Columbia University Press, 1977).

William Oddie, *Dickens and Carlyle: The Question of Influence* (London, The Centenary Press, 1972), p.41.

George Orwell, "Charles Dickens", *The Collected Essays, Journalism and Letters of George Orwell*, eds. Sonia Orwell and Ian Angus (London, Secker and Warburg, 1968: 4 vols.), I, 413-460.

Wilfred Partington, "The Blacking Laureate: The Identity of Mr. Slum, A Pioneer in Publicity", *The Dickensian* XXXIV (June, 1938), pp.199-202.

Hesketh Pearson, *Dickens: His Character, Comedy, and Career* (London, Methuen, 1949).

Una Pope-Henessy, *Charles Dickens* (Harmondsworth, Penguin Books, 1970; originally published 1945).

Victor Sage, "Dickens and Beckett: two uses of materialism", *Journal of Beckett Studies* number 2 (Summer, 1977), pp.15-39.

Andrew Sanders, *Charles Dickens: Resurrectionist* (London, Macmillan, 1982).

F.S. Schwarzbach, *Dickens and the City* (London, The Athlone Press, 1979).

Evelyn M. Simpson, "Jonson and Dickens: A Study in the Comic Genius of London", *Essays and Studies* XXIX (1943), 82-92.

Michael Slater ed., *Dickens 1970* (London, Chapman and Hall, 1970).

Michael Steig, "Dickens, Hablot Browne, and the Tradition of English Caricature", *Criticism* XI (1969), 219-234.

_____, *Dickens and Phiz* (Bloomington, Indiana University Press, 1978).

Taylor Stoehr, *Dickens: the dreamer's stance* (Ithaca, N.Y., Cornell University Press, 1966).

Stephen Wall, ed., *Charles Dickens: A Critical Anthology* (Harmondsworth, Penguin Books, 1970).

Alexander Welsh, *The City of Dickens* (Oxford, Oxford University Press, 1971).

Alvin Whitley, "Hood and Dickens: some new letters", *Huntington Library Quarterly* XIV (1951), 392-3.

Angus Wilson, *The World of Charles Dickens* (Harmondsworth, Penguin Books, 1972).

Edmund Wilson, "Dickens: The Two Scrooges", *The Wound and the Bow* (London, Martin Secker and

Warburg, 1941).

Section B: Works relevant to the grotesque

Richard D. Altick, *The Shows of London* (Cambridge,
Mass., Harvard University Press, 1978).
Friedrich Antal, *Hogarth and his Place in European
Art* (London, Routledge and Kegan Paul, 1962).
— Mikhail Bakhtin, *Rabelais and his World*, transl.
Hélène Iswolsky (Boston, Mass., M.I.T. Press, 1968).
Jurgis Baltrusaitis, *Le Moyen Age Fantastique*
(Paris, 1955).
— Frances K. Barasch, *The Grotesque: A Study in
Meanings* (The Hague, Mouton, 1971).
Gyles Brandreth, *Discovering Pantomime* (Aylesbury,
Shire Press, 1973).
Thomas Carlyle, "Preface and Introductions to the
Book called German Romance", *Critical and
Miscellaneous Essays* (London, Chapman and Hall,
1903; 3 vols.); vol. I.
— Arthur Clayborough, *The Grotesque in English
Literature* (Oxford, Clarendon Press, 1965).
John Clubbe, *Victorian Forerunner: The Later
Career of Thomas Hood* (Durham, N.C., University of
North Carolina Press, 1968).
Nicole Dacos, *La Découverte de La Domus Aurea et la
Formation des Grotesque à La Renaissance* (London,
1969).
M. Willson Disher, *Clowns and Pantomimes* (New York,
Blom reprints, 1968; first published in 1925).
Pierre Duchartre, *The Italian Comedy* (New York,
Dover Press, 1966; first published in 1929).
George E. Duckworth, *The Nature of Roman Comedy: A
Study in Popular Entertainment* (Princeton, N.J.,
Princeton University Press, 1952).
Christian Enzensberger, "Die Fortentwicklung der
Romantik am Englischen Beispiel", *DVjS* 1964, 534-60.
— Donald Fanger, *Dostoevsky and Romantic Realism: A
Study of Dostoevsky in Relation to Balzac, Dickens
and Gogol* (Cambridge, Mass., Harvard University
Press, 1965).
Willard Farnham, *The Shakespearean Grotesque*
(Oxford, Oxford University Press, 1971).
Eduard Fuchs, *Die Karikatur der Europäischen Völker
vom Altertum bis zur Neuzeit* (Berlin, A. Hofmann,
1901).
M. Dorothy George, *Hogarth to Cruikshank: Social
Change in Graphic Satire* (London, Allen Lane, 1967).
_____, ed., *Catalogue of Political and Personal
Satires preserved in the Department of Prints and
Drawings in the British Museum* (London, 1949).

Ernst Gombrich, "Leonardo's Grotesque Heads: Prolegomena to their Study", in A. Marazza, ed., *Leonardo, Saggi e Richerche* (Rome, 1954).

_____, *Art and Illusion* (London, Phaidon Press, 1962).

_____, *The Heritage of Apelles: Studies in the art of the Renaissance* (London, Phaidon Press, 1976).

John Harvey, *Victorian Novelists and their Illustrators* (London, Sidgwick and Jackson, 1970).

Draper Hill, *Mr. Gillray the Satirist* (London, Phaidon Press, 1965).

Michael Hollington, "The Fantastic Paradox: An Aspect of the Theory of Romantic Realism", *Comparison* no. 7 (Spring, 1978), pp.33-45.

John Dixon Hunt, "Dickens and the Tradition of Graphic Satire", *Encounters: Essays on Literature and the Visual Arts* (London, Studio Vista, 1971).

Christopher Hussey, *The Picturesque: Studies in a Point of View* (London, Frank Cass and Co., 1967; new edition).

Lloyd N. Jeffrey, *Thomas Hood* (New York, Twayne Publishing Co., 1972).

Lee Byron Jennings, *The Ludicrous Demon: Aspects of the Grotesque in German Post-Romantic Prose* (Berkeley, Cal., University of California Press, 1963).

Wolfgang Kayser, *The Grotesque in Art and Literature*, transl. Ulrich Weisstein (New York, McGraw-Hill, 1966).

Frances Donald Klingender, *Hogarth and English Caricature* (London, 1941).

Reinhard Lengeler, *Tragischer Wirklichkeit als Groteske Verfreundung bei Shakespeare* (Cologne, Böhlau Verlag, 1964).

José Lopez-Rey, "Goya's Caprichos: Beauty, Reason and Caricature", in Fred Licht, ed., *Goya in Perspective* (Englewood Cliffs, N.J., Prentice Hall, 1973).

David Mayer, *Harlequin in His Element: The English Pantomime 1806-36* (Cambridge, Mass., Harvard University Press, 1969).

Charles Mitchell, ed., *Hogarth's Peregrination* (Oxford, Oxford University Press, 1952).

Maximilian Novak, "Gothic Fiction and the Grotesque", *Novel* XI (Fall, 1979), 50-67.

Ronald Paulson, *Thomas Rowlandson: A New Interpretation* (London, Studio Vista, 1972).

Robert L. Patten, ed., *George Cruikshank: A Revaluation* (Princeton, N.J., Princeton University Press, 1974); especially Ronald Paulson's essay,

"The Tradition of Comic Illustration from Hogarth to Cruikshank".

J.C. Reid, *Thomas Hood* (London, Routledge and Kegan Paul, 1963).

John Ruskin, *The Works of John Ruskin* (Library Edition) eds. E.T. Cook and Alexander Wedderburn (London, George Allen, 1903; 39 vols.).

— Arieh Sachs, *The English Grotesque* (Jerusalem, Israel Universities Press, 1969).

Ronald Sheridan and Anne Ross, *Grotesques and Gargoyles: Paganism in the Medieval Church* (Newton Abbot, David and Charles, 1975).

Walter Sorell, *The Other Face: The Mask in the Arts* (London, Thames and Hudson, 1973).

Leo Spitzer, Review of Wolfgang Kayser, *Das Groteske: Seine Gestaltung in Malerei und Dichtung*, *Göttingische Gelehrte Anzeigen* CCXII (1958), 95-110.

Philip John Steed, *Mr. Punch* (London, 1950).

G.B. Tennyson, *Sartor Called Resartus* (Princeton, N.J., Princeton University Press, 1965).

Christian Thomsen, *Das Groteske im Englischen Roman des 18ten Jahrhunderts* (Darmstadt, Wissenschaftliche Buchgesellschaft, 1974).

_____, *Das Groteske und die Englische Literatur*, Darmstadt, Wissenschaftliche Buchgesellschaft, 1977).

Peter Tomory, *The Life and Art of Henry Fuseli* (London, Thames and Hudson, 1972).

Howard P. Vincent, *Daumier and His World* (Evanston, Ill., Northwestern University Press, 1968).

— Thomas Wright, *History of Caricature and Grotesque*, with an Introduction by Frances K. Barasch (New York, Ungar Reprints, 1968; originally published in 1865).

Section C: General and Miscellaneous

Jonathan Arac, *Commissioned Spirits: The Shaping of Social Motion in Dickens, Carlyle, Melville and Hawthorne* (New Brunswick, Rutgers University Press, 1979).

Charles Baudelaire, 'Quelques Caricaturistes Français', *Oeuvres Complètes* ed. Ruff (Paris, du Seuil, 1968).

George J. Becker, ed., *Documents of Modern Literary Realism* (Princeton, N.J., Princeton University Press, 1963).

Kirk H. Beetz, *John Ruskin: A Bibliography, 1900-1974* (Metuchen, N.J., The Scarecrow Press, 1976).

Walter Benjamin, *Charles Baudelaire: A Lyric Poet in the Era of High Capitalism*, transl. Harry Zohn (London, New Left Books, 1974).

_____, *Gesammelte Schriften*, eds. Tiedemann and Schweppenhäuser (Frankfurt am Main, Suhrkamp Verlag, 1974; 5 vols.).

_____, *Reflections*, ed. Peter Demetz (New York, Harcourt Brace Jovanovich, 1978).

C.P. Brand, *Italy and the English Romantics* (Cambridge, Cambridge University Press, 1957).

Jerome Buckley, *Season of Youth: the 'Bildungsroman' from Dickens to Golding* (Cambridge, Mass., Harvard University Press, 1975).

Peter Burke, *Popular Culture in Early Modern Europe* (London, T. Smith, 1978).

Gerta Calmann, "The Picture of Nobody: An Iconographical Study", *Journal of the Wartburg and Courtauld Institutes* LX (1960), 60-104.

Kenneth Churchill, *Italy and English Literature* (London, Macmillan, 1980).

Pierre Citron, *La Poésie de Paris dans La littérature française de Rousseau à Baudelaire* (Paris, les Editions de Minuit, 1961; 2 vols.).

Peter Conrad, *The Victorian Treasure-House* (London, Collins, 1973).

H.W. Donner, *Thomas Lovell Beddoes: The Making of a Poet* (Oxford, Oxford University Press, 1935).

H.J. Dyos and Michael Wolff, *The Victorian City: Images and Realities* (London, Routledge and Kegan Paul, 1973; 2 vols.).

Peter Fairclough, ed., *Three Gothic Novels* (Harmondsworth, Penguin Books, 1968), with an introduction by Mario Praz.

Avrom Fleishman, *The English Historical Novel: Walter Scott to Virginia Woolf* (Baltimore and London, Johns Hopkins Press, 1971).

Lilian Furst, ed., *European Romanticism: Self-Definitions* (London, Methuen, 1980).

Alethea Hayter, *Opium and the Romantic Imagination* (London, Faber and Faber, 1968).

Robert Hewison, *John Ruskin: the Argument of the Eye* (London, Thames and Hudson, 1976).

Michael Hollington, *Günter Grass: The Writer in a Pluralist Society* (London, Marion Boyars, 1980).

Keith Hollingsworth, *The Newgate Novel 1830-47* (Detroit, Wayne University Press, 1963).

Jens Christian Jensen, *Caspar David Friedrich: Leben und Werk* (Cologne, Verlag M. DuMont Schauberg, 1974).

Volker Klotz *Die Erzählte Stadt* (München, 1969).

Roger Lauffer, *Lesage ou le Métier du romancier* (Paris, éditions Gallimard, 1971).

F.R. Leavis, *The Great Tradition* (London, Chatto and Windus, 1948).

Derrick Leon, *Ruskin: The Great Victorian* (London, Routledge and Kegan Paul, 1949).

Georg Lukács, *The Historical Novel*, transl. Hannah and Stanley Mitchell (London, Merlin Press, 1962).

Colin McCabe, *James Joyce and the Revolution of the Word* (London, Macmillan, 1978).

A.D. McKillop, "Charles Lamb sees London", *Rice Institute Pamphlets* XXII (April, 1935), pp.105-128.

Charles Maturin, *Melmoth the Wanderer*, ed. Alethea Hayter (Harmondsworth, Penguin Books, 1977).

Kathi Meyer-Baer, *Music of the Spheres and the Dance of Death* (Princeton, N.J., Princeton University Press, 1970).

Ellen Moers, *The Dandy: Brummell to Beerbohm* (London, Gollancz, 1960).

Marcel Poëte, *Une Vie de Cité: Paris de sa naissance à nos jours* (Paris, 1925).

S.S. Prawer, *Karl Marx and World Literature* (Oxford, Oxford University Press, 1976).

Arthur Hobson Quinn, *Edgar Allan Poe: A Critical Biography* (New York, Appleton-Century-Crofts, 1941).

Ann Radcliffe, *The Mysteries of Udolpho*, ed. Bonamy Dobrée (Oxford, Oxford University Press, 1970).

Nicholas Rance, *The Historical Novel and Popular Politics in Nineteenth Century England* (London, Vision Press, 1975).

Jean Paul Friedrich Richter, *Des Feldpredigers Schmelzle Reise nach Flätz*, ed. J.W. Smeed (Oxford, Oxford University Press, 1952).

Karl Riha, *Die Beschreibung der "Grossen Stadt": Zur Entstehung des Grosstadtsmotivs in der deutschen Literatur ca. 1750-1850* (Bad Homburg, Gehlen Verlag, 1970).

Jean-Jacques Rousseau, *Essai sur l'Origine des Langues*, ed. Charles Porset (Bordeaux, Guy Ducros, 1970).

Michael Sadleir, *Bulwer: A Panorama* (London, 1931).

Marc Shell, *The Economy of Literature* (Baltimore, Johns Hopkins Press, 1978).

Leslie Shepard, *John Pitts: Ballad Printer of Seven Dials, London* (London, Private Libraries Association, 1969).

Marianne Thalmann, *Romantiker entdecken die Stadt* (München, 1965).

E.P. Thompson, *The Making of the English Working Class* (Harmondsworth, Penguin Books, 1968).

Graeme Tytler, *Physiognomy in the European Novel: Faces and Fortunes* (Princeton, N.J., Princeton University Press, 1982).

Patrick Waddington, *Turgenev and England* (London, Macmillan, 1980).

René Wellek, *A History of Modern Criticism* (New Haven, Yale University Press, 1955-1966; 5 vols.), vol. 2.

_____, *Confrontations: studies in the intellectual and literary relations between Germany, England and the United States during the nineteenth century* (Princeton, N.J., Princeton University Press, 1965).

Ioan Williams, ed., *Sir Walter Scott on Novelists and Fiction* (London, Routledge and Kegan Paul, 1968).

Raymond Williams, *The Country and the City* (London, Chatto and Windus, 1973).

INDEX OF NAMES
(Contemporary critics' names are not included,
except in a few cases where the contribution to the
study of the grotesque is of obvious importance -
e.g., Mikhail Bakhtin, Wolfgang Kayser)

INDEX OF CONCEPTS AND THEMES
('grotesque' is omitted because of its ubiquity,
but compounds like 'grotesque realism' and
'terrible grotesque' are included)

SI